Strategic Management in Public and Nonprofit Organizations

Strategic Management in Public and Nonprofit Organizations

Managing Public Concerns in an Era of Limits

SECOND EDITION

Jack Koteen

PRAEGER

Westport, Connecticut
London

Library of Congress Cataloging-in-Publication Data

Koteen, Jack.
    Strategic management in public and nonprofit organizations :
managing public concerns in an era of limits / Jack Koteen.—2nd
ed.
        p.   cm.
    Includes bibliographical references and index.
    ISBN 0–275–95531–1 (alk. paper).—ISBN 0–275–95532–X (pbk. :
alk. paper)
    1. Strategic planning.   2. Nonprofit organizations—Management.
3. Public administration.   I. Title.
HD30.28.K67   1997
658.4'012—dc20   96–44678

British Library Cataloguing in Publication Data is available.

Library of Congress Catalog Card Number: 96–44678
ISBN: 0–275–95531–1
        0–275–95532–X (pbk.)

First published in 1997

Praeger Publishers, 88 Post Road West, Westport, CT 06881
An imprint of Greenwood Publishing Group, Inc.

Printed in the United States of America

The paper used in this book complies with the
Permanent Paper Standard issued by the National
Information Standards Organization (Z39.48–1984).

10 9 8 7 6 5 4 3 2 1

TO MY WIFE
GLORIA,
FOR HER SPLENDID ASSISTANCE

Contents

PREFACE   xiii

   A Strategic Response to New Realities   xiii
   Impact of an Era of Limits   xiv
   The Ripple Effect of Severe Limits   xviii
   The Promise of Strategic Management   xx
   What This Book Attempts to Do   xxi
   How the Book Is Organized   xxiii

PART 1   A FAR DIFFERENT STRATEGIC MANAGEMENT

1   *INTRODUCTION TO SECOND EDITION*   3

   Original Focus of Concern: Can It Be Done?   3
   New Trends in Effective Practice   7
   New Chapters Added; Others Substantially
     Modified   12
   Updating Developments That Affect Strategic
     Management   13
   Underlying Beliefs: A New Paradigm Emerging   15

2   *STRATEGIC MANAGEMENT EXPLAINED*   20

   A Quick View of Strategic Management   20
   Evolution of Strategic Planning   22
   Fundamental Shift of Responsibility   23
   Characteristics and Aims   25
   How It Pays Off   29

PART 2 APPROACHES TO STRATEGIC LEADERSHIP

3 *CHIEF EXECUTIVE AS GENERAL MANAGER OF*
   STRATEGY   35

   Forging Strategic Capability   35
   Need for Help from Entire Organization   37
   Playing Multiple Roles   38
   Getting Personally Involved—Visibly   41
   Establishing a Proper Climate for Strategic
      Management   42

4 *CHIEF EXECUTIVE AS MASTER OF CHANGE*   44

   Successfully Meeting the Challenge of Change   44
   Ways of Responding to Environmental Change   45
   Building Blocks for Strategic Change   49
   Applying the Renewal Factor: The Waterman Project   50
   Becoming an Informed Opportunist   52
   Leading Others to Get Extraordinary Things Done   54
   Practices and Commitments Common to Successful
      Leaders   55

5 *CREATING A COMPELLING VISION OF THE FUTURE*   58

   How Vision Helps Leaders Create a Better Future   59
   Some Criteria for Making Visions Work   59
   Communicating Vision   61
   What Makes a Good Visionary Executive   62

PART 3 ESTABLISHING A STRATEGIC MANAGEMENT
         SYSTEM

6 *DESIGNING AND STARTING A STRATEGIC*
   MANAGEMENT SYSTEM   67

   Descriptive Model of a System   67
   Factors That Influence Systems Design   72
   Design Alternatives   74
   Focus on Management of Strategic Issues   77
   Preparing to Start Formal Strategic Planning   80
   Empower a Planning Team   80
   Research Insights on Planning Abandonment   82

7 *ORGANIZING A STRATEGIC MANAGEMENT SYSTEM*   85

   Guiding Concept: Raising the Quality of Strategic
      Decision-Making   85
   Planning Council or Executive Committee   87
   Chief Planner as Expert Advisor   90

    Strategic Management Support Group   92
    Strategic Operational Service Group   93

  8 *EVALUATING A STRATEGIC MANAGEMENT SYSTEM*   96
    Guiding Concept: Constant Learning, Continuous
        Improvement   96
    Ten Major Mistakes to Avoid   97
    Modifications on the Steiner Report Card   98

PART 4   SETTING THE STRATEGIC AGENDA

  9 *MAKING STRATEGIC ASSESSMENTS*   105
    What Is the Strategic Situation Audit?   105
    Assessing Program Performance   108
    Reading the Environment   111
    Analyzing for Strategic Implications   116

 10 *PREPARING THE STRATEGIC PLAN*   121
    New Versions Appearing   121
    Developing Components of the Basic Strategic Plan   122
    Defining Statements of Mission and Purpose   122
    Establishing Strategic Goals   124
    Expressing Organizational Values   129
    Setting New Strategic Initiatives   130
    The Implementation Matrix   131
    The Story of the Strategic Business Plan of the
        U.S. Navy Public Works Center   132
    Incorporating Special Features in an Expanded
        Version   133
    The Story of the Duke University Strategic Plan   135
    Stating Measurable Progress Indicators in Strategic
        Plans   137
    Providing Support Areas to Enable Plan
        Implementation   137
    Providing the Fiscal Outlook: Priorities and
        Constraints   138
    Devising Alternative Versions   138

PART 5   CHOOSING STRATEGIES

 11 *REINVENTING GOVERNMENT*   143
    Federal National Performance Review   143
    The Brookings Institution Appraisal   147
    A Critical Commentary on the National Performance Review
        Report   150
    Three Fundamental Approaches to Reinvention
        Undertaken   153

Varieties of Reinvention in the Agencies   156
The AID Story: A Reminder; Good Deeds Are Not Always
   Rewarded!   157
The Widespread Quality Movement in Government   158
A Serious Concern: Downsizing Government May Weaken
   Monitoring of Liabilities   160

12 STRATEGIC COMPETENCE IN NONPROFIT
    ORGANIZATIONS   162

The Strategic Response to Financial Stringency   162
The Arizona Study   164
Experience with Mergers   168
Transaction Survey of Cleveland Mergers and
   Consolidations   170
Growing Infrastructure of Professional and Technical
   Support   172

13 EMERGING INTERDEPENDENCE OF GOVERNMENT AND
    NONPROFIT SECTORS   175

A Masked Reality   175
Rise and Decline of America's Welfare State   176
New Perspective: Trilateral Interdependence of Federal, State,
   and Nonprofit Organizations   179
The Emerging Collaborative Model   183
Collaboration within Sectors   186

14 APPLYING POPULAR PRIVATE SECTOR STRATEGIES TO
    MANAGING PUBLIC CONCERNS   190

New Ways for Managing in the Public and Nonprofit
   World   190
Working with Total Quality Management   192
Improving "Customer" Satisfaction   197
Streamlining and Reengineering   204
Adapting the Enabling Role of Information
   Technology   208

PART 6 IMPLEMENTING STRATEGIC THRUSTS: USING
        MODERN PROGRAM MANAGEMENT METHODS

15 WHAT IS MODERN PROGRAM MANAGEMENT?   213

Source   214
Early Operational Concepts   215
Widespread Application   217
Increasing Strategic Role of Program Managers   219
Benefits and Pitfalls   220

16 *WHAT PROGRAM EXECUTIVES AND MANAGERS
    ACTUALLY DO*   224

    Who Are Program Executives and Managers?   224
    Basic Responsibilities   225
    Key Managerial Functions   226
    Performance Criteria   228
    Ten Important Learning Areas for the Modern Program
        Manager   235

17 *SETTING OBJECTIVES AND DEVISING ACTION PLANS*   236

    The Rise and Decline of the MBO Movement   236
    The Objective-Oriented Manager   238
    Benefits and Pitfalls   239
    Writing Meaningful Objectives   240
    Devising and Charting Action Plans   241
    The Importance of Gaining Agreement and Support   245

18 *DESIGNING PROGRAM/PROJECT PLANS*   247

    Rethinking Program Design   247
    What Does a Program/Project Plan Do?   248
    Components of Program/Project Design   248
    Design Format for Expensive Programs/Projects   250
    Preparing Simpler One-Page Program/Project
        Designs   253

19 *DEVELOPING PERFORMANCE MEASURES*   254

    Growing Attention to Performance Measurement   254
    The Mandate of Congressional Action   256
    Emerging Action Doctrine for Performance Measurement and
        Improvement   258
    Developing Performance Agreements with Senior
        Leadership   263
    Using Performance Goals and Objectives in Strategic Plans:
        The IRS Story   264
    Setting Performance Standards for Improving Customer
        Satisfaction   266
    The SSA Story   266
    Applying Best Practice in Telephone Service   268
    Establishing Performance Standards for Effective Local
        Government: The Allegheny County Story   269

20 *BUDGETING FOR PROGRAM ACCOUNTABILITY*   272

    Orientation   272
    Estimating Program Costs   276
    What to Expect from Central Staff Support   278

Useful Reminders for Effective Program Budgeting   280
Experimental Transition to Performance Budgeting   281

21 ORGANIZING PROGRAM AND RESPONSIBILITY
    STRUCTURE   283

Dividing Up the Total Program: Designing Program
    Structure   283
Using Traditional Concepts of Organizational
    Structure   287
Newer Organizational Thinking and Practice   292

22 USING TEAM STRUCTURES   295

When to Use Team Structures   296
Understanding the Team Approach   296
Guidelines for Designing a Team   300
Choosing Among Team Alternatives   300

PART 7 LEARNING FROM EXPERIENCE

23 CONTROLLING AND MONITORING PERFORMANCE   305
Why Control?   305
Use of the Traditional Control Matrix   306
What to Control: Elements   307
How to Control: Process Steps   309
Key Questions for Evaluating Control Measures   312
New Thinking: Are Controls Acceptable and Achievable in
    an Age of Empowerment?   312

24 EVALUATING PROGRAM PERFORMANCE IN A
    LEARNING ORGANIZATION   316
The What and Why of Evaluation   316
Performance Review and Appraisal   318
Design of Traditional Evaluation Studies   320
Analysis and Interpretation of Evaluation Findings   323
Preparation of an Evaluation Report   325
Creating an Organization of Learners   327

BIBLIOGRAPHY   333

INDEX   339

Preface

A STRATEGIC RESPONSE TO NEW REALITIES

New realities are forcing public and nonprofit organizations to change
drastically their traditional ways of doing business. These organizations
are seriously engaged in efforts to reinvent, restructure, and reengineer
with many new strategies borrowed from the private sector and the
global marketplace. In essence the new efforts focus on a bold mission
to deliver higher-quality service at less cost to a better-satisfied "customer," amid severe financial stringency and historic change.

This revised edition explains what is happening and why, provides
depth and perspective, and reveals some serious concerns. It describes
the compelling circumstances that create a difficult and demanding environment. The book indicates how strategic management can play a
significant role in developing a constructive response.

In just over a decade, strategic management has been adapted from a
business-sector model to become widely used for managing public concerns. It is mandated for use in all federal agencies in 1997; many states
and nonprofit organizations use strategic plans. But strategic management does not always achieve the results desired in the public or nonprofit agency. Making strategic management work effectively is a critical
need, particularly to enable it to serve the reinvention and transformation efforts under way in government and the nonprofit sector. The revised edition seeks to help with this difficult task.

A New Context

Public-interest decision makers and operating officials in both public
agencies and nonprofit organizations are caught in a series of powerful

forces that substantially affect how agencies conduct policy making, strategizing, and management. All around us we see a historic confluence of three major societal changes: growing complexity of public problems, severe financial constraints on efforts at their solutions, and popular pressure for rapid and profound change. These new conditions serve as constant determinants in policy and budget decisions. The pressure is great to cut back, delete, and limit; action favors the short term, the incremental, or the quick fix.

Events and dialogue in the political and professional arenas demand better government service for less, and yet insist on shrinking government. Under way is a historic shift of responsibility from Washington to the states and cities, often with insufficient funds. The call is insistent for the greater use of "charitable organizations," although interviews and studies indicate that executives of these organizations greatly fear that cuts in governmental financial support will undermine their efforts. Constantly, the press and media remind us that government must work better and must be leaner, smaller, smarter, faster, and cheaper.

These forces are the new realities. They make effective strategic planning in the context of strategic management—still in a formative stage in addressing public concerns—critically important for its promise in managing public concerns.

IMPACT OF AN ERA OF LIMITS

We now live and work in a period that historians may label an "era of limits." Financial stringency in the public and nonprofit sector poses constant constraints on what we can do. Events confirm that plans and promises frequently are cast aside as tight budgets are thrust upon us. This reality commands the attention of policy makers, decision makers, legislators, and service providers, as well as their "customers," all over the country. The repercussions of limited resources do not just affect government, religious, and nonprofit service agencies but also permeate to the highest levels of educational institutions. When the *New York Times* reported on its front page the resignation of Columbia University's president, it was also mentioned that "Mr. Sovern joins the Presidents of Yale, Chicago, and Duke who also have decided to step down in recent months each for a different reason but all citing the difficulties of leading complex institutions in a time of limited resources" (*New York Times*, June 7, 1992).

Financial Constraints

The national press constantly directs our attention to the most dramatic consequences of resource shortages. You read stories such as "Deficit Taking Toll on Big-Science Projects," which details the demise of the super-collider proton smasher and notes the continuing decline in authorized funds for scientific research that over a long time declined from 5.2 percent of the federal budget to 1.7 percent in 1993. The shift in priority was in favor of social programs like Medicaid, Medicare and Social Security that "ballooned to half the budget," reported the *New York Times*. But social programs are under the knife, as the quest to reduce government deficits and to balance budgets proceeds into the twenty-first century. No programs, however politically popular, escape the impact of the era of limits.

The consequences of limited resources strike across the board. A head of the Smithsonian anguished in his inaugural speech: "Clearly there are a lot of daunting challenges with this wonderful place, not the least of them that we've got a resource problem that is significant." In the arts, the chair of the National Endowment of the Arts called for a national partnership between commercial and nonprofit groups to deal with what she called the "financial crisis of the arts." She was quoted as saying, "It is unrealistic to get more public money in this time of budget cutting." She later was compelled to fight against major cuts and for the life of the agency.

The arts, the humanities, and the sciences are not the only recipients of tighter budgets and limited resources; also threatening are closings of Park Service campsites and cutbacks in school lunches, student loans, and scholarships. Certain are reductions in Medicare and Medicaid and welfare reform; the issue is how much to cut or how to cap the rise in costs.

Government's efforts to respond to unmet public needs has been further constrained by congressional requirements that new expenditures be accompanied by new revenues or by equivalent reductions in other programs. Additionally, the National Performance Review of Vice President Gore's efforts to "reinvent government" delivers on its promise to downsize the size of government with programs of cutbacks in employees—over two hundred thousand accomplished by early 1996—and in field offices, to the point that the federal government is as small as it was more than thirty years ago when John F. Kennedy was president.

Pressure from Public Demands

What is apparent is that vigorous public demand for services, particularly from organized special-interest constituencies, exceeds our supply of available resources—at all levels of society, from the nation's capital to each community. It was always so, but today's human problems are more visible, if not greater, with daily reminders in the media of poor children, the homeless, drugs and hunger, the mentally ill, prison shortages, joblessness, AIDS, and excessive regulation. Less obvious are the pressures of the organized special interests.

To our demand for limited resources, add the need for resources to redo and maintain the physical infrastructure of bridges and roads and the constant need for investment in human capital. These are our domestic needs; they do not include the overseas obligations of the only remaining Free World superpower.

Tough Choices

A limited supply of available money forces grim choices: what to do, how much, and for whom, and what not to do. Certainly we cannot allow what limited resources we have to flow only to the strongest self-interests and the most affluent and become callous to widespread human suffering and the deprivation of those left behind.

As Americans we agree that equity and fairness for all must be sought—continually. Yet, the setting of fair priorities is a difficult task requiring a delicate balance among citizen preference, expert judgment, and political power.

The Short-term Focus

Individual public and nonprofit organizations obviously have less to spend for meeting public needs. The social problems they confront are massive, and intended results are often difficult to achieve. How little we know for sure about how much in resources will gain a finite, measurable reduction in teenage pregnancies or drug addiction. What happens is that institutions and individuals focus more on the short term or the piecemeal or the more certain; change efforts tend to be incremental and incomplete, at best time-phased. Time horizons shrink at the expense of longer-term efforts to create a better future. We see this happening across the board in areas of health delivery and reform, in terms of prisons versus crime prevention, or in public education starved for tax dollars. These problems also affect many other public-interest programs: drug prevention and/or rehabilitation, welfare reform, the environment, the homeless, and the hungry.

Short-term horizons and partial solutions are understandably often necessary in these times, when financial resources for meeting unmet human needs are in such short supply. But short-term approaches too often occur in situations that clearly require a combination of short-term and longer-term efforts and that may cost much more if remedial efforts are postponed. As short-term decisions are made, serious societal problems are not resolved and in many cases grow worse. As the present outweighs the future, decline and deterioration of family and community continue.

As stringency of funds continues, the tendency is to avoid or disguise many serious problems, to gloss them over with appealing rhetoric, and to fail to search for root causes and outmoded core assumptions. Decision makers find it convenient and sometimes compelling to undertake short-term fixes and to apply superficial bandages. But serious problems worsen, in consequences and in cost.

The Complexity Factor

In public discussion we often fail to deal adequately with the complexity of many problems occuring nationally, whether it be health care, welfare reform, or crime. One dilemma is that people often want—and get—simple answers to problems that are not so simple. Detailed responses to intricate problems prompt public complaints about complexity, as is so prevalent in attempts to reform the provision of health care.

Responsible officials find that effective solution of complex problems demands certain amounts of bureaucratic resources and considerable attention. Needed, they claim, is a sufficient depth of analysis to find cost-effective solutions, over longer-term time frames. Such analysis requires sufficient staff time for monitoring and for making constant changes and corrections as experience indicates. Increasingly, we fail to do so, because it takes money, time, and effort that is said to be "bureaucracy" or "government"; these are considered automatic disqualifiers or "no-no's" in the minds of many.

But for effective problem solving, serious problems must be professionally and openly viewed as complex systems. Then our understanding increases; our time horizons tend to expand. In the systematic analysis of complex problems, we can uncover remedial efforts that present a wide range of choices. We need not be locked into current practice or outmoded assumptions.

The Prison Story: A Complex Problem. We can see the difficulty of resolving complex problems manifest in areas like crime, where the emphasis on immediate building of more prisons for the "warehousing" of inmates is given priority over longer-term social efforts—often deemed "wasteful pork"—when the focus is on crime prevention. President Catanese of Florida Atlantic University takes a constructive position when he describes the situation this way:

Like other public university presidents, I am angry and frustrated that tax dollars needed by higher education are instead being poured into the nation's increasingly desperate effort to control crime. . . . Building more and more prisons is at best a short term solution to our crime problem; finding approaches that will work over the long term is a far more complicated and perplexing business.

Do not misunderstand me. Criminals should be punished and kept in prison for their full terms. Prisons are extremely expensive to build and maintain, and the cost of warehousing inmates is skyrocketing. Our society cannot afford to underwrite the unlimited growth of its penal system. What else can we do? It is time for America's universities to take on the prevention and control of crime as a survival issue" (*Sun-Sentinel* [Ft. Lauderdale, FL], December 14, 1994).

Catanese then proceeds to discuss contributions that higher education can make in areas of education, research, technology, and in-prison programs. Government is usually expected to take the catalytic responsibility for focusing on serious societal problems. But we need not wait for government to take the initiative; what we need are collaborative efforts of government, the universities, and other nonprofit institutions to pursue common efforts in resolving complex problems.

THE RIPPLE EFFECT OF SEVERE LIMITS

What does happen in an era of limits is a vicious cycle. Events interact nationwide. Shortages and effforts to eliminate budget deficits at the national level curtail social programs and force down federal block-grant payments to states. The federal government, pressured by deficits and resource limits and advocates of "states rights," has transferred and mandated program responsibilities to state governments, but often without sufficient resources. These mandates in turn have raised state and city budgetary requirements and generated tremendous anger and protest at the state and local level. Although Congress has now legislated against "unfunded mandates," states and local agencies constantly search for resources to meet their increasing responsibilities.

The evidence of resource limits is extensive in the states. One review by the State Budget Officers Association highlights extensive cuts in needed and wanted services in fields like health and education. Prisons gobble taxes.

Large counties like Los Angeles are considering dramatic cuts in the nation's largest county government, particularly its services to the poor, because it faces the prospect of a huge budget deficit and its federal and state aid is declining (*New York Times*, June 19, 1995).

Limits are apparent in the cities, too. Declines in federal, state, and local aid have left cities like Syracuse "so starved for funds, that it is nearing a crisis" (*New York Times*, February 21, 1996). One solution suggested by the mayor of Syracuse is creating much concern. The mayor has proposed charging nonprofit tax-exempt institutions like churches, universities, and hospitals a "core service fee," a tax-like payment for such basic services as road maintenance and police protection. Such organizations have been tax-exempt for more than two hundred years. But cities like Syracuse, where 58.7 percent of the real property is tax-exempt, face serious budgetary shortfalls and are resisting the tax-exempt institutions.

Cities are pushed to find ingenious ways to make money. A *New York Times* article was headlined, "From Signs to Pistols, Cash-Short Cities Sell Past; Parking Meters and Fire Hydrants Raise Money for Municipalities." Cities have set up expresso bars in libraries and opened the "city store" to sell such items as old parking meters, vintage parking lights, and used manhole covers (to serve as coffee tables).

Nonprofits Suffer

As the federal government, states, counties, and cities confront resource shortages, they are less able to help the nonprofit sector in satisfying the citizenry's human needs. Thus the nonprofit organization is forced to compete for a smaller pie of resources from government sources. For some nonprofit organizations that are almost totally or largely (over 50 percent) dependent on government funding, the financial stringency is serious.

Many critics of government spending on social services ask the nation's charities to take responsibility for the poor. But the charities themselves fear that government spending cuts would jeopardize their ability to help the poor. According to a study by Lester M. Salamon of Johns Hopkins University and Alan J. Abramson of Aspin Institute, charity groups could lose tremendous revenues now earmarked for health, education, welfare, community development, and overseas relief if cuts proposed by Congress and the White House were enacted (*New York Times*, February 5, 1996). Estimates of proposed cuts in spending to large national charities are huge; Catholic charities would receive two hundred million dollars less from Washington by 2002; the Salvation Army is estimated to receive about fifty million dollars less in federal money. The Salamon/Abramson study estimates that to make up for cuts in federal spending, private giving would have to increase by 50 percent by 2002. Whatever the size of the cuts enacted, the impact will be substantial. The uncertainty will remain high; resources will remain short.

The many nonprofits that render service to the community rather than to members—and on average receive a third of their funding from government—are being compelled to compete more effectively for slimmer government contracts. Or, they need to go elsewhere for funds, either through raising fees or receiving increased levels of private and corporate grants.

When nonprofit organizations are compelled to establish fees or raise fees higher for service to clients, they may cut off service to those most in need. This moves the organization to commercialization for those who can afford to pay. In extreme cases, such behavior distorts the charitable mission of the organization, undermines its reason for being, and compels the board to confront the realities of resource limits.

Financial stringency forces the nonprofit organization to compete for additional support from foundations and corporate donors. Unfortunately, these funding organizations are finding their resources strained because the number of worthy claimants and their needs have increased. This demand forces tough choices on the foundations, as well as on corporate donors who are substantial sources of support for the nonprofits. It has become exceedingly more difficult to decide whom to support and for how much and who gets left out. Anyone who has read the angry responses by unsuccessful grant seekers to official rejections for grant requests will quickly appreciate the difficulties in the contemporary grant-seeking and grant-making process. Having played on both sides of the game, I have vivid memories.

Not all categories of charities fare equally in fundraising, according to a report of the American Association for Fundraising Counsel. Although charitable donations increased by almost 11 percent in 1995, to $143.9 billion, the biggest increase since 1986, donations to human service groups fell slightly, a decline of 3 percent after inflation, to such groups as the Red Cross and youth and family programs. Donations to arts, culture, and humanities groups, already faced with cuts in government support, were virtually flat after inflation. But gains in donations were experienced by public and society benefit philanthropies, a category that includes research and public policy organizations, community development organizations, and advocacy groups. Environmental groups also showed gains, which rose 10 percent after inflation.

THE PROMISE OF STRATEGIC MANAGEMENT

The challenge posed to our public-interest institutions is daunting: How do we do what we choose to do—within our limits—in ways that do it better and cost less and yet achieve higher levels of quality for a more satisfied constituent, client, or "customer," as Vice President Gore calls them in the program for "reinventing government."

A Major Tool for Change

Strategic management is being thrust into a major role for meeting the challenge. As it is increasingly accepted and now congressionally mandated for all federal agencies and is in wide use in states and nonprofit agencies, experts anticipate that strategic planning and management offer great promise in the management of public concerns. It offers compass, process, and strategy to deal with transformations compelled by a difficult environment, where rapid and profound change is under way and where uncertainty is the norm.

When it works well, strategic management attempts to keep strategic intentions within the practical limits of what can actually be achieved; and with performance measures it can provide warning signals when action is off course. It brings coherence to the multiple, sometimes contradictory strategies for better achievement of intended results. It counters the prevailing tendency to concentrate only on short-term time horizons without taking adequate longer-term measures. It probes complex problems in modes and time frames appropriate for their solution and allows us to begin to understand that not all problems are solvable, at least not in the here and now.

The Task Is to Make It Effective

In the private profit-oriented sector the threat to survival compels the effective use of strategic management in fundamental decision-making and execution. But in government and independent-sector nonprofit agencies, success or failure is less obvious in the absence of a bottom line. Yet we witness the beginning of a widespread movement to practice the private-sector strategic planning model that gives some semblance of compass and bottom line. We do find emerging a measure of competence for strategic process, strategy formulation, and plan execution in a number of government and nonprofit agencies. But strategic competence certainly is less than universal. The task under way is to broaden, deepen, and render effective the strategic response capability.

WHAT THIS BOOK ATTEMPTS TO DO

Communicate New Management Thinking

The agenda of the revised edition is to capture and blend the essence of new ways of managing and transforming the public and nonprofit organization. This book selectively identifies and explains pioneering but applicable private-sector management behavior; it also includes the time-tested management fundamentals of a vast number of concepts and practices developed and used over the last several decades.

The revised edition retains its aim to be comprehensive in scope and to reflect the "cutting edge" in management technology. It makes the new strategies in use more easily accessible and affordable to those responsible for doing business in the public and nonprofit world.

Explain Strategic Management

The revised edition discusses newly emerging and more effective practices of strategic management for individual nonprofit and public organizations. The new strategic management provides coherence and ways to operationalize the many new strategies emerging into wide use. In effect, strategic management has the potential to become the central integrating mechanism—loosely referred to as the "institutional brain and mind" for the modern public and nonprofit organization.

What strategic management does is to enable the organization to absorb the stimuli that signal changing environmental conditions that affect organizational performance. Then it guides internal performance assessment to identify strategic issues that require priority attention. It resolves the priority issues by mobilizing the tools of power: expertise, resources, and approvals for action. Strategic management thus becomes a crucial instrument for enabling an organization to make faster and sounder decisions that help it adapt to new realities.

Help to Create the Strategy-Competent Organization

As we move into the twenty-first century the strategy-competent organization will lead the way. It will possess the skill to choose and execute a bundle of strategies that can transform its internal behavior to fit a rapidly changing and often hostile environment. Ideally, it will have the capability to reframe its mission, sense its external threats and opportunities, and revitalize its internal strengths and weaknesses. It will renew, upgrade, and up-skill its human resources; realistically it will plot its financial outlook. And it will aggressively work to satisfy better its constituencies with higher-quality services. It must do all this in an environment of limited resources and still be able to respond with fairness and integrity, or change until it does.

The book's immediate target is to help forge the strategic competence of managers and executives who are busily engaged in meeting the many demands for transforming their organizations. They are being urged to provide quality services in smaller organizations that work better with less. They are being asked to operate through decentralized operating units closer to the people and still must understand and connect with top management's fast-moving strategic directions, values, and initiatives. They are being told the ultimate aim is to win customer respect and confidence from an often nontrusting and suspicious clientele. The new demands for improvement are certainly stringent, but they are necessary.

Be User-Friendly

The book sincerely seeks to ease the task of educators and trainers to help busy strategic managers, who understandably find their responsibilities increasingly difficult and complex. It strives to be operationally useful and yet be professionally sound. It enables practitioners and educators to be informed and updated on recent management developments and enduring trends in timesaving ways and provides pathways to further information on research and practice. The content of the book presumes little or no technical background or general expertise in management. The only prerequisite is real need—current or prospective—for strategic and managerial skills, and an interest in making a difference toward quality and excellence. The book's frequent reference to the needs and perspectives of practitioners and their agencies enables educators to help students ease, almost prematurely, the transition from study to reality in the working world.

A special aim is to help executives and managers be familiar with and learn to use a newly expanded menu of available strategic options adapted from the business world that better achieve desired and measurable performance results. The desired outcome is for executives and managers to be better able to lead or to participate effectively in a more agile but selective and decentralized strategic management process.

The book in complete form, or by selective use of separate chapters as supplementary handouts, serves as a valuable and affordable resource guide to provide depth and perspective for designing new courses or customizing existing ones. This is evidenced by the schools and centers that have adopted the book as text and used it for supplementary materials.

HOW THE BOOK IS ORGANIZED

No single best way exists to organize a management book. To make it most understandable and operationally useful, two organizing concepts are used. One way follows the logical flow in sequence of the major interactive components of strategic management as a process. The other approach focuses on specifics of strategic content. Both approaches are useful and necessary, though they may seem contradictory and distracting to the reader. They are separate sides of the same coin.

Knowledge in this book is of two types. One consists of practical technology and guiding concepts that indicate how leaders, executives, and managers and their organizations should behave. The other consists of conceptual insights and descriptive narrative of how organizations actually do behave. Both are intended to be operationally useful for enhanced understanding and ease of application amid the complexity and chaos of the real world.

After a new introduction and a revised preface, the book is organized into seven parts:

Part 1 discusses the introduction of strategic management, which was born and bred in the profit world and in the military, into the realm of public and nonprofit affairs. "Can it be done?" was a serious query in the last decade. With qualification, the answer was "yes—but." Now that strategic management has achieved widespread acceptance and is being made mandatory for all federal agencies, the concern is not whether but how to do it most effectively. The emphasis is on assuring that plans and strategic intentions, when formulated, can and will be implemented to achieve desired performance results.

In a separate chapter, sometimes used as supplementary handout training material, strategic management is explained in brief. What it can do, its evolution, and its characteristics and payoff are discussed.

Part 2 discusses new approaches to strategic leadership. No longer can leaders be solely concerned with the technical data and skills for making strategy; they must also master the skills and techniques for anticipating and producing constructive change. This means being skilled with people, vision, and values, as well as systems and structures. This expanded view of the chief executive as leader of strategy and master of change translates into a set of performance roles that creates a clear expectation of what is necessary at the top to achieve effective strategic management. The remainder of the book serves to set forth the strategies and instruments that enable the chief executive and organization to carry out the performance roles with greatest effectiveness.

Part 3 focuses on establishing and starting a strategic management system and how to make it work. This part of the book highlights a priority concern: how to make strategic thinking and acting an accepted and self-sustaining way of doing business in an organization.

Part 4 provides the basis for setting the strategic agenda. It indicates how to make strategic assessments that identify the major issues confronting the organization. This activity provides the basis for setting strategic directions and formulating strategic initiatives. It underscores the vital necessity of being acutely aware of what is happening in the environment that might seriously affect what the organization does and how.

Part 5 is completely new. It discusses current efforts and the main strategies for reforming government and transforming nonprofit organizations. It also explains the approaches of a number of popular private-sector strategies currently being applied to government and the nonprofit sector. The changing government–nonprofit sector relationship of greater interdependence and collaboration is explored.

Part 6 explains the use of program management methods for implementing strategic goals and initiatives. A new chapter reports on the thrust of developing measurement standards and benchmarks in the quest for better performance results.

Part 7 describes traditional and newer views of learning from experience. It explains emerging approaches to create an organization of all learners in what are being called "continuous learning organizations."

Part 1

A FAR DIFFERENT STRATEGIC MANAGEMENT

1

Introduction to Second Edition

Since the issuance of *Strategic Management for the Public and Nonprofit Organization* in 1989, much about strategic management has changed. Though the main structure of the strategic management system for the public and nonprofit organization remains solid, a number of significant changes have evolved in how it is perceived and practiced. New patterns of thinking about strategic planning and its broader framework of strategic management shift its purpose and quicken the tempo of its process. New ways expand its content, strengthen the strategic role of program managers, sharpen the roles of its leaders, and embrace new strategies adapted from the private sector.

It is too soon to declare the decline of bureaucracy as we know it. But evidence suggests we witness the beginning of new and distinctly better ways of managing in the public and nonprofit sectors. A new strategic management, reflecting an updated business model, has begun to play a major role in changing how government and nonprofit organizations work. Improved are most of the components of the strategic management system: strategic process, strategy content, implementation, and strategic governance.

ORIGINAL FOCUS OF CONCERN: CAN IT BE DONE?

When the book was first issued, from the perspective of a thoughtful practitioner, the prime focus of concern was whether or not to introduce into nonprofit or public affairs a model of strategic planning that was born and nurtured in the military and private-sector organizations. "Can it be done?" was a serious query. Long experience with forms of planning in the United States and abroad and educated intuition said "yes—but," and recent evidence is still supportive of that conclusion. The second concern was directed at the query, "If it is to be done, how do we provide greater assurance that plans, when formulated, will be implemented and that desired results will be achieved?"

The few public and nonprofit agencies that initiated strategic planning at that time experienced understandable difficulty in pursuing the full spectrum of strategic management that linked the setting of directional goals and plans to desired results. It is "understandable" because the lack of adequate implementation was almost universal in the author's experience with national development planning and agricultural-sector planning in the third world and with forms of planning in the United States. That is why the book concentrates so heavily (almost half) on implementing methods.

Recent evidence tells us that the lack of implementation still remains a significant problem but that it is receiving greater attention. This is clearly revealed in Vice President Gore's report on the National Performance Review (1993) of the federal program to "reinvent government," or REGO as it is called. Some progress on implementation is being made, in such areas as the expanded strategic role and enhanced skills of decentralized program managers, better program and project design, and improved performance measurement and accountability. More needs to be done.

The Situation—Then

When the original edition of this book was issued (1989), formal strategic planning offered more promise than certitude in results. In retrospect, my own lectures to working officials seemed almost proselytizing in tone: "Try it—it will help you," and I sometimes frankly added, "maybe." True, the World Bank at that time asserted with conviction that strategic planning was the most advanced form of planning and applied to public and nonprofit sectors. But there was little objective evidence of benefit. Only a sparse community of organizations without the traditional "bottom-line" and practicing strategic planning existed to serve as role models. Literature on strategic planning addressed directly to the public or nonprofit world was limited; it was necessary to adapt the literature and experience of the business community.

Presentations to American nonprofit board members and government officials in attempts to introduce formal planning often provoked strong skepticism or cynicism; similar presentations to foreign officials from the third world often encountered deep and polite silence. A most convincing point to pragmatic top officials that transcended geographical and cultural boundaries did not relate to planning's technical merit or its ability to enable the achievement of results. Rather, the convincing point was a practical one: Such planning would impress donors and better enable them to secure financing and mobilize resources.

Today's Widespread Use of Strategic Management

Strategic planning in the government and nonprofit sector is now widely practiced. Slowly but steadily, strategic planning—adapted from almost universal practice in the private sector under the label of strategic management—entered into the realm of public concerns of government and the nonprofit sector. In less than a decade, formal strategic planning has moved from a pioneering adventure in government, as in the federal Internal Revenue Service or the state of Ohio, and in nonprofit organizations, such as the American Red Cross, to widespread practice.

In the late 1980s, the federal Office of Management and Budget could identify only two federal agency strategic plans, and one was classified and not available for professional scrutiny. The Government Performance and Results Act (1993) mandates that by 1997 strategic planning is required in all federal government agencies. Many state agencies operate with written strategic plans; even small states like Wyoming use them.

In the nonprofit sector, one study (Stone 1991) reveals that of a sample of 44 nonprofit organizations, randomly selected from 104 arts nonprofits and 36 nonprofits serving the mentally retarded, only 8 had not engaged in formal strategic planning. Another study (McNurty and colleagues 1991) reveals that in its survey sample of almost two hundred nonprofit agencies more than half of the agencies used many specific strategies to combat financial stringency and uncertainty.

Shifting Direction of Purpose

The primary purpose that organizations select to focus their strategic management system is shifting in emphasis and direction. Traditionally, the fundamental purpose tends to be process oriented, that is, to facilitate the introduction of a formal strategic management system to coordinate the use and flow of strategic planning process and decision centers. This is done to link the essential functions of strategic governance, performance assessment, decision-making, strategy formulation and content, implementation, and learning from experience. A central feature is the development of a written strategic plan.

But in practice, a distinct change in purpose is emerging. The new emphasis focuses on the choice and use of specific strategy content to enhance an institution's performance; there is relatively less attention to formal process. Strategies are specifically designed as levers of change to better achieve targeted, needed results. In many cases, the compelling need is for strategy to assure survival, to adapt to chaos and crisis, or to achieve stability in periods of severe financial stringency and rapid change. As in business, nonprofit and government strategies are increasingly being designed to "transform" an organization to reframe its direction, change its culture and behavior, elevate its quality of product and service, satisfy its customers, and restructure how it operates. Just a few years ago, the conventional wisdom was to forget strategic planning under conditions of crisis. Today, strategic planning is "for all seasons, and all types of weather." Merely its form, content, and pace change.

Pursuit of Specific Strategies

In practice today, serious attention is paid to formulation of particular strategies and to whether they work. The new mantra is Strategy is results; it works or changes. This concentration on the content of specific strategies and their outcomes dominates the system's strategic management system. In effect, strategy content assumes greater importance than process, though process and supporting structures remain essential. The new strategic content appears to be an adaptation to severely limited resources and rapid and profound directional and policy change. Strategic management is adjusting out of necessity to a new set of compelling realities.

An examination of the efforts to "reinvent government" and "transform" the nonprofit organization reveals that identifiable strategies are steadily being pursued and skillfully applied. The strategies seek new ways to enhance quality performance at less cost in public and nonprofit agencies and to increase substantially their customer satisfaction. The popular mandate is "Do more, better, smarter, with less." The intent is to enable the organization to adapt to tight budgets and rapid change and yet to be responsive to the popular will.

Extensive Problems Have Arisen in Practice

With the increased use of strategic planning in organizations dedicated to public concerns, strains and difficulties in its practice have begun to be observed. Although the promise of strategic planning is widely accepted, achievement of beneficial program results remains elusive for many. Vice President Gore's report on the first phase of the National Performance Review (1993) of federal agencies pursuant to the president's effort to "reinvent government" reveals that of the 103 strategic plans reviewed, only nine were able to achieve intended results.

Anecdotal experience from administrators in nonprofits reveals similar difficulties. Too often the traditional nonprofit strategic plan contained a series of noble goals and generalized directions that were incorporated after extensive deliberations by committees, that some executive directors labeled the "challenge" or rationalized as "essential communication." But the plans often displayed little connection with program budgets and operations because implementation was neither seriously expected nor prepared for. A rigorous study (Stone 1991) documented that in its sample of nonprofit organizations practicing strategic planning almost 25 percent decided to abandon the practice and discussed the prevailing characteristics of planning abandonment.

Current Concern: How to Do It Effectively!

Widespread practice of strategic planning and its attendant difficulties shift our attention from a prior concern about whether to practice strategic planning. Much discussion originally focused on explaining to skeptical minds what strategic planning was all about, how a business and military model could work in a nonprofit world without a "bottom line," and what it aimed to accomplish. Now the focus is on ways to do it most effectively to achieve desired results. The priority issue now is no longer "if" but "how," and more often "why."

NEW TRENDS IN EFFECTIVE PRACTICE

Recent experience in the 1990s demonstrates that strategic management in the public and nonprofit sectors has begun to evolve and adapt to a turbulent environment of rapid and profound change in a period of severe financial stringency. Emerging are six new major patterns of change and a number of updating developments. Many of the new themes for change reflect the mission of progressive for-profit business firms: achieve higher quality product and service to better serve and satisfy customers at less cost, in down-sized and streamlined organizations. What appears to be happening is that the government and the nonprofits, with an interval of cultural lag of a decade or two, have begun in earnest to reflect new paradigms of managerial behavior in the business community. And yet the unique conditions of operating openly and entrepreneurially in the public interest without undue risk are generally being met.

The Major Trends

The trends and developments discussed in the second edition have been selected because they contain strategies, techniques, or approaches that meet three criteria:

Value. Provide beneficial value to a public or nonprofit organization and are ready for immediate application by practicing managers;

Current Practice. Are currently in extensive practice in many public and nonprofit organizations, verifiable by professional documentation; and

Durability. They satisfy experienced professional judgment that they represent a reasonably long-term directional trend that offers a glimpse at how progressive organizations will operate in the early twenty-first century.

Trend Number One: A significant pattern is the widespread presence of a full menu of available strategy choices that are used to "reinvent government" and "transform" the nonprofit organization.

A number of public and nonprofit organizations demonstrate a new mode of strategy competence. They exhibit the ability to select and execute a variety of strategic choices that change the organization's internal behavior to respond to a changing environment, whether it be opportunity or threat, and thereby achieve a substantial degree of success.

These organizations use strategies of many types as levers of change, which enables them to cope with environments of severe financial constraint and rapid and profound change. They select strategies to shift direction, increase revenues, decrease expenditures, and create specific change. In times of shifting directions, they use strategic goals and objectives to take positions and forge consistency for specific strategic actions, especially for organizations that operate in multiple locations.

The full menu of strategic options is important because no single strategy is sufficient by itself or useful forever in its application. Strategies most often work in concert with other complementary or subsidiary strategies; they often are used in time-phased sequence. Practicing managers are being trained to apply skillfully a bundle of strategies, many adapted from the private sector but appropriate for organizations seeking to serve the public interest with fairness and equity.

Many of the strategies are already in place in federal agencies, in some local governments, and in a number of nonprofit organizations. They run the gamut from Total Quality Management, Enhanced Customer Satisfaction, Productivity Enhancement and Cost Containment, Process Reengineering, Decentralizing Outreach Measures to Move Closer to the People, Outsourcing and Privatization, Enabling Role of Information Technology, Strategic Alliances and Affiliations, Mergers, and New Modes of Strategic Governance, to Restructuring, Downsizing, and Streamlining.

Trend Number Two: A second development extends strategic planning beyond a preoccupation with setting forward-looking directional

goals and formulating strategies—which are solely measures of future intention—into the zone of implementation where results are pursued and accomplished. This shift reflects a renewed emphasis on performance improvement, measurement, and accountability as devices for the better achievement of desired results.

Not long ago, surveys by the Congressional Budget Office and the General Accounting Office, reported in an accompanying report to the National Performance Review (Office of the Vice President, 1993c), "suggest that strategic planning and performance measurement remain a veneer in most federal agencies, having little effect on program operations." Previous efforts to improve program performance (from the performance budgeting of the 1950s through the programming, planning, and budgeting of the 1960s to the zero-based budgeting of the 1970s to management by objectives in the 1980s) have each made incremental contributions to linking strategic intentions to desired results, but assessments indicate they have had a limited impact.

Some federal agencies are now making substantial progress with new approaches to planning and managing for results. For example the Internal Revenue Service has developed a strategic plan for 1995–2001 called its "Business Master Plan, Strategic Extract," with a strong customer-oriented mission, strategic objectives, explicit performance goals to measure results, recent accomplishments, and statements of expected benefits.

The success of Sunnyvale, California, back in 1973 in adopting comprehensive performance planning, measurement, and budgeting encouraged results-oriented performance management in other states and cities: Florida, Minnesota, Texas, and Phoenix, Arizona (Osborne and Gaebler 1992). Other countries—United Kingdom, Australia, New Zealand, Canada, Sweden—have increased their use of performance measurement to guide management and budgeting over the last decade (Office of the Vice President, 1993c).

Efforts to use strategic planning and performance measurement to improve results are strengthened by the passage and implementation of the Government Performance and Results Act of 1993. Signed by President Clinton, the law requires that all agencies define their long-term goals, set specific annual performance targets, and report annually on performance compared to targets. Called for are strategic plans, annual performance plans, and annual performance reports. The law begins with pilot projects in fiscal year 1994 and proceeds to government-wide implementation by 1999 and 2001.

Trend Number Three: A third trend of major import is the decentralization of strategic planning by the expanded strategic role and greater involvement of program managers.

This is noted particularly in federal agencies, by program managers who operate "in the front lines" down in the agency and out in the field. What was merely suggested briefly in the book's original version as effective management logic is now emerging as a significant trend. The benefits are expressed in comments by the operating program managers themselves. Some of my students who are operating officials tell me that they are beginning to play an expanded strategic program role as agents for management change and are being given training in strategic planning and implementing skills. They are the implementors closer to the people of overall strategic directions and specific strategic initiatives of their agency. They often either participate in the agency's formulation of strategic plans and directional goals as members of strategic planning teams or are solicited for their views about strategic plans. They claim that because they better understand front-office thinking and directions, they can implement plans more effectively. One beneficial result is that top officials can have greater assurance that their directional goals and policies will produce intended results.

Strategic planning can no longer be perceived solely as a topside concern of the front office and the top management team. It now more often involves a fuller and deeper strategy team that includes the program and technical managers throughout the agency who are responsible for carrying out major strategic directional change in the community where real results are to be achieved. Slowly, the "bureaucratic barrier" between the front office and operating officials is coming down, or being somewhat lowered.

Trend Number Four: A fourth but related pattern is the evolution of strategic process that is seeking—with difficulty but some progress— to become more agile, selectively targeted, and flexible.

Contemporary strategic process differs sharply in being more flexible, less formal, and faster paced than the traditional behavior of strategic planning. Traditional strategic process formally blueprinted a path to success and proceeded at a predetermined and sometimes tortuous review pace, with little deviation. Recent experience with the strategic planning process, particularly in the independent nonprofit agency, indicates that it moves more quickly, targets selective but specific strategic issues, and changes rapidly, if necessary, at any time without the necessity to await or complete annual or multiyear planning cycles. More than occasionally, the strategic process seems to be less tidy, with unseemly missteps and shifts apparent that are sometimes rationalized in the name of "flexible response" or justified in the struggle for just plain survival. One expert calls the less formal process "management by groping along" (Liebschutz 1992).

True, faster response quickens the time-consuming nature of formal strategic process, but there is a downside. Fast response also tends to undermine reflective deliberation and sound, future-oriented decisions. Fast response can weaken the capability for depth analysis that strikes at root causes and reinvents core assumptions, which is so vital in complex situations of rapid directional, policy, and program change.

Strategic process has learned the necessity for but has not always achieved the discipline to be selective and incremental and to be pilot-minded rather than completely comprehensive in its application. The popular expression is "focus and concentrate," but "try it, first." The current focus of strategic change is on fewer goals, at any given period of time. The intent is to pay most attention to selected programs that produce greater strategic outcomes for the common good, but the practice often is to respond to the stronger special interest or board pressure. The selective, leaner approach does enable greater speed and flexibility, and it certainly requires fewer resources, although the outcome may not always reflect the best public interest.

Trend Number Five: Many strategic plans have begun to expand beyond a traditional basic version of limited but common elements to incorporate additional strategic features.

Less than a decade ago, an examination of strategic plans in public and nonprofit agencies—the relative few that existed—displayed a commonality of limited components and content. With the experience gained in the wider use of strategic planning, plans have begun to differentiate and appear in several versions.

A Basic Version usually contains the traditional core of five common components found in a number of plans, labeled by some organizations as "strategic directions." A Basic Version can be found in organizations as different as the Maryland State Government of Administrative Hearings and the National Association of Realtors. The aim is to articulate the organization's strategic intention to create a better future; contained are statements of mission, goals and objectives, and values. The Basic Version sometimes defines a "vision" and usually incorporates new strategic initiatives. An action plan is occasionally contained.

A number of organizations now prepare an Expanded Version that incorporates one or more additional strategic features. The expanded features express such matters as characteristics of distinctiveness and competitive advantage, they may state measurable program progress indicators toward planned goals and objectives, they provide for supporting areas like computerization and library modernization, or they discuss the specifics of fiscal outlook. The new features do not replace but add to the traditional core of components in the traditional basic version.

Trend Number Six: Another significant pattern is the emerging inter-dependence and collaboration between government and the nonprofit sector.

We witness a watershed change away from the perceived image of a welfare state. The reality is a society that opts for pluralistic institutions operating collaboratively in both public and private nonprofit spheres to satisfy the human needs of the people. Government entities extensively use nonprofit organizations to get done what was often considered government work that extends in some jurisdictions to schools, prisons, and waste treatment. More often government employs purchase contracts with outside agencies to deliver public services at competitive cost, although not always with success. There have been instances where contracts are inadequately supervised, with many dollars of unallowed funds permitted.

The nonprofit sector's collaborative relationships with government are most evident at state and local levels in the delivery of human services, and sometimes with shared financing. The emerging phenomenon of government–nonprofit agency collaboration is not found only in America but reflects a trend of the global community. It exists in England, Sweden, France, and Germany; in Eastern Europe, as in Poland, Bulgaria, and Russia; and in Asia's Japan.

NEW CHAPTERS ADDED; OTHERS SUBSTANTIALLY MODIFIED

Five completely new chapters are added in the new edition. One new chapter describes and evaluates major strategic efforts that are being applied to "reinvent government" with a declared mission to make it work better, be smaller, move closer to the people, and cost less.

A second new chapter describes a number of strategies used in the nonprofit sector and the degree of their success to enable nonprofit agencies to confront financial stringency and rapid directional change in policy and program. This chapter also discusses a growing pattern of mergers and strategic alliances.

A third new chapter describes ways to apply some popular private-sector strategies already being undertaken with beneficial results in public and nonprofit agencies and explains their guiding concepts, approaches, and techniques.

A fourth new chapter explains the growing presence of collaborative relationships and interdependence within and between the public and nonprofit sectors.

A fifth new chapter explains the growing attention to program measurement in the increased focus on "managing for results." It discusses the purposes, requirements, and implementation of the Government Performance and Results Act of 1993, which mandates the establishment of strategic planning and performance measurement in federal agencies. The chapter describes and illustrates the widespread use of performance standards in strategic plans, in directly achieving customer satisfaction, and in improving local government.

A number of other chapters, for example, the "Chief Executive as Master of Change," have been updated and expanded to incorporate new developments. Some modified chapters have previously been used by trainers and teachers with permission of the publisher, as separate handout for teaching or reference material. Care has been taken to ensure that they are still designed to serve as convenient, less expensive ways to modernize, expand, and customize curricula of existing courses or new ones.

UPDATING DEVELOPMENTS THAT AFFECT STRATEGIC MANAGEMENT

Other modifications are contained in the new edition:

Shift in Doctrine and Practice of Management by Objectives (MBO)

One modifies the previously popular but now outdated Management By Objectives (MBO). The shifts in management behavior evoked by the explosion in use of Total Quality Management and the widespread use of strategic planning change but do not dismiss managing by objectives. My working official students confirm this. A Japanese official working for the U.S. Navy in Japan writes me, "They say Management by Objectives is too old. It is Total Quality Leadership now. To me, MBO still works." But many others resent the arbitrary way it is often practiced.

Explosive Spread of Total Quality Management (TQM)

Total Quality Management, spawned in the federal government years ago, moved to Japan with dramatic results. It reappeared as almost standard practice in American industry, has begun to invade government, and is gradually appearing in the nonprofit sector. A new culture of quality performance is permeating the American scene; training courses have multiplied.

Growing Concern for "Customer" Satisfaction

Many organizations in government and an increasing number in the nonprofit sector—reflecting a significant trend in the private sector—

have taken up the challenge to provide better, even superior, service to their customers. They do not experiment with bold new theory. Rather, they apply important lessons distilled from the best practice of American organizations that have begun to master ways to create high-quality customer service. In federal government agencies, widespread efforts are under way to carry out the vice president's mandate to make the government customer friendly.

Organizations of government, as is done in industry, have begun to use focus surveys that ask customers how they view their organizations' services. Employees are being trained to ask what problems their customers encounter and how they would like services improved. In a number of agencies the service goal is very high, equal to the best in business.

Focus on Process Reengineering

Another important development is the attention to redesigning processes as the basis for greater customer satisfaction, with less time, cost, and effort. Proving to be so valuable in business, process reengineering is widely applicable in the government and nonprofit organization. Originally heralded as revolutionary thinking in the business literature, but now more modestly proclaimed as experience accumulates, process reengineering revives, builds on, and substantially improves widely successful programs of procedural workflow analysis and work simplification so prominent in the federal government after World War II.

A New Age of Electronic Management

Government and gradually the nonprofit sector have begun to borrow the lessons and experience of industry in the acquisition and use of state-of-the-art information technology. Already achieved is a record of significant improvements in breaking time barriers in processing and transaction times, rendering easier access to valuable financial and performance data, communicating more easily between and among employees and customers, and generating savings.

New Thinking about High-Level Governance

Another shift is the new thinking about high-level governance. Increasingly recognized in the literature is the imperative that top leadership become less focused on the short term and more visionary, if the organization is to be effective in an era of rapid change and severe financial stringency.

Changes in Organizational Structures

Organizational arrangements are substantially changing. Pressures for faster change dictate reductions in decision response time, faster processing of services, and an ease of access to data among units, employees, and outside customers and suppliers.

Responsive patterns of organization are coming into wide use. Their visible characteristics are:

—flatter structures with fewer levels and a less pyramidal hierarchy that moves decision-making down closer to the scene of operations and accommodates the trend to empower employees to make more of their own decisions;

—fluid structures that are temporary and shifting; they take the form of time-limited projects and teams, alliances, and joint ventures. More often, staffing arrangements include temporaries, part-timers, flex-timers, and contractors. The changing structures all encourage flexibility to accommodate the need for constant adaptation to a changing and often hostile environment; and

—process-driven structures that focus on lateral integration and improvement of sequential activity. They enable the working together of units and individuals on processes in pursuit of quality, cost-effectiveness, and customer satisfaction.

Reconciling Tension between Creativity and Control

Organizations are learning to reconcile the tension between fostering innovation and creativity and the processes of control. Many organizations are broadening the traditional approaches of diagnostic control systems of the 1950s and 1960s to include a blend with less intrusive levers of control.

The Building of Learning Organizations

Another development is the effort to move beyond traditional program evaluations for learning from experience. Many organizations create what are being called "continuous learning organizations" that are better able to adapt to changing circumstances and implement strategic guidance.

UNDERLYING BELIEFS: A NEW PARADIGM EMERGING

Fundamental to the new pattern for strategic and managerial thinking and action in the public and nonprofit world are several basic beliefs—call them guiding premises—that are establishing a new mind-set about government and the nonprofit organization and their relationships.

Government Has a Role to Play

The president's State of the Union message to Congress on January 23, 1996, pronounced that "to improve the state of our Union, we must ask more of ourselves; we must expect more of each other, and we must face our challenges together. The era of big government is over. But we cannot go back to the time when our citizens were left to fend for themselves." The key, he believes, is that the "federal government should give people the tools and try to establish the conditions in which they can make the most of their own lives" (*New York Times*, October 8, 1996).

Fundamentally government can be used to strengthen the institutions of a civil society. But "good" government reflects the times and serves as an effective catalyst for response to a series of crises—political, economic, and moral—that confront the country (Dionne 1996). Government is vital especially in periods of confluence of "social change, moral crisis, and great economic dislocation and distress." These crises provoke problems that society faces and cannot resolve as individuals or separate institutions. Government need not always be the initiator or the complete response, but it can serve as collaborative partner.

Problems can be an inadequate quality of education; the high cost and lack of affordable access to health care; burgeoning disease rates; widespread distress from excessive unemployment or underemployment; the advent of global warming, toxic waste, and environmental degradation; military and social security; consumer protection; work and food safety; opposition to the subordination of government to corporate or other special interests; and "safety nets" for the most vulnerable in society. To solve these and other problems people must work together; government is a catalytic mechanism that offers potential fairness and integrity in doing so for all the people.

But government cannot seek to do everything for everyone. Recent thinking ascribes to government a prescribed role—some prefer to call it a limited role. As President Clinton proclaimed, "We can't look to government to solve all our problems. . . . We must know the limits of what government can do, as well as what government must do" (*New York Times*, December 12, 1992).

Congressional law and political and public pressure compel government limitations. In response to budget deficits and low public confidence in how it works, government has deleted and curtailed programs—even popular ones—restrained bold and expensive program initiatives, and struggles to assist somewhat those most deprived and left behind.

The essential focus is not on how to eliminate government, although it can be smaller and leaner, but how to achieve "good government" closer to the people and more responsive to their desires and needs.

Government exists to serve the people. It can be said that government works well when government decisions and rules and their execution are fair and just for all; when efforts to provide services are productive, effective, and efficient; and when its effort to resolve or ameliorate political, economic, and moral crises are effective. The true test is the popular satisfaction and well-being of the people; key values to achieve and sustain are trust, credibility, and competence.

How Government Works Is a Problem; It Must Do Better

Currently, lack of confidence in our governmental institutions is at an unacceptable level. True, some measure of cynicism toward government, with its horror stories in the press about ineptitude, are part of our American heritage, almost as American as apple pie. Unfortunately, dramatized newspaper items of waste generate grossly exaggerated images of governmental stupidity and broadscale waste. The criticism is vented at the people in government—its "faceless and mindless bureaucrats"—not at its systems, incentives, and ways of operating. But people are not sufficiently aware of current efforts to "reinvent government" and "transform the nonprofit" that introduce tested management strategies for total quality management, enhanced customer satisfaction, streamlining, and reengineering. The evidence testifies that the effort is seriously under way, with substantial progress.

Government Downsizing and Enabling Others to Do More

More often, governments are deciding to "steer, not row," and to assume the responsibility for providing services but to let others do the actual operations. Governments slim down as they learn to make the transition "from doing to enabling others" in a new downsizing mode that makes extensive use of private nonprofit entities and often of profit-seeking organizations as well.

Governments are sharpening their managerial ability to decide what services are needed and calculate their specific performance and cost requirements; they can decide whether it is more cost-effective and efficient to outsource or privatize and use external resources. More often, governments have begun to use competitive bidding for cost-effective outsourcing and contracting; they are better able to authorize and quickly deliver funds to collaborating contractors. They are learning to better monitor performance outcomes, although greater competence in supervising contractor outcomes will be necessary. Not all contracted-out activities have proved to be satisfactory, and some have been reversed.

A Professionalizing Nonprofit Sector

What is often overlooked in America's mixed economy is the rapid growth in size and professional capacity of the third sector—the non-profits—called by some the "independent sector." Nonprofit institutional resources are being tapped as partners and collaborators to decentralizing governments in the financing and delivery of human services, largely through contractual devices.

A sizable nonprofit sector now plays a significant role in financing and delivering social services. The sector has grown at a rapid pace, with thousands of new organizations emerging each year. The nonprofit organizations designated tax exempt by the IRS have increased in number to more than one million. This compares to the number of private organizations, about three million. The best estimates indicate employment of from 7.9 to 10.3 million paid workers, supplemented by a volunteer unpaid work force amounting to the equivalent of another 5.7 to 6.7 million workers. Though nonprofits own only 1.8 percent of the nation's assets, the numbers compare favorably with the 3.9 percent of federally owned assets and with the 8.5 percent of government-owned assets when you include state and local government (Hodgkinson et al., 1992b).

The professional growth of the nonprofit sector is remarkable in the last decade, with a proliferation of more than twenty-six academic centers, numerous professional national and international associations, and some nonprofit-friendly commercial publishers. You can find a series of professional journals and sizable consulting practices and teaching programs that meet the market tests of numerous clients and students.

Most significant is that the greater reliance of government on the non-profit sector is a global phenomenon, with diverse descriptions around the world, including third-party government, the enabling state, nonprofit federalism, indirect public administration, or the social economy. Whatever the designation, we witness the emergence of human services provided within the pluralism of diverse institutional forms in mixed economies of government, private, and nonprofit sectors.

The professional nonprofit sector has opened its windows to the world's experience. The new international research movement of the global community, with institutional arrangements such as the International Society for Third-Sector Research and its official journal *Voluntas*, provides an additional dimension to understanding the crucial social issues of our time and how they are being resolved (Hodgkinson et al., 1992a).

Moving toward the Synergy of a Trilateral Framework

In the twenty-first century, the emerging model of collaboration among federal, state, and local governments, working with a growing nonprofit sector, offers the potential of significant advantage for all parties. The promise is for greater service satisfaction, higher levels of quality, and cost-effective savings, despite the serious constraints of an era of limits with financial stringency and rapid change.

Opening up are opportunities for resource and experience sharing, program experimentation in limited-risk pilot phases, joint use of capital-intensive new technology applications, and the elimination of waste and redundancy. But this can be accomplished only to the extent that modes of partnership are pragmatic, professional, and problem-solving and collaboration sufficiently prevails over partisan and parochial political advantage.

2

Strategic Management Explained

A QUICK VIEW OF STRATEGIC MANAGEMENT

Strategic management has emerged as the most modern form of planning in organizations. It has changed how organizations plan and implement their strategies, although the "ideal" of strategic management is only partially realized in even progressive organizations. Strategic management has become an essential tool for organizations to learn and develop if they wish to forge a state of excellence and respond constructively to a rapidly changing world. This is the main conclusion of the World Bank's survey of the experience of ninety organizations, which directly interviewed strategic planning managers and selected executives and consulting firms (Hanna 1985). Most of the organizations selected were in the private sector, where most of the development of strategic planning has taken place. But the findings emphasize concepts and practices essential to the effectiveness of both public and private organizations.

In essence, strategic management emphasizes an ongoing process that integrates strategic planning with other management systems. It employs a strategic planning process that is externally oriented, issue focused, and opportunity seeking. It entails active leadership that can direct organization-wide systems of strategic management and be capable of mastering the events and consequences of rapid change.

Strategic management stimulates decentralization and delegation within a strategic framework for longer-term guidance; it emphasizes line manager responsibility for strategic development and implementation. Staff planners act as advisors and facilitators to line executives who are the essential strategists. Strategy-oriented managers bridge the gap between planning and implementation with the adaptive use of program management methods that translate strategic intent into action and evaluate its results.

The practice of strategic management stems largely from private-sector corporate experience over the last several decades. Top management began to manage strategically when they realized they could not make big decisions affecting the future based only on today's operating practice. If they wished to keep up-to-date with the faster rate of change around them, they were compelled to search for key trends and issues in the environment. From analyses of real-world events and patterns, they began to detect threats and opportunities that required current decisions to be made for the future. Corporate leaders struggled to understand and create a clear vision of what the future could be; many undertook bold strategic initiatives to get there and were successful.

To do this effectively, top executives had to rise above their segmented experience and training in operational areas in order to understand the broader picture of what was going on. A single, narrow approach was no longer the route to success. It proved inadequate to depend solely on better financial planning or improved forecasting of growth for next year. Likewise, to concentrate solely on externally oriented planning or to seek responsiveness to markets proved necessary but were insufficient conditions to success.

Rather, strategic management seeks to use and merge all necessary approaches and resources to reach strategic goals. By definition and practice, strategic management is a broad concept: it embraces the entire set of managerial decisions and actions that determine the long-run performance of an organization. Essential to effective strategic management is a continuing decision process that conjoins an organization's internal capability with the opportunities and threats it faces in its environment as it pursues its strategic initiatives.

Current research reveals that the trend to strategic management abandons unstated goals and intuitive strategies; the central feature is the strategic plan. Researchers assert that, without prior assessment, strategies cannot be pursued successfully when an organization grows larger, its layers of management increase, or the environment changes substantially. Written strategic plans describing goals, values, and initiatives are now commonplace.

The greater use of strategic plans and processes has placed a greater emphasis on strategic factors in the evaluation of a manager's performance. Many senior managers now understand that unless they demonstrate their ability to think strategically, their future careers will be limited accordingly. A similar trend is the tendency to push more strategic management duties down the hierarchy into the hands of operating program executives and away from centralized strategic planning staffs.

What is emerging is a strategic program executive able to formulate or participate in strategic processes, plans, and initiatives that serve as a framework to guide the usual program management responsibilities. This capacity will prove to be a premium quality for modern program managers and executives.

Types of Strategy

The average organization has three types of strategy: (1) organization-wide or corporate, (2) program, or (3) resource support. Sometimes, a fourth type of strategy addresses institutional or administrative concerns.

Corporate Strategy. This answers the big questions of organization-wide concern about mission, goals, values, and new strategic initiatives. It stakes the boundaries of what we do for whom and the major directions we take to improve our overall performance.

Program Strategy. This explores the strategic implications of a particular program, often limited to choices about a specific service or product. Program strategy is also concerned with goals, values, and environmental issues. But the concern is only for their relevance to a particular bounded and defined program.

Resource Support Strategy. The principal focus of resource strategy is to maximize the supporting resources essential to achieving a quality level of performance. The resources may constitute budgeted funds (revenues or expenditures), human resources (program executives), and/or technology.

Institutional Strategy. This focuses on developing the organization's capability to carry out strategic initiatives. Such issues may range from computerization and systems of budgeting and evaluation to the attraction and retention of outstanding executives.

The four types of strategy are sometimes represented as a hierarchy. More important, they tend to interact with each other. They must be cohesive, integrated, in balance, and certainly not in basic contradiction if the organization is to be successful.

EVOLUTION OF STRATEGIC PLANNING

Back in the formative and groping 1960s, the term "strategic"—if it was used at all—was often meant by researchers and corporate managers to describe long-range, longer-term, or comprehensive planning. Of course, this was an aspect of strategic planning, but it was an incomplete description. Top management planners worked on top-level corporate or organization-wide decisions. They focused on decisions that were broad in scope, relating to the longer-term direction and focus of the company and the way it uses resources. Thus, in the 1960s the term "strategic" meant longer-range rather than short-term, top management level of concern, broad in scope, and significant to the whole organization.

Later, in the 1970s, the planning specialist flourished. Strategic planning began to develop a structure, staffing, and technique. In firms such as General Electric, which pioneered strategic planning, graduates from the business schools clustered in staff planning offices near the chief executive and helped him formulate and control strategy throughout the organization. They used highly quantitative techniques and developed strategic planning manuals that were detailed and voluminous. During the period of specialization, strategic planning began to focus on what happened outside the four walls of an organization. Experts began to reorient strategic planning in ways that emphasize the special relationship between an organization and its environment (Steiner 1979; Ansoff 1979; Ohmae 1982). Strategic analyses often read events and trends in the environment and made assumptions about what would likely occur. The strategists were looking for the environment's probable impact on an organization's internal decisions and operations as well as what to do to influence the environment. In business transactions, for example, strategic planning often focused on calculating and gaining competitive advantage. But in the public sector and in many nonprofit organizations, planning studies tend to analyze the environment to identify and assess the "needs" of targeted clientele groups and the appropriate "service delivery" to satisfy them. Often the issue is what we do for whom, what it will cost, and how we can do it better. In recent years of large public deficits, the question has often shifted from "What can we do?" to "What can we curtail or eliminate, and what will we save?" The climate of severely limited resources will plague us for many years.

FUNDAMENTAL SHIFT OF RESPONSIBILITY

Strategic planning and management, its thinking and practice as well as the role and power of its practitioners, is in a period of fundamental change. The movement of power is away from the professional planner, who for more than a decade held positions of great influence over the strategic plan or blueprint. The General Motors chairman who had originally established centralized strategic planning in 1971 decentralized the responsibility to the operating division manager. It was made clear that "planning is the responsibility of every line manager. The role of the planner is to be a catalyst for change, not to do the planning for each business unit." (*Business Week*, September 17, 1984, 62).

This fundamental shift in who does strategic planning and management and how it is being done is taking place all over corporate America. In company after company, the often extreme power of professional planners has been taken away by the managers. Grandiose blueprints for success have been shelved in favor of more practical approaches that respond to the environment. The insights of experienced managers are being considered, even when they cannot be fully supported by the evidence of quantitative techniques.

The trend is to cut back on the number of central planning staff, have smaller planning staffs report directly to operating units, and operate in what is considered a "support" function. The cutbacks in many corporations have been substantial. The cutbacks represent a drastic shift in the roles of central strategic planning units, who were accustomed to preparing a "blueprint" and then presenting it to the operating unit.

As operating managers have taken back the enormous power accumulated by professional planners, the semantics of strategic planning has changed. What had been labeled strategic planning is now broadened to the term "strategic management." This new label is defined most often as the "formulation and implementation of strategic plans, and the orchestration and carrying out of strategic activities of vital concern to the total organization." The newer term "strategic management" stresses three points: that the strategic planner is clearly the advisor and facilitator to line management decision-makers; that the program executive, not the strategic planner, is the key strategist; that strategic planning is always integrated with other functions of the program management process—program design, organizing, budgeting, staffing, controlling, and evaluating.

We find that strategic management embraces all the managerial problems that arise when strategic plans require actions in other functions of the management process. For example, new strategic initiatives usually require budgetary and staffing activity. The term "strategic management" makes it clear that the plan is incomplete until it is carried out and evaluated. Thus, under the strategic management mandate, managerial attention must place its day-to-day operations into the longer-term strategic context of its changing environment. This means developing internal structure and other managerial elements of institutional capability to support the new strategic initiatives brought about by specific changes in the organization's environment. The newer semantics of strategic management merely accommodates the idea that a strategic plan is a "paper tiger" until the program management executives can and are willing to do all the things necessary to get it implemented.

Why the Shift?

Why have operating managers begun to take back the enormous power accumulated by professional planners? The more philosophical among us may be right when they assert that the current shift is merely

the regular ebb tide of organization dynamics, in which power central-
izes for a time and then decentralizes in a continuous cycle. But there
are discernable reasons for the shift. Most convincing is the fact that there
have been too many failures of strategy. The documentation is extensive
on successful strategies that have failed. There are other reasons cited
for the drastic shift.

First, a new generation now exists of top executives who are strategic
thinkers and believe their key subordinates should be too.

Second, the excessive reliance on quantitative technique demands too
much effort, time, and cost, but has not yielded the timely results needed
to cope with fast-moving change. As planners relied excessively on quantitative technique, they grew more ignorant of the real world of customer
expectations. Managers felt planners did not give sufficient weight to
their experience, even though it could not always be supported by numbers.

Third, there is strong resistance to a planning bureaucracy by program
executives and deep resentment of being told what to do by those with
little practical experience who are not responsible for the end result. Operating managers resent the intrusion on their busy schedules by demands for numbers, papers, and data.

CHARACTERISTICS AND AIMS

Great confusion often exists about what really constitutes strategic
planning and management. Understandably, the adjective "strategic"
has different meanings to different people. Some persons, for example,
equate the word "strategic" with the word "important." This is easy to
understand when you see "strategic" describe the $600 million comput-
ing programs by the Defense Department for achieving world leadership
in supersmart and superfast computers in the twenty-first century. This
program is indeed important by virtue of its cost, size, and significance.
But many things can be strategic to an organization and yet not be so
large in scale and cost. Actually the adjective "important" is a useful but
incomplete description of things "strategic."

A useful approach is to define strategic management operationally in
terms of what it is, what it aims to do, and how it benefits the organization. Additionally, the phases of strategic management can be listed
to indicate their main interactive functions in sequential flow.

We explain strategic management operationally because we do not
wish to be overburdened with a precise definition in a situation that does
not possess an exact, universally accepted definition. The strategic planning expert George Steiner reminds us that Confucius is reported to have
said that if he were made ruler of the world, the first thing he would do
would be to fix the meaning of words, because action follows definition.

This is sage advice, says Steiner; but if he were ruler, he adds, the second thing he would do is warn his people that spending too much time quarreling about precise definitions in imprecise situations is wasteful and misleading.

Characteristics of Strategic Management

Five points that follow will help us better understand the nature of the strategic management process.

Strategic Management Is Oriented to the Future. It enables you to guide and direct the future. You do not have to "stay stuck in the mud" if the wrong decision was made or the right one omitted; perhaps external conditions changed drastically.

As a process, strategic management assesses the situation at hand, internally and externally, designs a desired future, and identifies initiatives to bring it about. Or, it can deal with the "futurity" of current decisions by examining the consequences over time of an actual or intended decision that a manager is about to make. If the manager does not like what is seen ahead, the decision can be modified.

Strategic management also looks at alternative courses of action that are open in the future and makes choices that become the basis for making current decisions. It identifies opportunities, threats, or constraints that lie in the future and provides the basis for decisions that exploit an opportunity or avoid or minimize threats or constraints.

Strategic management does not attempt to make decisions in the future; decisions can be made only in the present. But it can indicate "options" that are possible future choices. Nor does strategic management attempt to blueprint the future in fine detail. It never develops detailed plans that are set in stone, to be used without change into the far distant future.

Strategic Management Is a Way of Thinking and Behaving to Make a Difference. The strategic mentality is goal-oriented; it does not get bogged down in trivial detail. It accepts the commitment to plan for the future and not be solely preoccupied with the here and now. Shifting one's time frame from the present to the future, and back again, is a strategic skill that can be learned and reinforced with experience. The strategic mind copes with change; it shifts rapidly from problem to remedial action. It strives to make a difference.

Strategic planners and managers must understand that strategic planning is integral to the practice of management for improved performance results rather than feel it is an isolated end in itself. Managers must really believe strategic planning is worth doing, or at least keep an open mind about it, rather than resent it as an imposed unnecessary burden on already busy schedules.

In no way does strategic planning attempt to replace managerial experience and judgment. Rather, it has the common sense to include experienced judgment even when the issues or answers cannot be supported in precise quantitative terms.

Strategic Management Is Continuous and Recurring. Strategic management efforts cannot be a one-time or stop-and-start activity. It must be a continuous process that accumulates experience and improves itself. It is useful to perceive strategic management as an organized process of systematic learning and guided change. One key reason for continuity in the planning process is that it responds to external conditions that are in continual flux, and therefore its plans and instruments must be continuously updated and readjusted. Outdated plans are worse than no plans at all.

Strategic Management Sets a Framework for Guiding Other Phases of Management. This includes guidance to such managerial functions as program design, program budgeting, structure, human resource development, and evaluation. It provides guidelines to direct resources and talent into the highest priority activity.

Strategic planning does not do the actual operational or implementational planning, but it does produce the guiding basis for action by setting of goals, strategies, policies, values, and indicators and standards for overall progress.

Strategic Management Is Not Easy to Perform; It Is Difficult and Demanding. It demands an intellectual effort and much discipline. Required is the will and skill to select future courses of action rather than waiting for events and crises to push us into poorly considered action. Many times, the course of waiting—because we are uncertain of what to do— may make us too late for effective action or may incur substantial negative consequences.

Often the making of decisions rests on incomplete data and insufficient knowledge about what will happen in the future. Yet there are times— most times, it seems—when the making of a decision cannot await complete data or the data are unclear and ambiguous. Resolving these situations in which you must work with considered assumptions, best estimates, or even educated guesses certainly takes a great deal of courage, and indeed can be risky.

Then why do organizations make strategic plans if they are so demanding, uncertain, and risky? The obvious answer is that the process must be worthwhile if so many organizations do it, and more are beginning to start strategic planning and management programs. The increasing trend toward strategic management is clearly evident; training programs have vastly multiplied.

Though strategic management is more predominant in business organizations, more institutions in the public and private nonprofit sector have begun to base their program decisions on planned strategic goals and objectives and show greater concern for their environment and its impact on their future. Most feel that the payoff for strategic management is substantial. But, according to the experts, the major reason for the expansion of strategic management may be a negative one: The absence of strategic thinking and action allowed for too many mistakes.

Aims of Strategic Management: What It Seeks to Accomplish

Strategic management is a deliberate effort to put purpose into group effort. It assumes that individuals working together in groups want to know where they are going and what they are expected to accomplish when they get there. As one wise expert with a delightful sense of humor said, If you don't know where you are going, how will you know when you get there; and if you don't know what to do when you get there, why bother to go?

Of the many aims of strategic management, the following five are fundamental:

Provide Strategic Direction. Strategic management aims to do three things in setting strategic direction: (1) it sets goals to determine where you want to go and what initiatives you should pursue to get there; (2) it indicates where you wish to concentrate your resources and talent by setting your sights on key result areas; and (3) it gives necessary top-level and organization-wide visibility and attention to the goals and initiatives being pursued.

Guide Priority Use of Resources. Resource scarcity will always be with us. There would be little need for planning if human, financial, and material resources were unlimited. But in the real world, this is never so. Modern program managers must formulate their plans with the wise and intelligent use of limited resources strongly in mind. Our aim is to assign resources to their highest-priority use in areas that can return the greatest results.

Set Standards of Excellence. Strategic management gives program managers the means to set standards of excellence and create a culture of shared values. The use of indicators or measures of progress makes it easier to control and evaluate action taken and indicate when progress is being made or delayed. This facilitates and assures the effective implementation of strategic initiatives and programs.

Cope with Environmental Uncertainty and Change. Although we are constantly reminded that the only certainty is uncertainty, with the exception of death and taxes, we can never fully prepare for unexpected events. But planning methods can be helpful in reducing the risk inherent in future change and for better coping in contingencies. One can prepare to meet changing conditions and be in position to capitalize on opportunity or minimize negative effects.

Though many persons seem to be negatively conditioned against any effort at forward planning, most people tend to be favorably disposed. Actually, preparation for the future is built into our American folk culture and expressed in often-used phrases such as "saving for a rainy day" or the Boy Scout motto of "Be prepared."

Provide Objective Basis for Control and Evaluation. The essence of strategic management is to establish directional goals, new strategic initiatives, and indicators of progress. This makes it easier to guide the program, keep it on track, identify problems in a timely fashion, and measure progress of accomplishment. Without the planning effort to establish guideposts of where you want to go, how to get there, and how to be reasonably certain that you have arrived at the right place, there is no objective basis for control and evaluation. Without a systematic planning effort, every evaluation will have to formulate its goals, objectives, and indicators after events have taken place. This would certainly bias the evaluation findings and undermine the effectiveness of evaluation activities.

HOW IT PAYS OFF

Large corporations almost always have some type of systematic strategic planning and management process. Many public and nonprofit agencies now use them, though their degrees of formality, flexibility, and simplicity may differ. The reasons that organizations initiate strategic management, of course, will differ from organization to organization as circumstances and personalities vary. But there are primary reasons why strategic planning and management pay off.

Discharges the Most Important Top Management Responsibility

Top managers must make strategic decisions about which problems or issues to confront and what service and product they will provide and to whom. They do this either by an intuitive "seat of the pants" reckoning or by more formal and deliberate analytical processes. In the larger corporations, top managers testify that they cannot do without some sort of systematic planning process. This type of strategy planning is equally important in the public and nonprofit realm.

Sharply Asks and Answers Questions of Major Importance

Strategic management deliberately asks and answers the key questions facing an organization in an orderly way with a sense of priority and urgency. Key questions include:

—What business are we in?

—What is our vision of the future?

—What are our underlying purposes, directions, and values?

—What do we do best?

—Who are our target clientele?

—How well are we performing? Do we have top-quality performance?

—Are we satisfying our key interests?

—Where do we want to go—in service, target group, or quality?

—How does the changing environment affect us? What changes in our decisions or operations are indicated?

—What opportunities or threats exist that we should exploit or avoid? What weaknesses should be corrected?

—Are we productive and effective in what we do?

—Do we learn from lessons of experience?

These questions are always difficult to answer. But data-supported answers, rather than "hunches," are an urgent necessity in order to succeed. Assumptions and even instincts are essential guides, but they must be tested and verified.

A rapidly changing environment is often a major factor in influencing the introduction of formal strategic planning and management in many organizations. It is obvious that we are living through a period when change in the basic modes of how we behave and work are in rapid flux—from changes in lifestyle and longevity to computerization and information technology. Large organizations feel that the changing times demand the use of strategic management to give their managers a better understanding of the complex world in which they must operate and to calculate the best ways to respond. This is also true for smaller organizations in the public and nonprofit sector, where time and resources are so limited and where time-sparing and simplified methods for strategic management are so vital.

Introduces a New Set of Tools for Making Decisions

Strategic management introduces some important decision-making tools:

Compels the Setting of Directional Goals and Objectives. Setting goals and objectives are a powerful and positive influence in improving group effort. They help individuals and groups know what is expected of them. If they participate in setting them, they will tend to "own them" and thus strive harder to accomplish them.

Aids in Reading the Future. Strategic management emphasizes reading trends of what the future may bring and poses a series of optional but alternative choices about a desired future on paper. One can calculate on paper the consequences of each option without the actual investment of either time or money or both.

Reveals Future Opportunities and Constraints. Strategic management identifies opportunities and constraints as part of its strategic situation audit. This enables the program executive to mesh experience and intuition with the systematic collection and analysis of data.

Uses the Essence of the Systems Approach

Strategic management looks at an organization as a system composed of many component parts. It enables top management to perceive the organization as a whole and the interrelationship of its parts rather than working with each part separately. This perception of the whole organization is important because each part of the organization does not necessarily contribute to the best total program. Some parts may be in conflict or competition with others; there may be gaps that diminish the best solution. For example, an excellent service may not reach its clientele because it depends upon another part of the organization for its delivery or servicing.

The systems approach also enables the application of a "synergistic effect," where combining and interacting two or more programs may provide a result greater than the outcome of both if handled separately. The common definition of the synergistic effect is "when 2+2 equals 5."

Forces More Objective Performance Assessment

Strategic management depends heavily on an objective assessment of performance. You must know where you are going before you can get there. Likewise, you must know where you are and how well you are doing before you can plan for the future. All this depends on a solid basis of goals, objectives, and indicators for sound assessment.

Exerts Positive Influence on Organizational Behavior

Strategic management provides a payoff to the behavior of the organization and its staff in several ways.

Communications Are Improved. The strategic management process rests on a flow of communications through the organization, as assessments are made and goals and strategies are formulated, reviewed, approved, and disseminated.

Managerial Training Is Improved and Opportunity Is Increased. Strategic management is a useful managerial training and development process that enables managers to know what is most important to an organization and what they have to know and do to make a greater contribution. Of course, making a greater contribution to an organization is an effective and dramatic path to higher responsibility and reward, with greatly enhanced career potential.

Greater Sense of Participation and Belonging. The process of participating in strategic efforts with other key executives who determine major directions and initiatives can provide a large measure of satisfaction and motivation. Modern managers tend to have a strong feeling for "being in on" the decision-making process that affects their future and determines what they must accomplish to make a contribution to the organization. This process opens up opportunities for a broad spectrum of executives and their staffs to be creative and be recognized for their contributions.

Part 2

APPROACHES TO
STRATEGIC
LEADERSHIP

3

Chief Executive as General Manager of Strategy

FORGING STRATEGIC CAPABILITY

Chief executives increasingly accept the responsibility for developing their entire organization's strategic capability. More leaders have begun to realize that an organization cannot be successful unless the chief executive gives strong, consistent support to effective strategic performance and makes sure that others in the organization understand the depth of his or her commitment. No longer can leaders sit back passively and allow changing events to engulf and endanger their organizations without disastrous consequences. This concern for strategic capability is beginning to emerge strongly in both the public and the nonprofit organization, whose performance record is not often known for its rapid and effective response to change.

Leaders of public and tax-exempt nonprofit organizations—whose primary function is to provide service to society—are being compelled to deal with the changing demands placed upon them by boards, legislatures, or clients. Doing so requires the strategic capability of whole organizations—no longer just a few individuals at the top. Thus, a chief executive becomes a "general manager of strategy," a position in which he or she deals with the management of a multitude of strategies that are formulated, executed, and evaluated throughout the organization. This is done with the aid of a host of managerial instruments: systems, task forces, meetings and forums, decision and policy support structures, and strategic plans. Long gone is the tendency of the chief executive and a few trusted aides to withdraw into an environment of isolation to master technical data and then come forth with strategic pronouncements.

Today, the pattern is for organizational heads to manage an organization-wide strategic process whereby the prescribed rules of the game are set by those who run the strategic management system. The challenge is to use strategic process as a potent means to institutionalize strategic thinking and action throughout the organization.

In the past, top general management often stressed the "minimal management concept" that evolved from the decentralization of managerial authority that swept American industry in the 1950s. This concept was that general management should delegate the maximum possible amount of work to operating levels. This was valid for its time when overcentralized, top-heavy hierarchies were the general rule. But accelerated rates of change demand faster response from institutions. Increased turbulence in the environment and the growing size and complexity of problems and pressures compel that decentralized program operations be accompanied by an increase in strategic work by general management.

Strategic activity and its management will continue to flourish, say some cynical management experts, because the idea of having a strategy is intriguing and fashionable. It suggests that preparatory work has been set for taking positive action against a known problem or opportunity. For many it promotes the illusion that events are under control. At a minimum, "having a strategy" implies that action is part of a coherent scheme that is based on an analysis of the entire situation. Realistically, strategy-taking in institutional settings has distinct limitations:

—the weakness or uncertainty of an organization's capability to mount and sustain a strategic initiative;

—the unfriendliness and unpredictability of hostile environments;

—the distinct possibility the strategy will not work for a variety of unanticipated reasons; and

—the concern that putting strategic initiatives into a long-term written plan may overlook unanticipated threats or opportunities.

Meaning of the Term "Chief Executive"

The term "chief executive" means the person who has the authority to manage an organization or a major component thereof. This authority may rest in one individual—such as the president or executive director—or it may be shared with a deputy or executive vice president. The organizational leader may be labeled director, chair, or head. Rarely in hospitals, universities, or art museums is the designation "manager" or "executive" used, although sometimes "administrator" is acceptable.

Managerial designations may actually be resented by professionals, even though much of their responsibility may be managerial.

The Dimensions of Strategic Capability

By strategic capability we mean the measure of effectiveness by which an environment-serving organization launches and supports particular strategic initiatives. The term "strategic capacity" refers to the volume of strategic thrusts that can be handled by an organization. The amount of strategic work that can be handled is determined by the significance of the new initiatives, the number of initiatives to be undertaken, the size of the strategic budget, and its risk to the success of the organization's future.

General management usually concerns itself with developing strategic capability in three dimensions:

Strategic Intentions toward the Future. This seeks to clarify the organization's mission, set strategic directions, shape shared values, and undertake specific strategic initiatives.

Strategic Decisions. These are the choices regarding elements of strategic thrust, whether it concern strategic directions or the launching of new initiatives.

Strategy-Implementing Actions. These are the program activities taken to implement strategic initiatives, as well as the institutional or administrative actions necessary to support the carrying out of strategic initiatives.

In effect, the main instrument for forging these dimensions of strategic capability in an organization lies in the design and operation of the strategic management system, with its central feature, the strategic plan.

NEED FOR HELP FROM ENTIRE ORGANIZATION

No doubt exists that the chief executive has prime responsibility for strategic planning and management. Equally obvious is that chief executives constantly face time constraints in their performance of a variety of tasks. They are busy people serving in many roles of both substance and ceremony. They serve as leaders of plans, people, and performance. They design the future and struggle to make it a reality, while working hard to reconcile conflict and dissolve resistance. They innovate, and then run around to mobilize resources to pay for it. In effect, they do what is necessary to get an impossible job done.

Despite harassing schedules, most chief executives accept that strategic planning and management is their prime responsibility. Of course, chief executives can and do share and delegate strategic planning and management to a chief strategic planner and key operating executives in order to obtain their special expertise and information. But the ultimate responsibility must remain with the chief executives. They must be the chief strategists and the builders of an organization's strategic capability. Only the chief executive has the power of decision to make major commitments of approval and resource; only people at the top have the overall perspective on an organization's performance in order to blend all components into a cohesive whole. Thus, a chief executive's need for help on strategic management is a function of compensating for limited time and gaining the advantage of specialized expertise and data from others in the organization or from qualified consulting arrangements.

Some particular types of help include:

a. The designation and role delineation of a chief strategic planner and staff who can assist in matters of substance, as well as in the design and operation of a strategic management system.

b. The design and operation of a user-friendly, innovation-producing strategic management system that institutionalizes strategic thinking and action as an accepted means of doing business in a self-sustaining way and empowers people to innovate in steady fashion.

c. The use of specially designed structures for policy and technical support located close to the chief executive, which can contribute to improved decision-making.

d. The use of teams or task forces, with participants drawn from wherever available in the organization, who possess the skills and expertise appropriate to an assigned task.

e. The use of small strategy starts that are lower investments and less risky, to "learn-as-you-go" and to get moving faster in new directions. These are akin to the pilot, test, or demonstration projects that have long been used in management systems, but their substance and mode of operation and evaluation is designed to help launch and support new strategic initiatives. The use of small strategy starts is a practical approach to setting up a working minilaboratory to provide real-life experience to a strategic concept at minimal cost and risk.

f. The creation and use of an in-house strategic-support consulting service that can provide advisory services to program executives at headquarters or to field offices and local chapters and affiliates. Some organizations charge reasonable fees for their internal consultative services to local chapters.

PLAYING MULTIPLE ROLES

No longer can leaders be solely concerned with the technical data and skills for making and managing strategy; they must also master the social skills for anticipating and producing constructive change. This means being skillful with people, vision, and values, as well as with systems and structures.

This expanded view of leadership by the chief executive, as manager of strategy, is carefully translated into an integrated set of performance roles. This creates the right mind-set, namely, fuller commitment and clear expectation of what is necessary at the top to achieve effective strategic management. The roles are listed and summarized. The remainder of this book serves to put forth the remedies and instruments that enable the chief executive and the organization to carry out the designated strategic performance roles with the greatest effectiveness.

Realistically, not all chief executives are aware of the multiple leadership roles required for effective strategic management of an organization. Nor are all chief executives comfortable and competent in their roles that deal with strategic issues and decisions. Some are particularly uneasy about being reflective and philosophical about corporate values and culture. Others obviously prefer the concreteness of operational actions and the quicker satisfactions of accomplishment in the short term.

The listing of roles that are indicated for the effective strategic leader is formidable and their performance almost impossible, as judged by the comments of astute, experienced observers. Summarized are some roles that constitute a comprehensive though idealized pattern of action that is desirable to move toward.

Architect of a Clear Vision of the Future

This role attempts to create the future by defining mission and setting directional goals in ways that impel individuals and organizations to pursue them aggressively. It answers key questions such as :

—Why are we here?
—Where are we, realistically?
—Where do we want to go?
—How do we get there?
—What do we want to change?
—What do we do for whom?

Visions, to be realistic, should be compelling, challenging but somewhat achievable, future-oriented, and "lived"—not just declared in a burst of rhetoric.

Molder of Organization's Values into Corporate Culture

This role involves the clear definition of an organization's values and beliefs and the doing of all the things necessary to assure that the organization operates by them. Most organizations profess a set of values,

but only a minority are able to share values among large numbers of
employees so that they are able to render outstanding quality service
over time. For a strong culture of values in an organization to be effective, it must be supported by commitment to common goals, competence
to deliver superior performance, response to external threat and opportunity, and consistency over time.

Key questions to answer include:

—Which values prevail and determine the organization's behavior?

—Do they work for the organization, or do they serve as serious constraints?

—What do we want to do about them?

—How do we go about it?

Director of System for Strategic Management

This role focuses on the prime task of forging the organization's strategic capability. It seeks to make strategic management an accepted way
of doing business. It ensures that an effective system for strategic management is designed and operated with its central feature of producing
and implementing a strategic plan. It ensures that the system is flexible,
innovative, user-friendly, and capable of expanding the access of ideas
to the tools of power: approval, resources, and expertise.

It further ensures that the system produces sound strategic decisions
with executive support and seeks to resolve conflict and resistance. It
enables the chief executive to be the chief decider of prime strategies and
be definitely "in charge."

It recognizes the imperative to establish a competent chief strategic
planner with adequate staff and to give them support to provide strategic assistance to all areas of the organization, not just to the chief executive.

Sage of the Environment

This role focuses on the organization searching the environment for
threats and opportunities. It involves detecting external forces, trends,
and issues and analyzing them for strategic implications that could have
an impact on internal decisions and operations.

It requires concerted effort to link with and establish contacts with key
actors and institutions in the community that need to be mobilized in
various ways to improve the performance profile.

This role also reflects the need to gain insight and knowledge of the
industry to which the organization belongs in such matters as its eco-

nomic and other behavioral characteristics, major trends, innovative thrusts, and common constraints.

Mobilizer of Major Resources

This role concerns big money, key persons, and major clients. It means attracting and retaining adequate financial support; it involves attracting, developing, and retaining outstanding executive personnel. New modes of leadership compel the chief executive to pay greater attention to people in efforts to empower them to be more innovative and give their best. This includes making the organization a great place to work in which the organizational staff climate enables all persons to realize their highest potential.

Ultimate Guardian of Top-Quality Performance

This significant role makes the chief executive the ultimate guardian for the organization's success. With the strategic vision and plan clearly in mind, the chief executive ensures that the systems of program control and evaluation work to indicate exactly where the organization stands with regard to its performance and success. Emphasis is placed on organized learning of the lessons of experience and maintaining a continuous thrust for constant improvement.

GETTING PERSONALLY INVOLVED—VISIBLY

The key to effective strategic management is to get the chief executive directly involved in the system. Some say the key executives and the people around them must make all the main strategic decisions with appropriate staff and organizational support, of course.

Generally, the chief executive tends to be more involved with strategic management when it is first introduced. But it is important to keep the chief executive involved consistently and to make the participation visible to others so as to display interest, concern, and commitment.

Chief executives should meet face-to-face with the key members of the management team to discuss their strategic plans, main initiatives, and the key issues of concern. This job should not be left to budget or planning directors, although they have a strong role to play in the strategic management system and can help plan for making the meetings productive.

An important aspect of getting involved personally is the two-way need for information about what is really happening. Getting "around and about" to ask pointed questions is very useful; chief executives should be prepared to listen and learn, as well as to serve direct notice

of essential values and concerns for excellence. Needed are communication mechanisms—whether they be seminars, meetings, forums, or
even memoranda and e-mail—to acquaint staff with top management's
views and reactions to the state of strategic affairs. An important component of the communication thrust—to inform executives of strategic
plans and thrusts and to gain their response and reaction—is the physical presence of the chief executive or high members of the staff at scheduled and well-publicized events.

A common theme of strategic communication—however it is expressed—is that strategic management is the route to excellence and success, both for the corporation and the individual. It is urgent that chief
executives put a personal imprint on the introduction and direction of a
new strategic management system. They must promote broad executive
participation in the design and operation of the system through task
groups and self-managing teams set up to deal with specific tasks or
problems. Additionally, the chief executive should be personally visible
in the granting of incentives and awards for successful strategic activity,
particularly in the event of open award ceremonies.

ESTABLISHING A PROPER CLIMATE FOR STRATEGIC MANAGEMENT

If the atmosphere of an organization is hostile to managing strategically, having an extensive pattern of doing things differently in longer
time frames, then strategic management is bound to fail. Chief executives
have a strong responsibility to ensure that key executives have a congenial and positive attitude toward strategic management in its response
to change and that they clearly understand what is involved.

Executives must be made aware of the longer-term implications of the
constraints and opportunities in the changing environment. They must
be made to realize that shallow thinking and "quick-fix" solutions are
not acceptable. Deadlines and resource allocations must be shaped accordingly.

Chief executives can be most helpful in impressing upon staff some
key requirements that strategic management imposes upon an organization, such as:

—the imperative to define a clear and confident view of the future, even when
   the situation is murky;

—a willing capacity to accommodate change and to be able to do things differently—often;

—the ability to be operationally pragmatic while in pursuit of an inspiring vision
   and not to be blinded ideologically;

—the ability to reconcile conflict and differences, and to work with others in teams in the pursuit of common goals;

—the continuous quest for constant improvement;

—the realization by each executive that strategic management is an integral part of the management job, not something done by those strategic planning specialists; and

—that the reward system provide incentives for executives to engage successfully in strategic work.

The chief executive should deliberately take steps to mute or change opposition and bias toward strategic management and seek to explain and convert to the strategic management cause. Many staff who resist formal strategic management give a number of operational reasons for their objections. They often say:

—"I don't have enough time to get ready for tomorrow's hectic schedule, so how do you expect me to prepare for the next three to five years?"

—"Strategic planning and management is too damn complicated."

—"Why should I do it when my division is doing fine?"

—"It's just too much extra paperwork."

But the chief executive should recognize there are more fundamental causes of opposition to strategic management. For example, strategic management highlights competing demands for resources. In some situations, the real pressure of solving immediate operating problems drives out efforts to take longer-term positions. Planning for the future involves great risk and uncertainty. Most executives would rather deal with shorter-term operating problems with which they are more competent and assured of handling well. It is hard for most executives to give up the known for the unknown.

4

Chief Executive as Master of Change

SUCCESSFULLY MEETING THE CHALLENGE OF CHANGE

The new view of leadership stops looking back at the "good old days," accepts the inevitability of rapid, often unexpected change, and does something constructively. A guiding concept is this: Position yourself to anticipate change, and become adept at inducing constructive change that can make a difference for your organization. Learn to recognize that the disruption and chaos ensuing from rapid change need not be hostile to your interests. Change can be converted to advantage—not easily, but many organizations and their top leaders have done so. They demonstrate the ability to absorb the shock from having to shift to new ways of doing things in response to a turbulent, changing environment. They foster innovation; they are able to expand the access of ideas to the tools of power; they seem to be masters of change.

That is why Peters (1988) emphasizes the importance of "learning to love change" and the excitement and exultation of working with new and different things. He proposes that everyone be evaluated on the question, "What have you changed lately?" and proposes creating a sense of urgency for change throughout the organization.

A caution to keep in mind: Emphasis on the urgency for change can produce a "whirling dervish" syndrome in which everyone works hard to be different. But the constant change may be in trivial activity and not add up to being strategically significant to the organization. The challenge is to ask the question, "Change for what; so what?" and ensure that the answer addresses prime strategic concerns that make a difference.

Most of the study of strategic planning and management focuses on the substance of what strategy to change and the process of how to do it. What is now apparent is that substance and process are necessary but insufficient for implementing strategy effectively. Now recognized is the need also to pay close attention to the behavior of leaders as they react and respond to the environmental turbulence of rapid change.

WAYS OF RESPONDING TO ENVIRONMENTAL CHANGE

Escalation of Turbulence

Growing turbulence in the environments of public and nonprofit organizations substantially affects their strategic behavior and decisions. Never before has America confronted such huge budget deficits that so severely constrain desired public expenditures. Nor have changing lifestyles ever before threatened so many of our creative youth with the scourge of AIDS, as yet with no known cure. Meanwhile, the abuse of drug substances seriously affects our urban crime rates and fills our prisons. Never before did high technology of healthcare for an increasing number of elderly citizens cost so much, and the need for high technology for the military reaches astronomical proportions. None of our public and nonprofit institutions is immune from the serious effects of environmental change.

Many organizations are now aware that the turbulent events of environmental change display discernible patterns: novelty, speed, predictability, and complexity.

Novelty. Many changes reflect a great newness or novelty in that they have not occurred before in human history. If a change has happened before, there is precedent and knowledge for handling it. But if the change is new, the response time for its treatment takes much longer. But many organizations now seek to develop the strategic capability to anticipate and deal with new responses to new environmental changes.

Speed. Many changes occur with an increased speed of unfolding and tend to grow rapidly in geometric proportions. The expansion of information explodes. The abuse of drug substances has become most pervasive at all levels of society and in almost all geographical regions.

Predictability. Many changes are predictable in occurrence and consequence. As changes occur in the environment they generate available knowledge. Over time and with diligent surveillance, it becomes increasingly clear what are the threatening implications or the possibilities of opportunity. The sensitivity for predicting change is not universal or even widespread. But experts do exist and can be identified. Futurists—those who work to understand and anticipate the future—and their organizations are on the rise, as evidenced by the World Futures Society.

Complexity. Many changes represent a high degree of complexity in that they are difficult and time consuming to analyze and respond to. The drug dilemma is a clear example of complexity in that it represents so many variables, most of which are beyond the control of the responsible agencies in or outside of government.

Scale of Turbulence

Ansoff (1979) describes the turbulence of the environment with a scale of change that indicates its nature in terms of its rate of transition, for example:

—steady turbulence, in which the environment remains in a particular pattern for some time;

—shift in turbulence, which is a rapid transition from one pattern to another; or

—drift in turbulence, in which there is a gradual shift from one pattern to another.

These several scales of turbulence provide insightful clues to response possibilities. Threatening situations, for example, may be brewing for a long time before being perceived and may unfold slowly over time, like the "greenhouse effect," the gradual warming of the atmosphere. Many scientists predict the greenhouse effect will cause the temperature of the earth's atmosphere to rise within a century to levels unreached in human experience. A report prepared for the Energy Department warned that carbon dioxide emissions—the largest single cause of global warming—would rise by 38 percent by 2010 if nothing was done. The knowledge of the gradual shift provides sufficient time perspective to mobilize the American response and to hold international conferences under the auspices of the United Nations Environmental Program to consider major global efforts to alleviate the situation.

Pressures for Strategic Response

A key strategic concern of chief executives and their policy-makers in modern organizations is whether, when, and how to respond to changing events of environmental turbulence and, of course, how much and with what expectation of accomplishment for the resources expended. These leaders are subject to many diverse pressures—political, social, technological, or economic. In a democracy, pressures may arise from anywhere, inside or outside the organization. They may be manifest by boards, legislatures, presidents or citizens, the scientific community, or executives or clients. Or, the impetus to respond may result from the understanding of significant issues raised in the strategic management process of various public or nonprofit organizations and then analyzed and responded to in an orderly manner.

Modes of Response Vary among Organizations

Organizations, like individuals, tend to react to change in a variety of ways. Management observers often comment on the extreme responses, such as organizations that are restless and aggressive in continuously seeking to maximize their strengths and success. They move from success to success, while adjusting to a crisis or adversity that confuses or paralyzes others. Others are passive, not quickly reacting to events, if at all, often waiting for a bit more data, and generally lurching from one event or crisis to another. An in-between mode is the adaptive organization that reacts to existing problems and develops strategies to move ahead in small, incremental ways.

These oversimplified extremes have given way to more penetrating analysis of an organization's strategic response behavior. Some key questions are asked:

Response Time Perspective. How does an organization respond to perceived threat or opportunity? Quickly, slowly, or not at all?

Change Propensity. How strong a signal is needed to trigger significant change?

Discontinuity Tolerance. How much deviation from past experience is acceptable from among action options for change?

Focus of Attention. How much attention and response is accorded to triggering internal or external events, including budget magnitudes?

Type of Response Behavior. How does the organization respond to external turbulence? Does it maintain a passive posture, at one extreme, with response limited to repetition of past experience? Or does the organization take a creative posture, at the other extreme, with the development of novel initiatives, never before tried?

Ansoff's Construct of Response Behavior

The work of Ansoff (1979) classifies the characteristics that best describe the common thread or pattern of an organization's strategic response behavior in serving its environment. Five categories of a profile are used: stable, reactive, anticipating, exploring, and creative. The first two are primarily backward looking; the other three are progressively future oriented and tend to have many similar characteristics. The latter group requires a high order of social skills.

Ansoff indicates that the strategic responsibility of general or top management is to be "tuned and responsive to the ambient environment, to identify and understand quickly the implications for change, to determine courses of action and guide their implementation."

Although organizations tend to display distinct behavioral patterns in their mode of strategic response, different strategic initiatives may require various modes other than the organization's usual pattern. For example, environmental events that trigger the "greenhouse effect" can only be met with forward-looking, creative, anticipating, and exploring modes of response. But events that trigger problems that are known, with known solutions, can be met with backward-looking, stable, or reactive responses and existing data.

The categories of the Ansoff profile of strategic response include:

Stable. This one tends to continue doing what the organization has been doing. Its problem-solving mode is primarily backward-looking. It looks to data of the past and past precedents. Its action mode is to repeat familiar experiences. Alternatives are considered one at a time, evaluated by past experience, and tested in practice. If the test fails, another alternative is introduced. The process stops after the first success—a problem-solving characteristic Herb Simon calls "satisficing." This satisfies adequately the immediate problem but offers no assurance that the best solution has been found.

Reactive. This one tends to make only small, incremental changes in doing things. It also looks to data of the past. Its problem-solving mode is to seek to correct deficiencies through systematic analysis of causes. The process is also typically "satisficing."

Anticipating. This one tries to predict problems. It is an analytic process in which an effort is made to identify all possible alternatives. The probable outcomes of the alternatives are analyzed, and the best is selected on the basis of explicit criteria. It bases the future on past trends using long-term planning and budgeting.

Exploring. In this one, a major effort centers on identifying the nature of the problem and identifying or creating new alternatives. The set of alternatives is never complete. When the needs for skills and expertise crosses organizational lines, formal organization is ignored in favor of teams or task forces. In contrast, stable or reactive responses follow the traditional hierarchy and problems are assigned to existing units. It performs trend analysis, strategic planning, program budgeting, and "what if" modeling.

Creative. This one tends to be similar to the exploring mode but goes further in its efforts to look for new solutions. It is willing and able to move in uncharted and untried directions. It employs the identification and analysis of strategic issues and brainstorming and fosters innovative and creative behavior.

BUILDING BLOCKS FOR STRATEGIC CHANGE

The essence of planned change or response behavior is creating, piece by piece, new views of an organization's vision of its future. Actually, change tends not to be revolutionary. Rather it stems from increments of action, partial commitments, or small lessons of experience. Change evolves from perceived meanings attached to the pressures and opportunities that present themselves. Change moves in those directions where events provoke pressures or offer opportunities. Change occurs when conflict and disagreement dissolve into consensus and other plausible alternatives become less attractive. Uncertainty and confusion convert to what appears to be clear-sighted strategies with clear themes that can be simply articulated. Change comes about to meet the interests of new players and new demands when they arrive on the scene.

The immediate stimulus for change emerges from the presence of a series of building blocks—the forces of change. These building blocks increase an organization's capacity to meet new demands and opportunities (Kanter 1983).

Lessons from Experience That Depart from Tradition

These are learned lessons that depart from established methods that appear to have substantial merit. These events and activities provide the foundation of experience for taking on new strategic thrusts of a larger nature. They may be unplanned events, or they may be planned pilot or experimental activity in search of greater experience and feasibility checking.

Crisis or Galvanizing Event

A second set of forces may be crisis, utter chaos, or a major galvanizing event that send sharp signals for immediate action. It may be a crisis of leadership, a major loss of grant or client, a significant economic decline, or even the good news of a major grant.

Strategic Choices

These choices for change stem from the strategic decisions made to solve significant problems or seize opportunities that present themselves in the second set of forces. Or they may result from a strong strategic leader who makes deliberate and conscious strategic thrusts and initiatives rather than waiting and drifting into new directions. More often, major shifts in direction actually stem from a series of prior choices and decisions that build the experience and consensus for making bolder decisions at a later point in time.

Individual Prime Movers Linked to Power

Any new idea or strategy, no matter how clever or responsive, cannot be translated into action without someone in power pushing it. This is a two-way process. Leaders must be on the prowl for new ideas and be able to identify and link up with the proponents. They must be prepared to provide the power tools of approval, resources, and expertise. On the other hand, individuals with ideas must be able to articulate in program terms their requirements for the tools of power. The strategic management system discussed later is a prime instrument for doing this.

APPLYING THE RENEWAL FACTOR: THE WATERMAN PROJECT

Most organizations are beset with dilemmas and conflicts. They constantly face uncertainties and hosts of problems. But some thrive on chaos. No matter how much change and environmental turbulence is encountered, some organizations not only survive, they flourish. They make change work to their advantage. They continuously adapt their strategies, bureaucracies, and cultures to adjust to crises that defeat many others. How successful organizations do this is the subject of an extensive research project by Robert H. Waterman, Jr., and colleagues, the findings from which are contained in the book *The Renewal Factor* (1987). The Waterman group talked to the executives of forty-five organizations from a list of five hundred companies and studied these organizations in depth. The core findings of the project identified and discussed why and how some organizations, and not others, possess the capacity to meet the challenge of renewal in the face of crisis and chaos.

The Waterman project found many examples of renewal in a wide range of organizations, including the Humana Hospital, a furniture factory, the puppeteers of the "Sesame Street" television show, and the city government of Scottsdale, Arizona. Others studied were independent grocers, as well as the big corporations IBM, GE, Ford, Citicorp, and Hewlett Packard.

The research project was geared toward learning from the best. The study proceeded to identify the organizations and the people who "do it right." They are the renewers. The lessons learned from the study about the renewal leaders and their organizations suggests eight themes, each of which is fully discussed in *The Renewal Factor* and briefly described here.

Informed Opportunism

The Waterman study makes clear that renewing organizations set directions for their companies, not detailed strategy. These organizations believe that strategic planning is great, as long as no one takes the plans too seriously. They perceive more value in the process of planning than in the actual plan.

Direction and Empowerment

The renewing organizations look at everyone in the organization as a "source of creative input." This management style motivates people in ways to gain their quality effort and commitment to implementation.

Friendly Facts, Congenial Controls

Renewing organizations are hungry for information. They are always making comparisons and rankings and taking measurements to provide context and meaning. They remove decision-making from the realm of opinion-giving. They do maintain accurate and timely financial controls and insist such controls allow them to be "creative and free."

A Different Mirror

The habit of breaking habits is always present in renewing organizations. This is absolutely essential for change and renewal. It comes from the ability to anticipate crisis and arises from a continuing willingness to confront real problems before they mushroom into crises. Their "mirrors" reflect the real thing, not only what they wish to see and hear.

Leaders of renewing organizations want to know what is happening; they listen and learn from almost everyone outside the hierarchy—politicians, customers and clients, suppliers, operating employees, and fund-granting organizations.

Teamwork, Trust, Politics, and Power

Leaders of renewing organizations frequently talk about teamwork and trust. They find that high levels of political conflict, a lack of teamwork, and the absence of values contribute to serious troubles. In fact, it makes deliberate change almost impossible.

Stability in Motion

Renewal requires a constant interplay between stability and change. Too much change that occurs too fast, without time for adequate absorption, can be destructive. Renewing organizations strive for a degree of fluidity and flexibility so that change occurs regularly. Yet, steps are taken to provide a sense of stability, to absorb the disruption of change.

Attitudes and Attention

The attention of management is necessary to assure employees that they mean what they say when they ask for quality, cost cutting, or whatever. Exhortation is not enough; words are less important than actions to show what management wants and for what they will give incentive and reward.

Causes and Commitment

Renewing organizations commit themselves to causes that give meaning to their efforts and get people enthusiastic. Quality is the most common cause. At Ford, it is employee involvement and quality. The cause that moved the San Francisco Symphony was its aspiration to be world class.

Management's visible commitment makes a cause creditable and real and induces people throughout the organization to contribute to the central purpose. Management's effort to gain commitment must come from positive values and not be seen as a cynical means to manipulation.

Although all the themes and lessons identified by the Waterman project deserve consideration, one of the themes is selected for further discussion here because of its special relevance to the use of strategic management systems. It is "the informed opportunist."

BECOMING AN INFORMED OPPORTUNIST

Opportunities are often elusive. To successful renewing organizations they often appear in disguise or unexpectedly. But they are seen and seized, although they may not be detailed in an organization's strategic plan.

When organizations seek renewal, their leaders realize that renewal progress does not unfold strictly in accord with a master plan. Of course, strategic process and plan are used, but they realize that strategic plans do not—and should not—limit the seeking and exploiting of opportunity solely to the rational and orderly strategic process. They leave room for fusing the rational approach to information accumulation with the spontaneous, random feel for opportunity. This, Waterman says, is a way of managing "informed opportunism."

In renewing organizations, information is appreciated for its potential for strategic advantage. Quality information leads to the right strategy. The combination of information with opportunity makes for a significant difference. Informed opportunists are prepared to know what and where are the best opportunities. They know where to look and what to look for.

Be Prepared for Stochastic Shock!

Many of us have seen our best programs—even those most soundly conceived and formulated—get blown apart by some unpredictable turn of events. The process is stochastic when it is driven by random events; stochastic shock explains the unanticipated event that can and did occur to disrupt and undermine our intentions.

Waterman (1987, 34) comments on the limitations of rational, planned strategy this way: "Most companies try to overlap a rational, linear, deterministic technique which they call strategy on an underlying process that is random, full of surprises . . . in other words, stochastic." The rational strategic plan will not work unless it contains sufficient flexibility and elbow room to "go with the flow." Strategic methods must be able to fit the unpredictable forces at work.

Although most people and organizations are not good at dealing with random events and probabilities or statistics, organizations must place a premium on leaving room for the unexpected. They must make their strategic plans broad, directional, and certainly not produce detailed strategies or complicated long-range plans. They can build flexibility by separating strategic planning from operational planning, but they must provide and maintain strong links and interactions between the strategic initiatives and the implementing program management.

Pragmatic Strategy: Combining Analysis with Intuition

Successful executives interviewed by the Waterman group were certain that instinct or intuition plays a large role in being an informed opportunist. They were not saying that intuition—hunches, instincts, or feelings—replaces rigorous analysis and quality information. Rather, intuition stemming from experience and good information is complementary and can move you away from or toward opportunity, and cannot be ignored.

LEADING OTHERS TO GET EXTRAORDINARY THINGS DONE

The book *The Leadership Challenge* (Kouzes and Posner 1987) discusses the practices leaders use and the commitments they make when they are at their "personal best" in leading others to get extraordinary things done in organizations. Starting with a research project, the authors surveyed more than 550 leaders with thirty-eight open-ended questions; conducted more than forty-two in-depth interviews, and received 780 completed two-page forms from other managers. Those interviewed and surveyed were middle- and senior-level managers in business, not-for-profit, and public-sector organizations. From an analysis of the data, a Leadership Practice Inventory was developed. Then over three thousand managers and their subordinates were asked to assess the extent to which they used the leadership practices "when they are doing their best" at leading others to get things done. They discovered that leaders do exhibit certain distinct practices, which do not seem to vary from industry to industry or from profession to profession. They believe that leadership behavior is not confined to a few charismatic men or women, but "is a process ordinary managers use to get extraordinary things done" and constitutes a skill learnable by anyone interested. The book is designed to help people enhance their leadership capabilities by "assessing their strengths and weaknesses as leaders, learning how to inspire and motivate others toward a common purpose, acquiring skills in building a cohesive and spirited team, and putting these lessons to use more regularly."

What Followers Expect of Their Leaders

What leaders do is only part of the story. What followers think about their leaders will determine whether individuals can serve as and be recognized as leaders. A study of fifteen hundred managers for the American Management Association asked, "What values—traits or characteristics—do you look for or admire in your superiors?" Of the 225 different ones identified, the most frequent cited characteristics were integrity—which is being truthful and trustworthy, with character and convictions; competence—which is being productive and efficient; and leadership—which is being inspirational and decisive and providing direction. A follow-up study of eight hundred senior public executives, alumni of the Federal Executive Institute, arrived at similar results, and rated integrity, competence, and leadership as the three characteristics most admired in their superiors.

The results of a subsequent study of over twenty-six hundred top-level managers to determine their view of superior leader characteristics reveals a striking similarity to the other studies. The authors conclude that leaders must possess these essential characteristics: honest, competent, forward-looking, and inspiring. Taken together, these characteristics add up to "credibility." Their word can be trusted, they will do what they say, they have the knowledge and skill to lead, and they are enthusiastic about the directions in which they are going.

PRACTICES AND COMMITMENTS COMMON TO SUCCESSFUL LEADERS

The leadership research data uncovered five fundamental practices, each of which contains two commitments that enabled leaders to get extraordinary things done. They are:

Practice 1: Challenging the Process

Successful leaders seek to change the present situation. They do not sit back; they innovate and experiment with new and better ways of doing things. Leaders accept the challenge to do what is necessary to get new services and processes adopted. They need not create new ideas, which can come from others. But they are effective at getting them accepted and put into practice. Leaders are not always perfect, but they do learn from mistakes.

The commitments made to support the first practice include:

Commitment 1: Search Out Challenging Opportunities to Change, Grow, Innovate, and Improve. People identified as leaders are associated with significant change whether it be winning wars, resolving crises, or political turnabouts. Managerially, leaders are associated with significant and successful changes in product, quality, customer satisfaction, process, or cost. They open up new doors that present challenges for doing one's best with skills and abilities that people do not always know they have. Leaders find the experience rewarding and exciting; they respond with intensity, determination, and commitment. Followers feel inspired, motivated, energized, and proud.

Commitment 2: Experiment, Take Risks, and Learn from Mistakes. Leaders experiment with new approaches to old problems. They systematically collect innovative ideas with mechanisms such as staff meetings, status reports, retreats, and even visits to places where best practices are employed. Leaders set up small experiments and initiate small-scale pilot or demonstration projects to diminish risk and gain experience. They honor and reward risk-takers and support them during difficult times.

Practice 2: Inspiring a Shared Vision

Leaders look forward to the future. They have a sense of what is possible and are positive that people working together for a common purpose can make a difference.

Commitments to support the second practice include:

Commitment 3: Envision an Uplifting and Ennobling Future. Vision gives direction and purpose to an organization. It is an ideal and unique image of tomorrow. It sets us apart and makes us feel special. Vision helps to decide what one wants the organization to do and be in the future. Record the vision on paper; test and change it to make it more achievable.

Commitment 4: Enlist Others in a Common Vision by Appealing to Their Values, Interests, Hopes, and Dreams. It is important to identify your constituents so that you can focus on their interests and know what appeals to them. Search out the commonality of their interests and aspirations and be effective in communicating to your audience. Make sure you are positive and optimistic. Reveal your enthusiasm, and avoid being tentative. Be genuine, and say only what you mean.

Practice 3: Enabling Others to Act

Leaders know that they need others to get things done. They actively seek partners in planning and executing. They are considerate of employee needs and sensitivities; they foster self-esteem and mutual respect. They promote collaboration and work hard to get people to work together.

The commitments to support the third practice are:

Commitment 5: Foster Collaboration by Promoting Cooperative Goals and Building Trust. The guidelines suggested for collaboration are: share the credit and always say "we"; create interactions to assure that you and others do not work in isolation; create a climate of trust by fostering openness and predictability about intentions and behavior to make people feel secure; focus on gains not losses, on opportunities not problems; and involve people in planning and problem-solving.

Commitment 6: Strengthen People by Sharing Information and Power, and Increasing Their Discretion and Visibility. The guidelines suggested are: get to know people and be sensitive to their needs; learn to be interpersonally competent and be serious in creating bonds of trust; share your power in the service of others by helping and supporting people; and keep people informed by making connections with people who can open doors, offer information, and provide support and backing when necessary. Help others make connections.

Practice 4: Modeling the Way

Leaders show the way. They find ways to demonstrate their philosophy, high standards, and values in ways that make their organization unique and distinctive.

The commitments to support Practice 4 are:

Commitment 7: Set the Example for Others by Behaving in Ways that Are Consistent with Your Stated Values. Put in writing the values you believe in and have them known in the organization. It sometimes is necessary to be dramatic in getting across fundamental values about the organization. Learn to be a storyteller and circulate the stories until they become legends. Do not fear being emotional to show that you really do care. People around you like to know the intensity of your commitment to values.

Commitment 8: Plan Small Wins That Promote Consistent Progress and Build Commitment. Make a plan with others to achieve exceptional results. Break the plan into manageable chunks that specify events and milestones to be accomplished. Take one step at a time and get it done. Make the progress visible to create positive momentum. Seek to give people choices in what they have to do and how, and get them to feel like "owners."

Practice 5: Encouraging the Heart

Leaders encourage, support, recognize, and reward their workers. They express pride in their work and organization and let others know. They display these commitments:

Commitment 9: Recognize Individual Contributions to the Success of Every Project. Develop measurable performance standards so that everyone will know when the job is accomplished well. Install a formal systematic process for rewarding performance.

Commitment 10: Celebrate Team Accomplishments Regularly. Recognizing team accomplishments highlights a key point that great performance is the result of many peoples' efforts. Create social support networks to facilitate people working together and provide the positive feeling of belonging to a larger enterprise.

5

Creating a Compelling Vision of the Future

The need for great leadership with vision is always with us. A state of crisis and chaos often seems to exist in some government and public-interest nonprofit agencies. Many organizations are incapable of coping with the expectations of their constituents. A credibility gap—an uneasy mistrust of all institutions, but particularly public-interest institutions—is a widespread, almost worldwide phenomenon.

People constantly challenge the performance of public institutions. They are spurred on by the pressure of advocacy groups, deep resistance to regulations, organized consumer and public interests, and a responsive media. We live in a time of contradictions when the public demands increased services and benefits, yet our leaders face the serious constraint of an obsession with "no more taxes."

Unfortunately, no certain understanding exists to distinguish effective leaders from ineffective ones despite the multitude of empirical investigations conducted in the last seventy-five years. It was once thought that leadership ability was a matter of birth; leaders were born, not made, was the conventional wisdom. This view failed to explain leadership. Other notions prevailed. One insisted that great events made leaders out of plain people; others claimed leaders possess certain types of "traits." But no leadership concept has stood the test of time in spite of voluminous literature.

New views of leadership have emerged that offer promise. Bennis and Nanus (1985) tell us in their book *Leaders* that effective leaders use vision as an instrument to move organizations and people toward future conditions. They create the promise of potential opportunities; they empower people to grow and change. They forge new cultures and strategies that focus direction and resources.

HOW VISION HELPS LEADERS CREATE A BETTER FUTURE

An exciting vision is a hallmark of leadership success. A forum on presidential leadership at Harvard's 350th anniversary credits former president Reagan's success in the White House to his clear vision for the country and an ability to communicate it to the voters. Studies of leaders credit a "vision orientation" for being a large factor in their success. Bennis and Nanus report, "Leaders articulate and define what has previously remained implicit or unsaid; they invent images, metaphors and models that provide focus for new attention. By so doing, they consolidate or challenge prevailing wisdom" (1985, 39).

Bennis and Nanus further suggest that leaders, in their vision orientation, concern themselves with basic purposes and general directions. They create new ideas, new policies, and new methodologies. People are compelled and attracted to the enunciated vision. It is not necessary to coerce people to pay attention to visionary leaders. Their intensity and commitment is magnetic; they draw in people to a movement. Essential to the attraction of attention by the use of vision is the "creation of focus." All ninety leaders interviewed by the Bennis group clearly knew what they wanted to achieve. They had an "agenda" with a strong concern for "outcome" and "results," and results get attention.

SOME CRITERIA FOR MAKING VISIONS WORK

What Is Vision?

Most of us dream about a future when people are more successful and happier. Most often, these fantasies have little relationship to reality. Most Americans think of "vision" as reverie or imagination. But unlike simple fantasies, the new approach to strategic leadership exploits "vision" to help define and create a better future using a panorama of facts, hopes, expectations, and opportunities.

In strategic terms, visions can help organizations know where they are headed and can set the basic directions and strategies to get there. Visions weave together the essence of the mission and values to be accomplished and the fundamental directions for change to take. The constant components of vision are mission, goals, and values that can serve as the adhesive to bring everybody together.

Criteria for Effectiveness

A number of criteria are emerging to guide the effective development
and execution of vision. Unfortunately there is not yet any definitive
empirical research to support the practical wisdom of the criteria offered.

Effective Visions Are Compelling and Satisfying. This is true not necessarily for everyone but for a vast number of the targeted group. Visions
do something for you and to you, and they try to obtain the best from
everyone. Visions can bring about confidence on the part of staff so that
they perform well and gain great satisfaction for their contribution. This
is especially true if individual contributions are directly recognized and
rewarded.

Effective Visions Pose Clearly Stated Challenges. They must challenge
what exists and seek to make a difference. They must be succinctly articulated with clarity that tells precisely and emphatically what is
wanted. They reflect a "stretch" beyond the current situation and reveal
distinctly favorable outcomes for the future. Though visions can never
be fully attained—they symbolize ultimate purpose and direction—they
must contain the possibility of sufficient progress to retain credibility.
Visions will not remain challenging if they do not make sense in terms
of the real needs and wants of the target clientele group. Visions grossly
out of touch with reality will wither and die.

Effective Visions Are Guideposts on Uncertain Terrain. In times of change,
disorientation and disorder can be overwhelming unless a clear vision
of a better future exists. Vision offers a beacon of light to guide decisions
and behavior. The key ideas that become guideposts seldom change
drastically over time, but can be modified and fine-tuned to reflect
changing experience.

*Effective Achievement of Vision Requires the Creation of Substantial Imple-
menting Capacity.* This is necessary to enable organizations to devise and
execute strategies. Whatever the vision promises, the capacity to deliver
must exist and be continuously replenished. Broken promises and the
inability to follow rhetoric with deeds seriously undermine credibility.

Effective Visions Honor the Past. Visionary leaders call for the creation
of opportunities in the future by recalling past greatness. It is important
to draw upon comfortable themes that make people confident in reaching for new directions. One useful concept is to stress continuity, even
though the vision may contain a sharp break with the past. Continuity
can be shown in many ways. Chief executives can use the appointment
and promotion of certain executives to reflect linkage with the past; they
may invoke great ideas and heroic personalities of the past. Much effort
is often taken to disguise threatening discontinuity to make the transition
more smooth.

Visions Must Be "Lived." Formal pronouncements may be doomed if they are not quickly followed by visible actions that indicate sincerity of commitment and possibility of progress. Visions can backfire and be counterproductive if the stated vision offers attractive promises but consequent action fails to produce as promised.

Visions can be outright dangerous if they are too risky, absolutely unattainable, or just downright impractical. Visions must be somewhat attainable, at least in part. They cannot remain rhetoric or pure exhortation. They must be lived or they degenerate into ignored slogans that can severely undermine strategic response capability.

New Vision Requires the Development of Commitment. Effective visions are able to mobilize acceptance and support to get people to make it happen. Large corporations have taken hordes of executives on five-day retreats to discuss their vision. Certainly it does not take that many days merely to share a succinct mission statement and a limited number of goals and objectives—if only that would do the job. The communication of vision—sufficient to garner commitment—takes time in ways that go far beyond extensive dialogue and exchange. It includes training that conditions behavior in support of new organizational values and offers symbols and rituals to reinforce the new vision. It may even include new recruitment and promotions, to put in place loyal supporters who are clearly committed to work for the new vision.

COMMUNICATING VISION

Visions Provide Meaning

Having a vision and believing in it is not enough. Without effective communication, nothing will be accomplished. Success requires the capability to communicate a compelling vision to others in ways that achieve meaning. This is the task of strategic leadership.

The issue is not whether one is being informed. Rather, the concern is one of communicating complex and abstract ideas so that the message and its intention are understood. President Reagan demonstrated a superior ability for making abstract topics come to life with anecdotal experiences and crisp "one-liners" such as "Government is the problem, not the solution."

The Bennis and Nanus interviews with ninety established leaders drew several fundamental lessons from their experience about communicating meaning. First, it is leadership that influences and organizes meaning for the members of the organization. Through symbols, actions, and words, leaders help members of the organization to understand the purpose and significance of what is being conveyed. Through such meanings, people are induced to support directional goals and strategic initiatives with, it is hoped, enthusiasm and commitment. Such communication exerts a kind of social control over the behavior of employees.

Second, the style and means by which leaders convey and shape meaning vary enormously. President Reagan used vivid images and human anecdotes to communicate. One of his budget messages made obvious the enormity of the trillion-dollar budget by comparing the number of dollars to the size of the Empire State Building. Some leaders highly personalize their visions with great visibility. Others may be taciturn and less charismatic, but they manage to get their message across better than the more articulate. They learn to make actions speak louder than words. They use extensive executive forums to arm surrogates with the written word to communicate meanings and to solicit reaction, response, and support. They put in personal appearances at these forums to lend an air of authenticity and authority and often to listen and learn the reaction and response of key executive staff.

Third, providing meaning to the staff of an organization extends beyond what is usually meant by communication. Conveying meaning is much more than "facts and knowing"; this information is often useful and necessary, but it is decidedly inadequate. Communicating meaning must provide direction and values; conveying vision answers the concern for knowing "why" rather than knowing "how." Providing meaning answers purpose and significance; in effect, it can enhance motivation and better morale.

WHAT MAKES A GOOD VISIONARY EXECUTIVE

The experts tell us that visionary executive behavior is distinctly different from that of the nonvisionary executive. The executive who is considered nonvisionary may be very productive and proficient in the tasks performed. But job conduct may not be strategic in the sense of creating a clear picture of a better future and guiding others toward that future state in ways that inspire superior performance. The nonvisionary executive solves daily problems, presents a reserved and "laid-back" response to people and ideas, pays attention to weaknesses and criticism, and talks about current activities.

In contrast, the visionary executive articulates philosophy, values, and ideas; is receptive, expressive, and supportive to people and ideas; pays attention to strengths; and talks about future goals and directions.

Hickman and Silva (1984, 160–61) reviewed research and literature and set out a ten-point composite of how an executive with vision

—searches for ideas, concepts, and ways of thinking until a clear vision crystallizes;

—articulates the vision into an easy-to-grasp philosophy that integrates strategic direction and cultural values;

—motivates employees to embrace the vision through constant persuasion and setting an example of hard work;

—makes contact with employees at all levels in the organization, attempting to understand their concerns and the impact the vision has on them;

—acts in a warm, supportive, and expressive way, always communicating that "we're all in this together, like a family";

—translates the vision into a reason for being for each employee by continually relating the vision to individual cares, concerns, and work;

—concentrates on the major strengths within the organization that will insure the success of the vision;

—remains at the center of the action, positioned as the prime shaper of the vision;

—looks for ways to improve the vision by carefully observing changes inside and outside the organization; and

—measures the ultimate success of the organization in terms of its ability to fulfill the vision.

Part 3

ESTABLISHING A STRATEGIC MANAGEMENT SYSTEM

6

Designing and Starting a Strategic Management System

DESCRIPTIVE MODEL OF A SYSTEM

Any model of strategic management as a system admittedly is an oversimplified portrayal of complexity found in what many call the "real world." Its main use is simply to increase comprehension of what takes place in actual organizations. This enables the players and students of strategic management to learn how to design and operate rules of the game.

The model is designated a "system" to emphasize its linkages and interrelationships among operating functions of a continuous process. The overall description is designed to sharpen perception of the system as a whole, as well as to help understand each of the system's interactive parts. Ideally, players in one function of the system can better relate to others in the system. Optimally, this produces greater teamwork and better end results.

Introducing strategic management into an organization provides a purposeful system that embraces the broad management processes of an entire organization. Strategic management operates with agreed upon purposes and a set of interdependent components that unfold in sequential phases. Relationships are explained; inputs, instruments, and outputs are usually specified in advance. The system is declared and authorized from on high. Rules of the game are prescribed, and a written strategic plan is employed as a central feature. More mature systems tend to link strategic plans with operational plans, with their constituent program and budget plans, and sometimes with manpower plans.

Strategic management as a system deals with how an organization responds to the events, threats, and opportunities of its changing environment. It works to set strategic directions and initiatives that move toward a desired vision of the future. As the system matures, it begins to extend beyond the declaration of intentions or challenges expressed by setting strategic directions and announcing bold new initiatives. Necessarily, the system pays greater attention to implementation of strategy through the organization's operating behavior or program management. The mature system treats strategic thrusts and operating program management as two sides of one coin. They are incomplete if they are separate.

In essence, the prime emphasis of strategic management is to focus on the making of strategic decisions and to assure that the right ones are made and made well or changed. A second emphasis is that operational activities should derive directly from the strategic decisions. Of necessity, they must interact and influence each other.

Variety of Purposes

A clear commonality of purpose for the strategic management system does not exist in public and nonprofit organizations. The reason is that individual organizations are different. They vary in size from small to large. The scale of turbulence and change in their environment varies; it can range from stable to a rapid shift of unanticipated and complex change. The nature of the problems they face may have long- or short-term implications. Their top managements possess different management styles of strategic response; they may be passive or aggressive. They may prefer to wait and react to events, rather than search and probe to anticipate them. These factors shape the design of an organization's strategic management system, but particularly they determine the purposes it selects for the system's focus. In recent times, as financial shortages threaten and profound changes in policy and program take place, greater attention focuses on the faster selection and flexible implementation of specific strategies, with relatively less emphasis on process.

Facilitating Strategic Planning. One fundamental purpose is to facilitate the introduction and use of strategic planning in an organization, with an essential output the development of a written strategic plan. The strategic management system is then geared to the development of a strategic plan that sets strategic directions and proposes strategic initiatives to be undertaken. Coordinated actions are then taken to realize the plan's implementation.

This purpose of facilitating strategic planning can be an opening wedge in the introduction of a strategic management system in an organization. For example, the federal Internal Revenue Service described the design of its strategic management system in this way in its initial introduction:

(1) The Strategic Management System is designed to facilitate overall planning for the Service. It provides the framework for a process to: (a) identify environmental changes and trends that will affect the Service's ability to carry out its mission; (b) facilitate consideration of these trends by the Commissioner and the Policy and Strategic Planning Council; (c) determine the Service's broad response to these trends, that is, the strategic directions in which the Service should move; and (d) formulate strategic initiatives to translate these directions into action.

(2) The System provides: (a) for a re-evaluation of the Service's Mission; (b) a structure for the development of the IRS Strategic Plan; (c) mechanisms for implementing the strategic initiatives; and (d) a process for keeping the Strategic Plan current (U.S. Treasury 1985 Sec. 210).

Mobilizing for Major Change. Another purpose aims directly at achieving major change or redirection for an organization. Organizations facing a sense of crisis or chaos require a strong but flexible strategic process that can mobilize the organization to move along new paths toward a better future. The strategic management system is geared purposely toward the deliberate change of strategy, program, and organization behavior more in keeping with the real and anticipated demands imposed by the environment. The continuing and rapid rate of environmental turbulence for some organizations necessitates a constant ability to adapt and respond. Their capability to think and act strategically is of paramount importance to survival and success.

Integrating Strategic Framework with Operational Plan. Another major purpose of the strategic management system is to serve as an integrating agent and mechanism for tying together the strategic framework of directions and initiatives with the implementing operational program and budget. In some instances, the financial and manpower plans are also subject to integrating scrutiny and action.

In effect, the emphasis on integration enables the organization to link strategic planning with the broad management processes of the organization. This places the organization's resource managers—such as those in personnel, budgeting, or finance—directly in context with the organization's strategic thrusts. Although conceptually sound in practice, the attempt to mesh staff resource managers with program executives in a strategic framework is never an easy task and is often fraught with conflict and difficulty. But it must be done.

Institutional Strengthening. In addition to the above purposes are a series of other purposes that primarily aim at institutional strengthening for strategic management rather than seek programmatic change. They

seek to use the strategic management system to train managers and executives, develop better communications, improve information, shift resources more easily, or devise better ways to detect internal strengths
and weaknesses and take corrective action. They set better indicators of
progress or establish more realistic goals and objectives.

Other purposes cited are to improve the ability to raise strategic issues
for action by top management or to teach how to conduct environmental
scans of potential opportunities and threats.

In summary, many different purposes can be selected for the employment of strategic management systems, though the primary emphasis
now more often focuses on the selection of specific strategies and their
effective implementation. Actually, not all purposes are mutually exclu-
sive; many interrelate or may be subsumed under others. They reflect
merely different emphases or partial elements and may be more appropriate for some organizations at varying stages in their organizational
life. What is clear is that the purpose or purposes selected and the emphasis placed upon them do determine the nature, scope, and operation
of the strategic management system.

Multiple Phases

The strategic management system is a recurring set of multiple phases
that set the rules of who plays, and how, in the strategic management
game. Though the system is potentially comprehensive in scope, not all
organizations contain systems that embrace all phases equally. Some organizations emphasize the formulation of written strategic plans, with
their attention to implementation a bit isolated from the strategic process.
The evidence is that the operational plan and program budget often
share only tenuous links with the strategic plan and process. Other organizations have begun to integrate their strategic framework with their
implementing program, budget, and manpower plans; and more agencies are stating their intention to do so.

The strategic management system possesses four identifiable phases:

Assessment of the External and Internal Environment. This embraces the
analysis and study of performance improvement, environmental trends,
culture of shared values, and institutional strengthening.

External environment means the factors—opportunities and threats—
that exist outside the organization and are not usually within the short-
run control of top management. The external factors constitute the context in which an organization operates. The task of reading the environment means identifying the set of external events and trends that can,
and do, influence strategic performance. It also means identifying and
linking with key actors and institutions in the outside community

that can affect the performance profile, such as clients, legislatures, boards, professional associations, and special-interest groups.

Internal environment means those factors—strengths and weaknesses—within the organization itself that are also not usually within the short-run control of top management. These form the context in which work is done; they include the organization's structure of responsibility and authority, culture of values, and human and financial resources.

Strategy Formulation. This phase guides the preparation of strategy and the strategic plan. It does these things:

—reviews and reaffirms the statement of mission;

—identifies significant environmental trends and issues;

—determines the fundamental values to emphasize;

—selects the major areas of concern to be addressed;

—sets the strategic directions to follow;

—selects the appropriate strategies; and

—develops strategic initiatives to carry out the directions.

Strategy formulation is a process for developing strategies and a strategic plan that deals with environmental threats and responds to opportunities in ways that accommodate an organization's strengths and weaknesses. This phase sets the strategic agenda by which major areas of concern are selected for concentrated focus and addressed. The ensuing strategic plan makes the deliberate transition from a statement of strategic intentions to the announcement of strategic action initiatives to be undertaken to move the organization toward the accomplishment of strategic goals.

Strategy Implementation. This phase develops the capability and ways to carry out strategic initiatives that offset the often prevalent inability in public-interest affairs to move from rhetoric to reality and action. It does the following things:

—establishes realistic objectives and progress indicators;

—designs strategy-implementing program plans;

—budgets for program and performance accountability;

—organizes with flatter, self-managing teams;

—develops strategic human resources; and

—estimates financial requirements.

During this phase, fact-finding surveys are usually undertaken to determine what means are necessary to put in place the essential institutional support needed to accomplish the intended directional goals and initiatives. The institutional support takes such form as staffing, structure, skill development, material procurement, facilities and space development, library support and computerization, consultative technical assistance, and financial requirements.

This phase is sometimes called the "tooling-up" or "get-ready" activity, which may also include a "dress rehearsal" of all key parties in their designated roles and tasks. Sometimes a pilot or demonstration project of lesser scope is initiated for strategic initiatives of large investments of money, or risk, and huge uncertainty. The smaller pilot project is designed for feasibility testing and for gaining experience prior to decisions for accelerated expansion.

Control and Evaluation. This learning phase monitors the organization's strategic performance so that desired results can be compared with what actually happens. Evaluation examines what you have been doing now and in the past, in order to improve the future. It does these things:

—establishes controls to provide timely feedback, and to keep planned actions on track;

—conducts evaluation studies;

—identifies lessons of experience and facilitates organization learning; and

—recommends readjustments in strategy and implementation.

In this phase, steps are taken to determine whether the strategic plan, in any of its components, needs to be modified and specific initiatives be curtailed or expanded.

FACTORS THAT INFLUENCE SYSTEMS DESIGN

Adapting to Uniqueness

Strategic management is, and must be, unique in each organization. There is no particular strategic management system that every organization can adopt. Rather, it must be designed to fit the unique characteristics of each organization and the diverse personalities of its key decision-makers. Differences in scale and size of the organization and in the services and products it provides make for many variations in the strategic management process. Some organizations tend to make strategic decisions in simpler modes than others that may have a more formal planning and review process. They might informally decide over lunch what other organizations would schedule for an all-day planning and review session. In some organizations, the scope of strategic planning and management is fully comprehensive of the organization's services and products; while in others, strategic management is limited to a major program or product or merely to one or two geographic locations. In some situations, the will to strategize and confront the future by top management may be less than adequate, or at least different. In some circumstances, the strategic plan is perceived as a "strategic challenge" rather than an integrative and implementing action instrument for the agency's management processes.

Each situation in its own way will determine the nature of the strategic management effort that can be tolerated. The experts seem to agree on one thing: There is no perfect fit for strategic management. Rather, it is a process to be designed and adapted to a particular situation. It requires that one be systematic in learning what makes it work and what it takes to make it work better for an organization. With that caution in mind, one should understand the determinants for designing the strategic management system and then consider some design alternatives.

System Determinants

Designing a strategic management system that is appropriate and fits the unique characteristics in an organization is never an easy task. Too often a system is quickly designed, goes through several years of disruptive trial and error, and then is abandoned. It may not be possible to design the perfect system, but it is important to keep to a minimum the disruptive major systemic changes that can occur in the early years of a system.

Five determining factors for system design stand out:

Size and Structure. The larger organization with multiple structural layers, extensive geographic dispersion, and many diverse organizational entities generally requires a more formally prescribed system of strategic management. This is necessary to be able to communicate and enforce rules of the game and to define and gain acceptance of strategic intentions and expectations throughout the organization.

Public organizations with decentralized field structures must provide for field guidance, gain their participation, and be receptive to the realities of clientele demands and changing demographics out in the community. Similarly, nonprofit national organizations with loosely affiliated—rather than closely integrated—local chapters must be able to provide strategic guidance to obtain cohesive, forward-looking programs, in tune with changing times. But the style in which strategic guidance is given will vary in light of the extent of authority and control that exists. It can range from mandatory to voluntary; in either event it must be pursuasive and competent. The headquarters of the American Red Cross demonstrates its sensitive understanding of affiliate behavior when it offers its local chapters a voluntary consultative service (for fee) for the development of strategic planning and management.

Turbulence of the Environment. The growing environmental turbulence and ensuing changes that face public and nonprofit organizations substantially affect when and how they respond and how they live with the consequences. If the changing events move rapidly, the organization must be able to respond in time. If the organization faces slow, drifting changes like the "greenhouse effect" of potential great significance, then there is more time to understand the threat, mobilize the technical and financial resources, and formulate a response.

If the challenge of change is complex and significant, with little precedent or knowledge to guide the strategic response, solving the problems with strategic thrusts will demand more formal systems of response, not casual ones. In effect, the turbulence of the environment determines the mode and design of strategic response. It shapes the response: slow or rapid, passive or aggressive, or reactive or anticipatory.

Previous Planning and Program Budgeting Experience. A complex and comprehensive system of strategic management depends on prior planning experience that aims at directing the future. It requires an acceptance of looking forward to a better future with a degree of confidence. The absence of program budgeting experience and system in an organization would make it very difficult to design a strategic management system that included phases of implementation.

Management Style. Systems of strategic management, with their scanning of the environment for trends and issues, depend upon a top management that looks forward to influencing the future. Additionally, strategic management thrusts are usually embedded in a strong culture of values. Organizations that are not able to think philosophically and conceptually in what they believe cannot perform well strategically.

Furthermore, a "laid-back," passive style of management that waits for events to happen before it reacts or that procrastinates in its response to external changing conditions will inevitably have trouble in the design and performance of a strategic management system.

Program Cost and Societal Consequence. The more expensive the program in terms of financial requirements and use of high-powered talent, the more justifiable the performance is of complex tasks, extensive analytical studies, and fact-finding explorations. Likewise, the more significant in consequence the programs and the greater the uncertainty surrounding their accomplishment, the more necessary a formal system is for strategic planning and management that demands considerable effort, review, and analysis.

DESIGN ALTERNATIVES

In designing the strategic management system, some alternatives must be adapted to the organization's unique conditions, and they are discussed in turn.

Completeness of the System

Starting out with a complete and comprehensive strategic management system that includes all phases, complete coverage of all programs and services, and all organizational entities is very demanding. Rather than designing a complete model when embarking on a strategic management system for the first time, an organization can review its significant threats and opportunities and can deliberately target its attention to a critical few areas of concern. It can then launch a limited number of strategic initiatives. Another alternative is to target selected programs or services and concentrate and focus in depth, or to target clientele groups or geographical locations.

The areas of concern selected must be of significant import to the success of the organization and warrant the distinct possibility of making a significant difference. Where there are only a critical number of areas to contend with, the system can be tested, experience can be gained, and lessons learned before the next cycle is commenced.

The trend is toward greater selectivity in picking problems or opportunities and gaining a quicker response to shifting external conditions—whether it be constraint or an emerging opportunity. This underscores the importance of not being burdened by efforts to be complete and comprehensive at the expense of flexible, quick responses to rapidly changing events.

Not all organizations undertake the full scope of integrated strategic management phases, including implementation. When an organization focuses primarily on strategic planning, it tends to treat separately its annual and budget planning cycle from its development and use of a strategic framework. In these situations, the program budget can be isolated from strategic guidance; this could undermine an organization's capability to respond to its changing environment. It can make strategic implementation difficult to accomplish.

Depth and Sophistication of Analysis

It is very easy to overload the system with ever-increasing requirements for data and their analysis in order to support key strategic decisions. Extensive demand for decision support—understandable when consequences are substantial—can be extremely consuming and expensive. The question "When is enough?"—in terms of data and its analysis—has no easy answer. It seems prudent to be selective and less comprehensive in the number of strategic concerns to pursue at one time and thus to be able to pursue the priority areas in sufficient depth. This removes a great deal of uncertainty surrounding the launching of strategic initiatives. You can never be sure, but being well-informed lowers the risk.

In some organizations, the number and nature of reviews and analyses tend to be excessive, with negative results of time delay, wasted effort, and often unnecessary confrontation and antagonism. Experts urge the avoidance of perfunctory reviews by multiple layers of structure in the name of good communications that contribute little to the particular strategic issue or decision being faced.

The tendency is emerging to avoid the "paralysis by analysis" syndrome by developing a bias toward action. In this situation, you move faster by learning as you go by starting lower-risk projects. These are controlled, pilot, or demonstration activities that "hedge bets"; risks are minimalized until enough experience is gained. The strategic leaders who advocate a bias toward action insist that all analysis is incomplete. They claim you can only diminish the uncertainty of changing conditions by supplementing planning with organized learning from diminished-risk projects before undertaking full-size programs.

Sometimes, the analytical process contains what is called a "contention system." Rules for dissent are formalized; staff take positions on matters that arise and do so in writing. This creates an institutionalized environment that provides an open forum for disagreement and clears the air of festering dissent.

Degree of Formality

Strategic planning and management processes can be highly formal and ritualistic, or they can be casual and loose with few written requirements. The emerging cliché "the less paperwork the better" does not help very much. Experience indicates there is practical wisdom in putting in writing, for all to know, the essentials of the strategic management process: key issues and decisions made, and the assignment of responsibilities for implementation and evaluation. In fact, the requirement for sound strategic decisions—because so much is at stake—is clear justification for a formal process of carefully assigned tasks, their prescribed review and analysis, and clearly designated focal points of approval.

A certain amount of paperwork, ritual, and routine is necessary in any social system that aims to harmonize the efforts of diverse groups at many levels of an organization. The crucial issue is to be sensitive to the time when widespread feeling among staff is that the system's requirements are so burdensome and stressful that they defeat the basic aims of producing innovative ideas to advance an organization's strategic goals.

Time Horizons

Many strategic plans cover a five-year period, although in a number of organizations the strategic time period is anything more than two years. The strategic plans emerging in public agencies do not always contain the definite time limits of private-sector plans or those of large nonprofit national organizations. They tend to be multi-year, with financing indicated for specific time periods because of funding limitations.

For example, an American Red Cross strategic plan (1987) covers the period FY 1987–88 to FY 1990–91; the strategic plan for the State of Ohio (1984) targets the "Eighties and Beyond."

Extent of Participation and Involvement

Despite the added complexity, experts strongly recommend open communication, its free exchange, and extensive involvement and participation of concerned parties. This fosters innovation and greater acceptance of change. But open communication does have a high cost in time and effort.

The strategic management process usually calls for an input of ideas from a wide spectrum of concerned parties inside and outside the organization and provides opportunity for their extensive participation and involvement. In some instances, reactions may be solicited from important donors, clients, funding organizations, or professional groups. Representatives from the community may be solicited for their concerns and interests.

The chief executive officer (Petersen 1988) of one regional organization offered this frank comment on participation and involvement in its strategic planning process:

The process of accumulating information, developing responses, reviewing conclusions with a variety of boards and committees involved, and producing the final document was far more involved than anyone anticipated. Communications had to include, in addition to our Board, seven Regional Boards, six Standing Committees, and from one to four committees for each of the seven Boards. In addition we had to keep our staff involved at all levels. The necessity for that kind of information exchange is one of the significant differences between our kind of nonprofit operation and a for-profit organization.

FOCUS ON MANAGEMENT OF STRATEGIC ISSUES

Reasons for Strategic Issues Management

Strategic issues management is a core concern of the strategic management system. The first reason for issues management is to focus management attention on resolving strategy-derived issues as they arise from implementing a selected strategy initiative. Previously, it was expected to revise strategies annually. But strategies are long-term affairs and can take several years to implement. Annual revisions were too disruptive and not practical, taking too much time with too little result. Consequently revisions tend to be made on a two-year basis. In the strategy review process, the identification of key issues and how they are resolved becomes the crux of the process.

A second reason for issues management is to resolve issues derived from the environment. These emerge from the process of environment scanning, identification of trends, or the detection of threats or opportunities. In many organizations, these kind of issues arise during the conduct of the situation audit or WOTS-UP analysis—an acronym for Weaknesses, Opportunities, Threats, or Strengths.

A third reason for the significance of issues management has been the occurrence of unexpected and surprise events that impact solidly on the organization and require attention. These so-called stochastic events occur at random and are often unanticipated. Their speed and novelty make them difficult to handle on a regular, scheduled time cycle. Provision must be made to enable issues to be identified and resolved off-cycle and as they occur, if they are sufficiently significant to require quick resolve. A prudent course of action is to prepare for the unexpected.

Organizations find it necessary to have an orderly process for issue identification, analysis, and management. Top management, in effect, becomes the issue management team, with the planning staff geared to do the staff work. In some organizations, the planning council or executive committee sets the key issue agenda and is the forum for the discussion and resolution of key issues. Rules of the strategic management system should define the process whereby issues are identified, reviewed, and decided.

Defining the Strategic Issue

Strategic issues vary from organization to organization and in point of time. But the sources of information about potential strategic issues are generic; they are the trends in the external environment (particularly the threats and opportunities), trends of strengths and weaknesses in the internal environment, and trends in organizational performance. Large organizations develop capabilities and extensive networks for systematically scanning the environment, assessing performance, and monitoring institutional strength. All organizations are alert to trouble spots, serious problems, or emerging opportunities. How they do it—and how well—is part of the strategic challenge.

These are some criteria that can be used for identifying and screening strategic issues for top management consideration:

—current or potential impact on organization performance, or any phase of the strategic process-strategy development, revision, or implementation;

—urgency in significant consequences and speed of occurrence; and

—impact or interdependence with other issues.

The Strategic Issues Management Process

Strategic issues management identifies, assigns priorities, and manages the analysis, review, and resolution of major issues, while addressing prime strategic concerns of an organization. It calls for early identification and fast response.

Strategic management calls for periodic review and updating of current issues. It does not wait for normally scheduled reviews or assessments. It can happen at any time. This necessitates a positive, aggressive search for emerging threats or opportunities and then quickly screening them for top management's attention.

Strategic issues management demands a quick response and entails the identification of a staff group to be responsible for soliciting issues from throughout the organization. It consolidates and screens the issues. The staff group may convert the issue to a standard format for the presentation of options and recommended actions. Often, teams or project task forces are temporarily established to examine those issues that cross organizational and functional lines, as many strategic issues do.

The ultimate responsibility for managing the strategic issues process belongs to top management. This is the source of power that has the authority and resource to initiate prompt action if necessary. Large organizations designate their executive committee or planning council for this task, with essential staff work performed by the office of central planning. Sometimes, several strategic management committees are formed, enabling separate committees to be established in functional or geographic areas that can take action in their respective areas. But usually, the strategic issues management committee cuts across hierarchical or functional areas and can assign the issue to an established unit or create a new task force or project team. Progress from the unit or team is reported directly to the designated top management center for strategic issues management.

Strategic issues management is integrally linked to the strategic management system. Generally, most strategic issues are generated through the periodically scheduled planning process and are incorporated into that process during its various phases. But the nature of strategic issues management insists that high-priority issues—wherever and whenever detected—must be able to move from detection to review, analysis, and approval in rapid time, and off-cycle from the scheduled strategic process.

The first prerequisite to successful strategic issues management is that it be an arm of top management and that top management give it full support and be involved. To enhance top management's acceptability, it may be necessary for members of the top management group to have a voice in ranking which issues should be addressed. Most importantly, the chief executive plays the crucial role in selecting and confronting the issues of greatest importance to the organization and not just those favored by several of the senior staff. The task of forging the strategic issue agenda is crucial to the long-term success of an organization.

PREPARING TO START FORMAL STRATEGIC PLANNING

Clarify Who's in Charge and Who Gets Involved; Build Support

The decision to start strategic planning in an organization can easily be made by the chief executive. The responsibility for strategic planning belongs to the chief executive, who may feel it is his or her prerogative to start. But recent evidence suggests that for sustained use of strategic planning the decision to start should rest on a strong coalition of commitment and sympathy for formal planning between the board chair and the chief executive (Melissa M. Stone 1991). It is urgent the chair and the chief executive share a positive consensus of support for the demands and promise of formal strategic planning. A strong coalition gives legitimacy to the process and encourages others to give it their best effort. The board chair and chief executive should be visibly involved in all major strategic decisions. Furthermore, the decision to start should not be made in isolation from the key executives within the agency, the influential members of the board, and those outside the organization who have a strong stake and influence in the organization—major donors, funding authorities, and parent or supervisory entities.

EMPOWER A PLANNING TEAM

The presence of a planning team serves to design and guide the effort to initiate, operate, and evaluate strategic planning. The team is advisory; it advises and recommends; the chief executive and top management team decide. In organizations with a governing board, the board is involved in all the major policy decisions.

The Planning Team's Role

The planning team serves as a staff arm to the chief executive for the design of strategic planning process, its plan of action, and the monitoring of progress and results. The team does not do all the planning for the organization and then sit down and prepare the strategic plan. Rather, the team sets up the process, devises the action plan, and sets the rules of the game for itself and others to play. Components of the process and action plan are assigned to individuals or teams, whether it be a recommended mission statement or an assessment of program performance; progress is then reviewed. Members of the planning team are expected to be helpful to members of the organization with assigned planning tasks for questions of substance, process, and possible outcomes. It is not unusual for planning team members to do some of the planning work and drafting, either as individuals or in task groups, particularly in smaller organizations.

Team Composition

Team members, often about four to six, are selected to reflect a balance in types of organizational expertise:

—topside executive with organization-wide perspective;
—planners with understanding of planning process and methods;
—experienced functional and technical experts that can help to assure sound substance; and
—experienced budget and management officials to relate monetary and managerial processes and substance to the plan's strategic plans and initiatives.

Primary Functions

Although the primary responsibility of the team is design of the planning process and its assignment and monitoring of planning tasks throughout the organization, other functions can be assigned:

—provide essential data and special studies when needed or assign to others wherever it can be best handled;
—supplies information on significant trends and issues arising from the environment;
—educates and trains personnel in strategic planning;
—reviews, consolidates, and evaluates proposed strategic directions and initiatives;
—prepares strategic plan guidance on the proposed submissions of the components for the strategic plan;
—serves as a facilitative and coordinating link to implementing management systems; and
—monitors action plans of approved initiatives for their implementation, reviews

progress and problems, and reports periodically to the planning council or other policy-level group about planning issues and progress.

In the larger agency, there often is a permanent chief planning advisor, who personally is on the planning team, and may be elected its chair. The office of the planning advisor may provide the secretariat for the planning team and do much of the staff work assigned to the team. The chief planning advisor, where one exists, is not a substitute for the planning team. Rather, the planning advisor is the key planning resource to the organization and the planning team. The planning team is a device that deliberately blends the expertise of top management perspective with operating functional expertise and with planning process and substance. This better enables the linking of process with the substantive achievement of desired outcomes and results—a fundamental aim of effective strategic planning and management.

RESEARCH INSIGHTS ON PLANNING ABANDONMENT

An article in the *Harvard Business Review* (Unterman and Davis 1982) asserted that nonprofits were probably a generation behind the strategic planning stage of development by for-profit organizations. Playing "catch-up," today's rapid pace of starting strategic planning has begun to show signs of difficulty. One indicator is the significant number of cases in which formal planning has been halted or abandoned (Melissa Stone 1991). In one survey, a sample of 44 selected randomly from a set of 104 arts nonprofits and 36 nonprofits serving the mentally retarded reveals that twelve organizations had abandoned or halted formal planning, while eight had no formal planning.

Characteristics of Organizations with Formal Planning

Research findings reveal that agencies that practiced ongoing planning or were beginning to plan were more likely to have a specific pattern of characteristics than those that had abandoned formal planning after an initial experience with the process. The characteristics are:

—a well-understood mission, that is, a general consensus about its general purpose and direction;

—a board that concerns itself with higher-level policy issues, such as goal attainment, rather than preoccupation with daily operational issues; and

—a board that has clear decision-making structures.

In the sample group organizations that had clarity of mission also tended to have boards that were concerned with policy matters and were structured for making decisions.

There is no certainty whether the revealed characteristics will guarantee sustained, effective planning. Stone's findings do suggest that it is prudent to assure that the characteristics are present in the organization. Apart from their importance to strategic planning, experience and current doctrine support the "primacy of mission" and a "dynamic board" as being hallmarks of excellence in nonprofit organizations (Knauft, Berger, and Gray 1991).

Characteristics of Planning Abandonment

Those organizations that had abandoned formal planning or have no planning were conspicuous for their lack of the three characteristics. Additionally, two other characteristics prevailed:

1. The organizations were more likely to have executive directors who described themselves as "entrepreneurial" or "going where the opportunities are." These executive directors were often negative about the effectiveness of long-range planning. One said, "When I've seen elaborate planning, things accomplished took longer and were not as exciting as when they are entrepreneurial. They became more bureaucratic." These managers preferred to make major decisions by themselves or with few staff members.

2. The organization was more likely to be a collection of individual interests rather than an organization with a broad organizational mission. For example, the founder of several arts organizations were artists, devoted to their art careers, but with little concern for management or their boards. In other instances, organizations working for group homes for the mentally retarded were often dominated by family members of clients, who preferred to deal with daily operational issues. In one case the board had vetoed a recommendation to set up a long-range planning committee. Its members felt that "such a committee was superfluous" because some of the founders made all the major decisions.

Organizational Context: External Norms and Pressures

Many, if not most, organizations that adopt formal planning and professional management methods are pragmatic. They respond to external norms and pressures—whether from a major donor, grantor, management assistance agency, or even the head of fundraising who feels it gives greater credibility and attractiveness to potential fund-raising sources. Major sources of funding by government entities expect "its contractors to be professionally managed" at both the board and staff levels.

Response to an individual board member is insufficient stimulus to start or sustain strategic planning without gaining a coalition of board and agency management support. If the individual board member were to leave, the lack of in-depth support could undermine sustained continuance for formal planning.

In certain instances of arts organizations, it was found that having corporate executives on board planning committees facilitated the positive coalition for planning by both board and staff management. As one manager said, "This plan was done because we got a committee and a chair that knew what planning was, and knew how to do it." But findings revealed that business representation on the board was not a sufficient condition; it was not significantly related to whether formal planning was started or abandoned. More pointedly, the findings suggest the value of having on the board members who are knowledgeable of and sympathetic to formal strategic planning and professional management processes and who can act in coalition with a similarly disposed executive director.

7

Organizing a Strategic Management System

GUIDING CONCEPT: RAISING THE QUALITY OF STRATEGIC DECISION-MAKING

The crux of strategic management is the ability to make and implement sound strategic decisions in a timely manner. Too often, the experts complain, strategic planning results in little more than "window dressing for poor thinking." When this occurs, the executives involved become disappointed, frustrated, and even scornful of the strategic process.

At best, people are reluctant decision-makers, institutions are worse, and public institutions are almost impossible. So often decisions are avoided, delayed, or kicked under the rug. When major issues are finally decided, it is often under conditions of conflicting demands and pressures, if not strong protest and sharp disagreement. The problem is compounded when the decision flounders in its implementation follow-through.

The dilemma of decision-making can be substantially resolved by a strategic management system that can satisfy certain conditions with special organizational arrangements.

Essential Conditions

To raise the quality of decision-making in a difficult environment, the following are some of the essential conditions to be satisfied:

Top Management's Visible Commitment and Involvement in the Strategic Management System and Plan. Without top executives' strong and consistent support, there can be no effective strategic management or strategic plan. Chief executives must be visibly involved—often in face-to-face meetings—with the organization's major strategic issues and decisions.

Chief executives usually take charge of developing the capability for strategic management. As part of this responsibility, they ensure proper system design for strategic management and designate the chief planner and how his or her planning role is to be played.

Informed, Coordinated Decision Support for Key Strategic Issues. Strategic decisions taken at the highest echelons of an organization are often complex, far-reaching, and vital to the organization's success. They merit the closest scrutiny and require the access to a supply of studies and data pointing out justification, benefits, and consequences—positive and negative.

For strategic decisions to be sound, and their implementation effective, they require the combined wisdom of three kinds of expertise: topside general executives with an overall perspective of the whole organization, planners with an understanding of planning process and technique, and functional experts who can determine technical soundness of decision substance. These combinations of expertise are embodied in the use of top-level planning councils and executive committees. Additionally, the legislature or the board provides guidance about the interests of the community and supplies a general guardianship of organizational performance.

Another essential condition for quality strategic decision-making is that key strategic issues affecting an organization be identified, analyzed, and submitted to the highest echelons of an organization. Vital to the success of decisions regarding the resolution of key issues is the quality of decision-making procedure and staff work that is developed. Usually the office of the chief planner serves as the staff arm of the top strategic committees and councils to perform the necessary analyses and provide the required documentation.

Integrated Implementation of Strategic Decisions. It may be stating the obvious to say that decisions are not self-implementing. But too often decisions flounder and are less than successful because of a lack of adequate provision for their implementation. Deliberate steps must be taken to assure that strategic initiatives are translated into an integrated form of program design or modification, staffing requirements, and funding. In some situations of high uncertainty and major risk, smaller starting projects of a pilot or demonstration nature can be used as learn-as-you-go before major investment commitments are undertaken.

Operational Support for the System. The strategic management system requires continuous attention and servicing to keep it functioning well. A host of operational matters are involved. The plan must be kept updated. A handbook that describes the strategic management system and prescribes rules and roles for its operation must be developed and maintained. Training and educational programs have to be designed, programmed, and executed. In the larger public organizations, the pre-packaging of hiring qualified contractors to render quality consulting service more quickly on a when-needed basis must be accomplished.

Special Organizational Arrangements

Meeting the conditions essential to the quality of decision-making in a strategic management system can be substantially assisted by special organizational arrangements. Strategic management by its very nature cuts across functional and organizational lines. It aims to provide a co-herent strategy for direction, focus, and new initiatives. In traditional managerial thinking and practice, such aims are usually the role of top management structure. But the practice of strategic management leads to greater knowledge of the external forces that have an impact on the decision-making and operating of an organization. Making sound deci-sions that deal with the complexity, novelty, and speed of these external forces necessitates the emergence of new structures and changed think-ing about current ones.

The new or adapted structures give visibility and direct attention to efforts to raise the quality of strategic decision-making. They designate focal points of authority for review and approval. They assign new roles that cut across traditional organizational boundaries and promote a re-sponsibility for the organization as a whole, rather than a composite of many independent feudal entities. They create expectations of quality decision-making and establish procedure to achieve it. Such structures can mobilize expertise whenever and wherever needed, regardless of organizational boundaries and levels of hierarchy.

Descriptions of four special organizational arrangements follow. Some stand as separate entities; others may be internal units of other structures that perform the necessary supervision and administrative support.

PLANNING COUNCIL OR EXECUTIVE COMMITTEE

Focus on Quality of Decision-Making

At the core of the strategic management system is its ability to render timely and sound decisions related to the most urgent strategic issues and concerns, that is, whether they constitute constraints, threats, or op-portunities. This is the role of the planning council or executive com-mittee. In large nonprofit organizations there may also be an executive committee at the board level. The composition of such councils or com-mittees is usually the top management team, with the chief executive as "chair," the deputy as vice chair, and other members being chief counsel, planning chief, and other designated top policy-making assistants.

Primary Functions

The planning council or executive committee is responsible for these kinds of activities:

Selecting the Key Strategic Issues for Resolution. The committee sets the strategic agenda for the organization that is selective and flexible. Being selective means that not all issues must be considered at the planning council level, only those deemed most urgent to the organization's successful future. Being flexible means that issue agendas are not confined only to those contained in the strategic plan. Issue agendas for an organization are not set in stone; issues must be identified, submitted for decision, and resolved whenever they are deemed important to the organization and not necessarily in accord with a prearranged schedule.

Considering Possible Courses of Action. The council or committee makes decisions, selecting the best course of action based on the information provided. It ensures that decisions are made in the context of environmental trends and events and internal strengths and weaknesses.

Coordinating and Securing Agreement Where Required. This may involve communicating with elements outside the organization's jurisdiction to secure their cooperation wherever they influence or are influenced by the organization's operation. Such activity may involve securing agreement, enhancing understanding, or gaining active assistance in pursuit of a common strategic purpose.

Establishing Means of Resolving Conflicts. This may involve the active identification and analysis of conflicting points of view, pressure points, and their protagonists and antagonists. It could involve negotiation and compromise.

Obtaining External Assistance—Financial or Technical. There may be situations where major additional assistance is necessary and high-level intervention is required to get authorization and funds.

The Internal Revenue Service describes the role of its policy and planning council:

The Planning Council is chaired by the Commissioner. Members are the Deputy Commissioner, the Chief Counsel, the Deputy Chief Counsel, and the Associate Commissioners (Data Processing), (Operations), and (Policy Management). The Planning Council serves as a forum for discussion of policy and strategic issues to assist the Commissioner in making policy decisions. Issues are proposed for Planning Council consideration by any Service executive. Moreover, all employees are encouraged to raise issues to keep the Strategic Plan current (U.S. Treasury 1985, Sec. 220).

Importance of Decision-Making Procedure

For most decisions—other than those with single objectives such as making money or gaining votes—social scientists find it difficult to determine if the decision has worked out well, particularly decisions in the public and nonprofit world. The results of most decisions include some benefits gained and some undesirable losses realized. Often, quantitative values are assigned—though subjectively—to the balance of benefits and losses, sometimes related to costs. Almost every executive has had to submit a cost-effectiveness justification for a proposal. Decision-making experts consider such ratings of "doubtful validity because they are subject to a variety of errors deriving from face-saving distortion and rationalization" (Janus and Mann 1977, 10–11). Janus and Mann suggest a preferable way of predicting whether a given decision is likely to lead to satisfaction or regret. From the extensive literature on decision-making, they have extracted seven major criteria that can be used to determine whether decision-making procedures are of high quality. Though they concede systematic data are not available, they claim that satisfying these seven "ideal" criteria will enable the decisions to have a "better chance than others of obtaining the decision-maker's objectives and of being adhered to in the long run."

To the best of his or her ability and within his or her information-processing capabilities, the decision-maker:

1. thoroughly canvasses a wide range of alternative courses of action;
2. surveys the full range of objectives to be fulfilled and the values implied by the choice;
3. carefully weighs whatever he or she knows about the costs, risks, and negative consequences of each alternative;
4. intensively searches for new information relevant to further evaluation of the alternatives;
5. correctly assimilates and takes into account any new information or expert judgment to which he or she is exposed, even when the information or judgment does not support the course of action initially preferred;
6. reexamines the positive and negative consequences of all known alternatives, including those originally regarded as unacceptable, before making a final choice; and
7. makes detailed provisions for implementing or executing the chosen course of action, with special attention to contingency plans that might be required if various known risks were to materialize.

Janus and Mann's working assumption is "that failure to meet any of these seven criteria when a person is making a fundamental decision (one with major consequences for attaining or failing to attain important values) constitutes a defect in the decision-making process." They further assume that "the more defects, the more likely the decision-maker will undergo unanticipated setbacks and experience post-decisional regret." The rigor of the recommended criteria with its implied high cost in time and effort may help to explain why so many decisions end in setbacks and regret.

CHIEF PLANNER AS EXPERT ADVISOR

The Facilitative Approach

The primary role of the central planner is to serve as advisor to decision-makers, the prime client being the chief executive and top assistants. The planner advises and recommends; the chief executive decides. Chief planners must be qualified to address key issues that are important to decision-makers. They must be able to provide policy and strategy alternatives, recommendations, and estimates of consequences that are timely.

Although planners are always expected to be technically competent, they must also be sensitive to the real world's demands of political, economic, and social pressures put upon decision-makers. There are situations where the technical perception of planners can be at variance with the seasoned judgment of high-level decision-makers. Some decisions— or lack of decision, or its delay—may appear to the planner as sheer irresponsibility or an avoidance of a painful choice to ward off tomorrow's consequences. But the high-level decision-maker may perceive the situation as keeping faith with political promises or reducing political risk and gaining positive consequences.

To state that there are two sides to decision-making is often gross simplification. For each strategic choice, there may be several premises and several alternative conclusions; each choice may entail combinations of fact, value, and doctrine. Mature perspective is required of chief planners in order to discriminate among technical factors and the pressures of environmental demands. In some situations, the planner is asked to help in the process of negotiation and compromise. In any event, the chief planner must be able to retain the trust and support of the chief executive.

How planners perform their advisory role is a crucial element in the effectiveness of their working relationships with executives. At progressive organizations, reported in a survey by the World Bank in Washington, D.C., planners described their role as "process facilitators who help foster change in the consciousness of others" (Hanna 1985, 48). They exert their influence by generating new ideas, information, perspectives, knowledge of external trends and significant issues, and experience with planning processes and techniques. Their advisory role is similar to independent professionals in a consultant-client relationship.

Some planners prefer to provide solutions and write planning documents. Sometimes this is necessary and warranted. But the most effective role of planners is to assist executives by providing them with data, and sometimes the assistance of others, for making their own decisions. It is increasingly recognized that planners are acting to facilitate the thinking and action of management, rather than planning for others or providing their own solutions. The planning role is becoming one of advisor and catalyst for strategic thinking and is a stimulating source for anticipating and facilitating constructive change.

Functions

Provides Essential Data and Special Studies. This information may be supplied on a periodic basis or upon request.

Supplies Information on Significant Trends and Issues Arising from the External Environment. Planning offices, in effect, can become the chief executive's "eyes and ears" to the outside world. They may organize an organization-wide network of trend identification and analysis, with a periodic journal to communicate trend findings.

Designs and Evaluates the System. The central planning office usually designs the details of the strategic management process, sometimes with the aid of outside consultants.

Educates and Trains Personnel. It is common for workshops and seminars to be conducted on-site or in nearby universities to help executives do their strategic work and particularly to prepare their strategic submissions in the prescribed manner. In some organizations, such as the Internal Revenue Service, educational stipends have been granted for the study of strategic management. The limitation of university study for participants from public and nonprofit organizations has been that the content of courses and literature in strategic management has been oriented to the profit-seeking private sector. This is changing with the availability of books and journal articles on the growing experience of strategic planning in the public and nonprofit sectors.

Reviews, Consolidates, and Evaluates Proposed Strategic Directions and Initiatives. Central planning staff usually do the staff work essential to the consolidation, review, and approval of the components and composite strategic plan, prior to their submission to the approving authority (the planning council or the executive committee). The authority to change, modify, or stop strategic proposals varies from organization to organization and needs to be clarified to avoid sharp conflict.

Prepares Strategic Plan Guidance. The office of chief planner prepares or consolidates for the chief executive the guiding message to the organization on the proposed submission of the strategic plan. Guidance may offer significant overall trends, constraints, or opportunities affecting the strategic plan submissions of the various organizational entities and line-of-service groups. In some instances, the guidance may present for reaction and reaffirmation the statement of mission, fundamental organizational values, and the essential strategic focus and priorities.

Conducts Evaluations of Strategic Performance and Develops Indicators and Measures of Strategic Progress. The work of evaluation and development of indicators of progress is usually done with the participation of teams of agency executives and sometimes with the help of outside consultants.

The central planning office of a large national nonprofit organization, the American Red Cross, offers consultative field support in strategic plan development to its local affiliates. In one mode, it provides consultative technical assistance in a facilitative manner by phone or through the mail. It offers suggestions on strategic process, plan development, or ways to organize board planning committees. In another mode, staff from the central planning office work out jointly with local executives a local chapter's strategic plan. In other instances, it offers full service for a modest fee to develop a local chapter's strategic process and plan with use of an assigned project leader and several central staff in active collaboration with local leaders and staff.

STRATEGIC MANAGEMENT SUPPORT GROUP

Focus on Implementation

The strategic management support group, chaired by the chief planner, is established to assist the chief executive in ensuring follow-through on the implementation of all initiatives in the strategic plan. The group is composed of the chairpersons who have been designated to be the action officers for each of the approved areas of strategic initiatives. They are responsible for developing action plans and the implementation of specific initiatives. In the Internal Revenue Service, the chairpersons are in charge of teams of individual executives who have been designated to implement specific strategic initiatives. Action plans and subsequent progress are discussed at meetings of the support group. Support group designees are usually key executives with some program responsibility in the initiative area, who possess the pertinent background, knowledge, and understanding that underlie the particular strategic initiative.

The support group, as an extension of the planning council, is intended to reduce the workload of the planning council, whose members have duties that are very demanding. It brings together key executives with major strategic plan responsibilities to follow through and monitor the implementation of approved initiatives, review activity, and report progress on implementation to the planning council or executive committee.

One agency involved in strategic management, the Internal Revenue Service, asserts that key executive attention is critical for effective implementation, particularly in the initial operational stages of an approved initiative. The use of a special organizational arrangement provides a visible means for ensuring that initiatives are accomplished in a timely fashion and, when necessary, will enable changes to be made quickly. It demonstrates clearly to everyone concerned that the organization is making a long-term commitment to strategic management.

Functions

A strategic management support group:

1. Provides a forum for dialogue and issues on the implementation of strategic initiatives;
2. Focuses responsibility and accountability for the implementation of specific strategic initiatives;
3. Serves as a coordinating and facilitative link to other management systems;
4. Monitors action plans of approved initiatives, reviews progress and problems, and reports periodically to the planning council; and
5. Submits issues arising from implementation to the planning council for resolution.

STRATEGIC OPERATIONAL SERVICE GROUP

Focus and Function

The focus of the strategic operational service group is to service the strategic management system with several activities essential to its operation and maintenance. The group may be an integral part of the office of the chief planner. Its functions include:

1. Devising and maintaining an issuance and instruction handbook on how strategic management works in the organization;
2. Taking or coordinating measures to keep the plan current that may involve the use of trend analysis and issue papers;
3. Conduct a continuing orientation and training program in strategic management; and
4. Making available prescreened, qualified contractors on a quick response basis, as and when needed, to help in the development or implementation of strategic initiatives.

These functions are described as follows:

Use of a Strategic Management Handbook. The need to inform and guide the staff on how to go about the task of strategic management is well served by a compact, well-organized, widely distributed loose-leaf handbook. This handbook serves as a key tool in increasing awareness and commitment to the practice of strategic management. It must be well documented and fully understood by managers and executives at all levels. It can be supplemented by group seminars and workshops.

The handbook describes the strategic management system and its central component, the strategic plan, and the roles and rules whereby strategic management is practiced in the organization. The handbook contains a personal message from the chief executive and is distributed widely throughout the organization. It contains ways for keeping the plan current and indicates how to modify and update the handbook. Responsibility for the handbook may be assigned to the office of planning.

Keeping the Plan Current. The handbook indicates ways to keep the plan current. It prescribes the importance of identifying trends and developing issues of long-term significance to the strategic management of an organization. The Internal Revenue Service has a well-organized system for performing trend analysis and preparing issue papers. Trend analysis consists of identifying trends, gathering and organizing data, interpreting trends as to their impact, and formulating alternative responses for high-level consideration. Issue papers may be a relatively brief two or three pages in length. They contain this kind of information: statement of issue to be considered, an analysis of trends involved, and if possible, recommendations for a higher authority to consider. Detailed background and justification material may accompany an issue paper. The planning office will usually review the issue paper for coordination and completeness before being presented to the planning council or executive committee.

Continuous Orientation and Training Program. Extensive orientation and training efforts for almost all employees with various roles and responsibilities in strategic management are well justified. It is vitally important to stimulate awareness, commitment, and competence in thinking and acting strategically.

In the initial period of establishing a strategic management system, mass orientation seminars should be convened to hear the chief executive and the top management team explain what they mean by strategic management and tell why it is important to the organization and to each staff member. Other types of seminars can instruct staff how to be competent and comfortable in using strategic management methods in the conduct of their jobs. These seminars can be conducted by a combination of outside consultants with employees representing both the functions of staff planning and operational executive experience. Some organizations do a needs analysis of the organization that details what training is needed by whom and indicates the priority interests of employees.

Adding a series of books on strategic management to an organization's library is a wise investment. Some organizations, such as the federal government, pay the costs for employees to attend relevant courses at universities. The United States foreign aid program pays the costs for foreign officials of third world countries to attend courses in strategic management in the United States.

Readily Available, Prescreened Technical Assistance. Large public organizations, with all the talent they possess, still find it necessary and cost-effective to contract for technical assistance in their management practice. They find it advantageous to have readily available, prescreened qualified contractors to perform quick response services on a when-needed basis. They advertise for, screen, and hire in advance of work to be performed a number of qualified firms. This is done on the basis of a broad scope of work so that the contractors can respond quickly to requests for specific services. The Internal Revenue Service calls the prescreened services "task order contracts," and the Agency for International Development calls them "Indefinite Quantity Contracts." Both processes are in accord with federal procurement regulations.

8

Evaluating a Strategic Management System

GUIDING CONCEPT: CONSTANT LEARNING, CONTINUOUS IMPROVEMENT

Developing an effective strategic management system is never a one-time effort. Rather, constant learning and continuous improvement is the guiding concept. This learning mode starts out with a carefully considered design format that is adapted to local organizational conditions that exist at the time. Then the design effort continues to search for an "adaptive redesign" that readjusts the system to make it more attuned to the changing needs and interests of the organization. This constitutes an organized learning mode where one can continue to learn more about what is being done so that one can do better.

Extent of Institutionalization

The essential concern for evaluation is to discover the extent to which the strategic management system has become institutionalized, that is, an accepted and effective way of thinking and acting strategically on the organization's priority issues. The ideal expectation is that the system encourages individuals throughout the organization to react and adapt constructively to constantly changing conditions. In doing its strategic work, the organization scans the environment and identifies key issues, establishes strategic directions, embodies and promotes specific values, and moves forward by undertaking strategic initiatives. Meanwhile, top management visibly takes on the crucial task of developing strategic capability and improving strategic performance. Ensuring that these conditions prevail in the organization is essential for the system evaluation process.

Does the System Work? How Well?

The evaluation process must pragmatically determine whether the system works to promote the intended level of strategic performance. Otherwise, the system may become bureaucratically rigid, lessening flexibility to change directions whenever necessary despite what the strategic plan states. Evaluations can also render the system "user-friendly" to ensure that the burden of strategic work does not exceed the level of employee tolerance. Dissatisfaction with the system's requirements can promote discontent and low morale, thereby undermining the creative effectiveness of the system.

TEN MAJOR MISTAKES TO AVOID

More than two decades of experience with strategic planning systems have revealed a great deal of dissatisfaction. Lessons have been learned about what is to be done and how, and what should be avoided. Steiner (1979), an eminent authority and author on strategic planning and management, sent a questionnaire to six hundred companies and received one-third in usable replies. The questionnaire contained fifty pitfalls—summarizing a vast collection of dissatisfaction, mistakes, and lessons of experience with strategic planning. The pitfalls listed in the questionnaire ranged across the spectrum of strategic planning. It described problems in getting started and problems related to the nature of strategic planning. Other pitfalls had to do with the process of strategic planning and using strategic plans.

Of the fifty pitfalls listed, the ten major avoidable mistakes were:

1. top management's assumption that it could delegate the planning function to a planner;
2. top management becoming so engrossed in current problems that it spends insufficient time on long-range planning and the process becomes discredited among other managers and staff;
3. failure to develop company goals suitable for formulating long-range plans;
4. failure to ensure the necessary involvement of major line personnel in the planning process;
5. failure to use plans as standards for measuring managerial performance;
6. failure to create a climate in the company that is congenial and not resistant to planning;

7. the assumptions that comprehensive planning is something separate from the entire management process;

8. the injection of so much formality into the system that it lacks flexibility, looseness, and simplicity and restrains creativity;

9. failure of top management to review with departmental and divisional heads the long-range plans that they have developed; and

10. top management's consistent rejection of the formal planning mechanism by making intuitive decisions that conflict with the formal plan (Steiner 1979, 294).

One limitation of this ranking is the questionnaire's focus on strategic planning rather than the fuller phases that extend to implementation. Even so, though the listing derives from firms in the private sector, the pitfalls are pertinent to organizations in the public and nonprofit sector. It will be invaluable when similar surveys are conducted for public and nonprofit organizations that operate strategic management systems.

MODIFICATIONS ON THE STEINER REPORT CARD

Designing a strategic management system can be complex and difficult; evaluating its effectiveness is equally so. No one is ever happy with any bureaucratic routine, no matter how urgent or valuable. Lingering frustration and dissatisfaction will undermine system performance and may eventually lead to the system's abandonment or disintegration. It is prudent to make sure that the system and its prime users are compatible in expectations for what the system can do and its results.

Steiner (1979) also devised an evaluation questionnaire that applied primarily to private-sector organizations. Most of the questions are valid for public and nonprofit organizations, although the shift in thinking from strategic planning to strategic management suggests additional emphasis on plan implementation and on the extent to which planning is linked to other management processes.

The main elements of evaluation as used in the Steiner evaluation schema, with two others added, follow.

Overall Managerial Perceived Value

This element seeks to learn what the chief executive and other major line managers think about whether the system helps to carry out their strategic responsibilities more effectively and is actually useful to them. Questions can be used to ferret out whether the benefits are perceived to be greater than the costs and the attendant physical and mental effort involved. Evaluation questions about the system can focus on potential benefits: Does the system sharply raise and answer issues of major importance, for example, does it relate to underlying purposes, strategic direction, basic values, services rendered, and target clienteles? Does the system compel the setting of strategic directions and the taking of strategic initiatives? Does it reveal future opportunities and serious constraints? A general question to determine the degree of satisfaction with the current system could be "Are any major changes needed in the strategic management system?"

Production of "Correct" Substantive Answers and Results

This element focuses on perception of the substance of strategic management. Evaluation questions can cover the satisfaction level with the entire range of end-product components of the strategic management system, including:

—development of organizational mission statement;

—identifying future major opportunities;

—anticipating future major threats;

—appraising organizational strengths or weaknesses;

—clarifying priorities;

—setting strategic directions;

—formulating strategies;

—undertaking strategic initiatives;

—mobilizing means of implementation: funds, staffing, and facilities; and

—preventing unpleasant surprises.

System Design

This element focuses on the determinants that condition the design of a strategic management system and render it unique and appropriate to an organization's circumstances. The primary question concerns the extent of top management's commitment and support for the strategic management system.

—Does the chief executive give visible, personal attention and effort to the system?

—Does the system establish realistic decision processes and focal points?

—Do the central planners work well with top management and with other managers throughout the organization?

—Do the central planners provide facilitative advice on strategic management and the development of a strategic plan to local affiliates or other organizational units?

—Do the strategic management committees and councils work well?

Strategic Management Processes

This element seeks to ascertain the effectiveness of the processes of strategic management with its central feature of strategic plan development.

—Is the amount of time and nature of effort given by the chief executive to strategic management substantial or perfunctory?

—What is the extent of acceptance or dissatisfaction of managers with strategic management processes and work requirements?

—Is the process sufficiently flexible to permit issues to be identified and decided whenever needed, regardless of what is contained in the plan?

—Is adequate attention given to indicators and measures to evaluate progress?

—Is there an adequate flow of ideas to decision centers from inside the organization and external committees?

—Are there too many layers of review? Are the reviews and analyses prescribed by the system excessively time-consuming and sufficiently productive?

Yield of Valuable Ancillary Benefits

This element focuses on assessing the extent to which the system produces ancillary benefits. The strategic management system is geared primarily to fulfill specified major purposes, such as facilitating strategic planning, selecting effective strategies, or causing major redirections or substantial renewal. Additionally, the system can yield other, perhaps less urgent but still substantial, benefits that tend to deal with the institutional strengthening of an organization essential for strategic performance. Such benefits can consist of these types of activities:

—improved communications;

—improved managerial systems;

—greater sense of participation;

—improved managerial training and expanded opportunities for manager's contribution and promotion; and

—improved coordination of organization programs and operations and enhanced cooperation among operating divisions and levels of hierarchy.

Integration of Planning with Other Managerial Systems

The transition of strategic planning to strategic management in organizational practice makes it clear that planning alone will not produce the necessary mobilization of resources and expertise to respond to and implement strategic thrusts. Planning processes must be deliberately linked to other managerial processes so that strategic decisions can translate into operations throughout the organization. Progressive organizations, according to a World Bank survey, have integrated their planning processes with other managerial systems: organization structure, resource allocation, program management, evaluation, communication and information systems, and performance and reward incentives.

Key questions can be used to ferret out the extent of, and need for, greater integration of strategic planning with operational and budget plans, and other related managerial systems: Does the strategic framework in the plan directly relate to an implementation profile of resource allocation, implementing programs, and human resource requirements? Are changes in the system needed to improve strategy implementation by further integrating planning with other management systems?

Adequacy of Servicing the System

This element seeks to determine the quality of operational support and service given to achieving the effectiveness of the system. Some key factors to be checked are:

—the quality of the issuance and instruction handbook on strategic management;

—the adequacy of the measures and process to keep the strategic plan current and up-to-date, such as the use of trend analysis and strategic issues management;

—the quality of orientation, training, and education for developing strategic management capability; and

—the adequacy of making readily available qualified contractors to provide, on a when-needed basis in short-order fashion, technical assistance to meet an organization's needs for developing or implementing strategic initiatives.

Part 4

SETTING THE
STRATEGIC AGENDA

9

Making Strategic Assessments

Few managers are aware of the great changes taking place in the real world that seriously affect the performance of their programs and operations. Some changes occur rapidly; others seem to stretch out over years. How to learn about these changes in time to counter their negative affects or exploit an emerging opportunity is a major concern for the program manager. The process by which this is done is called "strategic situation auditing."

WHAT IS THE STRATEGIC SITUATION AUDIT?

Operationally, the strategic situation audit is an analysis of performance and whatever seriously affects it, in order to provide a basis for making strategic decisions and for preparing the strategic plan. The aim is to make a significant improvement in the way an organization provides quality product and service.

There does not appear to be any consensus on the precise content of the situation audit. In this book we discuss three important content areas from which individual organizations can custom design what is most appropriate for them: performance, environmental impact, and strategic implications.

An audit, to be most effective, should be limited in scope or concretely targeted to a particular organization unit, or program, or several of them. But the audit should never attempt to analyze the total organization. Trying to analyze everything, and all at once, dilutes the ability to get the analytical job done in time to take opportune action.

Strategic audits can be conducted on a formal, systematic basis or handled very informally. They can be structured and prescribed, or they can be handled simply by individual managers talking in a free-wheeling manner with colleagues and subordinates over breakfast or lunch.

In some organizations, the audit is very complete and comprehensive; in others the process is loose, unstructured, and partial. In practice, both modes of audit can and should occur simultaneously. Many organizations blend formal and informal approaches with a tendency to move toward more systematic but targeted assessments, leading to preparation of a strategic plan.

Purpose of the Strategic Audit

The major purpose of the strategic audit is to identify and analyze the key external events and trends that have a potential impact on current or future performance. This means identifying the external forces before their serious impact is felt. No organization can identify every bit of information that influences strategic decisions. But each organization must learn to look for those factors in the changing environment that are of the greatest interest to them, which could have the greatest impact.

A second purpose is to provide a forum for sharing and debating divergent views about the noted environmental changes and their possible impact. Ambiguities and uncertainties in the environment can be made more explicit and assessed.

A third purpose is to guide the quality of intellectual thinking associated with the strategic audit to stimulate creative and innovative approaches. It is urgent not to permit the auditing activity to degenerate into a routine bureaucratic exercise that generates a great deal of paperwork and elegant analytical technique but does not add much more in the way of new and exciting initiatives. The wise role of strategic leadership is to create the climate conducive to creative change and stimulate staff to do their best in finding exciting answers to harassing problems.

Content of the Strategic Audit

The strategic audit covers in content whatever is necessary to tell us where we really are in relationship to the outside world. It takes a sharp picture of how well we are doing now and what may happen to us in the future. Generally, the diagnostic content includes these elements:

Performance. An analysis of data about past and present performance and any existing forecasts and projections; sometimes it also includes an analysis of institutional and managerial support, such as structure, system, and top management commitment.

Environmental Context. An identification of trends, forces, and events having a potential impact on the formulation and implementation of strategic directions and initiatives.

Strategic Implications. The analysis of strengths and weaknesses of an organization and the threats and opportunities that exist in the organization's environment.

Recent thinking refines and extends strategic analysis to examine issues of comparative advantage, investment and disinvestment, and damage control (Kearns 1992). Sophisticated analyses of strategic issues can adapt the private sector techniques of portfolio analysis with use of the Growth Share Matrix developed by the Boston Consulting Group, wherein products or services with strong competitive positions are labeled "stars" and are nurtured, or "cash cows" and are "milked." Other products or services may be labeled "dogs" or "question marks" and are targeted for phasing out or removal.

Process of the Strategic Audit

As a process, strategic auditing is a recurring activity that must be staffed, scheduled, and organized. Working methods must be designed and tested; staff must be trained in their use. Obviously, staff cannot be fully engaged in their regular professional duties and work overtime on strategic analysis. Schedules must be rearranged, and workload burdens be reallocated, so that strategic analysis is made a regular part of program management work. This requires top management understanding and support.

When strategic audits are to be performed, a series of steps must be planned and implemented:

—Undertake performance analysis;

—conduct an environmental scan;

—build a strategic situation data base;

—perform a strategic implications analysis;

—derive a set of strategic planning issues;

—set strategic goals to channel change into the most productive areas;

—choose appropriate strategies; and

—design new strategic initiatives to start necessary action.

Each of the steps is described and discussed in the following sections of this chapter.

ASSESSING PROGRAM PERFORMANCE

The assessment of performance is designed to provide an objective basis for answering this crucial question: How well are we really doing? And will we continue to do so? To answer the question, we propose that three elements of performance be subjected to analysis, and a "profile of supply and demand" be developed, as follows:

—Supply of outputs of product and service.

—Market demand for product and service.

—Resources mobilized for use in providing product and service.

Profiling Supply and Demand

A "first cut" at the supply and demand situation is to take a focused picture or "profile" of the products and services provided and to whom. Compiling a profile of benchmark data of the current situation provides a firm basis for determining what can or should be done to improve performance.

Developing the profile starts by clarifying terminology and asking these basic questions:

—What are the services and products that constitute the output of the particular program? This we call *supply*.

—To whom are they provided? This is the *demand factor* or *market segment*. What are the client's key characteristics?

—When and where are they provided, and at what cost, if any? This is the *delivery factor*.

—What (and how many) resources are required and used to provide current supply and meet demand?

—What changes in the current situation are indicated? Why?

Useful Checklist for Supply/Demand Profiling

To provide a solid set of answers to the above questions, we have developed a checklist of further questions to guide an investigation. These questions are merely suggested guidelines to get you going in the right directions and in no way should prevent you from probing other areas that may be directly relevant to your situation. Unfortunately, it is often necessary to answer questions by asking more questions, if we really mean to probe deeply enough to arrive at reliable and proper answers.

Product and Service (Supply and Delivery)

—What quality P and S do we provide? Characterize level of quality and reliability or consistency.

—Which are in most demand? Why? How do we know? Do we have a competitive advantage? Are we distinctive?

—Which do we prefer to supply? Why?

—Are new P and S planned or desired?

—Are the P and S adequately available, accessible, and affordable to clients?

—Identify key people who can and do affect supply and rank them (if possible) in terms of their power to start, stop, or modify any changes to be made.

Client or Beneficiaries

—Who are our clients or beneficiaries?

—What are their characteristics? How do they know about our P and S? What do they consider to be primary value?

—What new markets should we serve?

—How do our clients see us? Are they satisfied?

—What do they think we do well or poorly?

—How can they register complaints? Does it matter if they do?

Resource Mobilization

—What budgetary resources are available? Are they adequate?

—What is current staffing? Vacancies? Turnover?

—Is current equipment adequate? What is needed and why?

—Are facilities adequate and sufficiently modern?

—Do staffing shortages exist, or do we have excess personnel?

—Are staff qualified and well-trained? Is further training indicated?

—Do we use flexible, temporary staff arrangements?

Assessing Balance: A Basis for Strategy Building

To build an effective performance strategy, one seeks to assure the balance of the components of supply, demand, and resource. The first concern is to determine in which component the major problems reside. Is demand insufficient, that is, you do not have enough clients, even though the identified need is large and supplies are available? Or is demand greater than supply? Perhaps the big bottleneck is lack of adequate resources, people, or equipment to satisfy pressing demand.

The next step is to analyze the situation in terms of its most pressing problem in order to develop an appropriate strategy for its corrective action. Are you building primarily a supply, demand, or resource strategy? The reason you want to know this is that corrective strategies, to be effective, must address different aspects of performance depending on the nature of the problem. Also, the expertise to take corrective action resides in different places. The power to take action also rests with different people in the hierarchy. For example, when demand is high but people and equipment are inadequate, it may be possible to convince top management, which controls resource flow, to remedy the situation. But if available supply is high and demand is low, then attention must flow to investigating clientele behavior and directing efforts to influence and increase demand. The strategic-minded manager wants to work on the most serious problem and not be distracted by a host of smaller problems that may not make a significant difference.

Clients may often fail to respond because of an unwillingness or an inability, or both. If so, incentives or information may be useful to generate demand. Sometimes a negative image of the product or service may inhibit demand. Or clients may feel the product does not meet their need, or expectation, even if it does. One must be aware that clients often respond in what seem like nonrational ways, in that they behave in ways that are counter to their own best interest. It is wise to realize that in many situations feelings are facts, and must be accommodated.

The concept of balance is derived from system-thinking and is an obvious and simple one, despite the elegance of its label. What it means is that an adequate amount of resource must be mobilized if we wish to provide a specific supply of product and service. Both the amount of resource and the supply of product must match but not be excessive to the demand by targeted clientele. If not, there will be serious imbalance with negative consequences. You could be wasting money and time and may be undermining the success of your program.

For example, in the field of family planning, merely having on hand an extensive supply of contraceptive devices is a necessary condition, but it is insufficient for success. An adequate demand for the contraceptive's use must also exist, together with essential acceptance, accessibility, and affordability.

Of course, perfect balance may never be achieved. But one seeks to maintain the best possible balance over time to accommodate changing conditions. Thus, we are concerned not with a one-time check, but a continuous process of finding out what is happening, and learning how to be responsive to needed change.

Useful Checklist for Balance of Supply, Demand, and Resource

—What are the operating goals and objectives for the program?

—What are the most urgent problems?

- A supply problem?
- A demand problem?
- A resource problem?

—What factors seem to create the problems?

—Which imbalances are occurring? What consequences?

—Can supply and its resource requirement be deferred or time-phased till a different demand is effectively expressed?

—What specific interventions are indicated? To whom?

—Where are the power points and decision-makers to alleviate the problem?

—What measures are needed to win their support?

READING THE ENVIRONMENT

The task of reading the environment means identifying the set of external events and trends that can and do influence the outcomes of program performance. Environments and programs constantly interact with each other. Programs most often draw their inputs of resources from the outside, such as staff, equipment, and finance. They depend on the market for money and people, which of course is constantly changing. At the same time, the outputs of supply depend on changing conditions of demand and what clientele need and want.

Managers are always looking for reliable data and signals from the outside community that can help them make their strategic decisions. As a general rule, these are some elements of the environment that require special attention and indicate frequent need for intervention and linkage. They are defined as follows:

Detecting Forces and Trends. The identification and analysis of trends and events, or any external force, that can influence the performance elements of a program's supply, demand, or resource is necessary. Part of the analysis should focus on the way the data are collected to assure their continuing timeliness, efficiency, and effectiveness.

Assessing Complexity and Risk. The systematic examination of the size and spatial coverage of a program and its degree of homogeneity or diversity of its clientele or product is required. The extent of stability or turbulence or uncertainty in the environment is also covered.

Identifying Influential Actors and Institutions. The identification and linkage with key actors and institutions whose support and action need to be mobilized to improve the performance profile is important.

Calculating Competitive Advantage. The identification of strengths and core competences that give you competitive advantage over other providers of service and product is necessary.

Detecting Forces and Trends

Most program managers agree on the importance of scanning the environment, but few understand how to go about it. Even when they do, it is difficult and time-consuming to compile and analyze relevant data. Yet the job must be done, or programs will run the risk of failure, as changing conditions undermine program performance and affect ultimate survival. The issue is not whether to do it; it must be done. Rather, the issue is to do it efficiently and effectively.

The environment is a big area; but it does contain different segments of behavior that may be relevant. Some are political, where conditions are set by government policies or rules or by decisions government officials make. Others are economic, which set the conditions of employment, inflation, or interest rates. Others are social-cultural, which set the conditions of lifestyle and determine how large segments of the population live and behave toward each other. Another segment of the environment pertains to technology, which determines how we go about the technical part of business and influences the choices suppliers of goods and services make, as well as the choices of clients.

Of course it is not possible for any program manager to scan the entire range of environmental behavior. A manager looks at professional or trade journals, reads daily newspapers, has lunch with colleagues, and attends conferences. Actually many large corporations hire special services that do systematic scans of the environment and provide special analyses for their clients. Some recent best-sellers offer the major findings of recent change; one identifies the "megatrends."

Our scan of the environment looks for those conditions that can influence client demand or can affect the way we supply product or mobilize resources. We seek to learn of significant events or trends that may impact our decisions or indicate the need for changes in the way we do our business. In larger organizations where the external trends are so important, they organize within the organization to go about scanning the environment in the most efficient way. The Internal Revenue Service recognized the need for a trend coordinator to establish good communications channels and minimize the undesired duplication of effort.

Examples of Impacting Trends. An excerpt from the American Red Cross corporate plan illustrates one national nonprofit organization's use of impacting trends in their strategic planning effort:

Community Volunteer Services

There are three trends that are developing within the country generally that will affect this activity. There are (1) a continuing and expanding need for services for and by older persons, an age group that will comprise approximately 42.7 million persons by the year 2000, including 7.8 million veterans; (2) a decided emphasis upon services for and by the handicapped as a result of the White House Conference for the Handicapped and current and proposed legislation; and (3) the expansion of the hospice movement which will encompass a wide variety of volunteer service needs. In the next two years, efforts will be concentrated upon development of needs assessment, program development and program assessment tools to assist chapters in the provision of the above needed services in their communities (American Red Cross 1978, 7).

Assessing Complexity and Risk

We must assess the complexity of the environment with which we deal to better understand the risks we are taking. The environment is considered complex when these conditions exist: When the program's scope and size are large and its geographic dispersion is great; when there is great diversity among the clientele; and when much uncertainty exists about client response, economic or political conditions, or supply considerations.

The greater the complexity of the above conditions, the greater is the risk in undertaking new initiatives. It is therefore necessary to examine these conditions carefully before any new strategic action is taken. Several main ones are discussed below.

Scope. The size or spatial coverage of a program indicates the scope of its environment. If the program is limited to one local area or is a "pilot" project with specific boundaries, it is unnecessary to consider complex national circumstances. Regional or local conditions prevail. As the program expands beyond its limited scope, it becomes more difficult to provide adequate supply and mobilize demand from remote points. Many programs become national ones, but rarely do they start full blown without some pilot or demonstration experience. Decisions about what programs to expand and how fast requires systematic strategic analysis, with a heavy input of implementation or "get ready" preparations.

Diversity. No program is ever completely homogeneous. Its clientele usually fall into categories, though one category may predominate at a particular point in time. It is important to know who are your clients and what are their primary characteristics and needs, if you wish to service them properly. You will discover that diverse clientele groups may possess different needs and wants that may be in conflict. The government attempt to meet the needs of small business or the small farmer can be very different from attempts to help the large businessman or large farmer. Their needs and capacity to absorb help are vastly different.

Uncertainty. Environments are seldom stable; conditions continue to change. Our concern is to determine how frequent are the changes, how drastic, and with what degree of predictability. The greater the uncertainty—whether it be political, economic, or social—the greater is the need for strategy to be flexible and rapidly responsive to emerging changes. The search for information in uncertain environments is a difficult one. It may be necessary to mobilize networks of institutions to collaborate on data accumulation and communication. Clientele participation to obtain timely feedback should also be considered.

Identifying Influential Actors and Institutions

The environment contains not only impersonal forces that affect program performance but also key persons and their institutions who can affect the supply and demand of a program's service or product. Of course, clientele groups are the most influential actors, but often they are the most ignored. There also are the government and legislative leaders who can influence legislation and policies or adjudicate rights and privileges. Then there are those who can influence the mobilization of resources, whether they be top managers, or board members, or controllers, or private bankers, or even private foundations. Whatever the sources of major influence upon your program, it is important to identify them and systematically to canvass their interests and expectations. Then, consider the best arrangements and linkages to mobilize their influence in your program's behalf.

Calculating Competitive Advantage

Whether you are in government, business, or the nonprofit independent sector, you must compete for limited resources and clients. This concept is well accepted in the business sector's practice of strategic planning. Some experts, such as Kenichi Ohmae, the Japanese strategic planning authority, feel competitive advantage is the prime purpose of strategic planning.

In the public and nonprofit sector, competition is also most relevant, though it may be somewhat differently applied. The most obvious aspect of competition is the quest for resources, whether it be from individual, corporate, or foundation sources or even the United Way. It is therefore important to know what is your relative position with regard to your competitors—the conditions in which you compete—and what is your competitive advantage or "competitive edge." Although difficult to do objectively, it is most useful to rank your product and service by its characteristics and costs against those with which you compete to determine your competitive advantages. If the ranking is not favorable to you, then you have the basis for some key strategic decisions.

Checklist for Reading the Environment

Detecting Forces and Trends

Which forces and trends influence your program's performance?

—Are they political, economic, social-cultural, or technological?
—Which are the most significant?
—How do they impact on your program?
  • Do they affect client behavior?
  • Do they affect supply of service or product?
  • Do they affect resource mobilization?
  • Do they suggest new technology or equipment?

How efficient and effective is the search for relevant information?

—Who is responsible for collecting external information?
—Is a coordinator needed? Why? What would it do?
—In what ways can collection and analysis of data be
  done better?

Assessing Complexity and Risk

What is the scope of the program in terms of its size, spatial coverage, and cost?

—Is it local or national?
—Is it a "pilot" for possible expansion? Or is it developed on a national or international scale?

What is the diversity of the program in terms of its type and mix of service and product and categories of clientele?

—Are the products and services closely related?
—Are clients homogeneous or diverse in terms of age, education, economic level, or ethnic origin?
—Does the diversity indicate any needed change in product or service or suggest a preferred clientele group?

How certain are environmental conditions?

—Is there political, social, or economic stability or turbulence?

—Is the pace of change slow or rapid?

—What "readiness for change" exists in the decision-making group? Do they acknowledge that problems require action?

—What can be done to fortify against or hedge disruptive change?

Identifying Influential Actors and Institutions

Which actors and institutions are most important in affecting demand, supply, or resource mobilization of particular program service or product? In what ways?

—Do they exert control or influence over your program?

—Do they support your program, or are they hostile?

—What measures can be taken to gain their constructive support or be able to minimize their hostility or negative interference?

Calculating Competitive Advantage

Who are your key competitors?

—In what conditions do you compete?

—What is your competitive advantage or disadvantage with regard to your main competitors?

—What measures must be taken to build competitive strength and advantage?

—What is necessary to do to get the measures for building competitive edge understood and accepted by the strategic decision-makers?

ANALYZING FOR STRATEGIC IMPLICATIONS

What Is WOTS-UP Analysis?

This section is a crucial one. It focuses on how to analyze for strategic implications the data accumulated from the several elements of the strategic audit: the performance analysis and the environmental scan. The resulting data are subjected to a search for strategic issues that stem from two sources. One is an analysis of strengths and weaknesses of the organization as they affect the program and its provision of quality service and product. The other source for strategic issues or implications is an analysis of the opportunities and threats the program faces from its external environment.

The aim of strategic implications analysis is to identify significant strategic planning "issues" that indicate an area where action needs to be taken but requires prior approval from higher management. Each "issue" should be characterized by its primary nature as to whether it signifies a threat or weakness or a strength or opportunity. This process thus produces a definitive list of strategic issues and describes the remedial actions proposed. The label "WOTS-UP Analysis," as used by Steiner (1979), is an acronym for its content: Weakness, Opportunity, Threat, Strength. Often the strategic implications analysis provides the basis for setting key directional goals and undertaking new strategic initiatives in the organization's strategic plan.

We now seek to clarify the key components of strategic implications analysis, or "WOTS-UP" analysis.

What Are Strengths and Weaknesses? Strengths are internal competencies possessed by the organization that increase its ability to perform as intended. They are often compared to the competencies of competing organizations or to outstanding examples of achievement and excellence, particularly as they exist in other organizations with similar product or service. Strengths may be based on capabilities, contacts, and motivations of an organization's staff. In simple terms, strengths are what they know and what they can do. Strengths may also take the form of vast financial resources, lean or flexible organization structure, or responsive management systems.

On the other hand, weaknesses are attributes of the organization that tend to decrease its competence in comparison with its competitors and diminish its ability to provide quality service and product.

Every organization is a combination of strengths and weaknesses, but management tends to be more aware of their strengths and less knowledgeable about their weaknesses.

What Are Threats and Opportunities? Environmental analysis also determines the threats faced by the organization and the opportunities available to it. A threat is a reasonably probable event that, if it were to occur, would produce significant damage to the organization. An opportunity, on the other hand, is a combination of circumstances that, if accompanied by a certain course of action on the part of the organization, is likely to produce substantial benefits. In business, threats are often defined as the organization's competitors. But in the nonprofit world threats may stem from an impending funds cut from a major donor or legislature.

Opportunities are often thought of in terms of new technologies or gaps of unfulfilled market demand. Identifying the opportunity allows you to determine what you want to do and when. This opens up a series of tasks in strategic planning, program planning, and budgeting. In fact, opportunities engage the full spectrum of program management work.

There are some problems in doing strategic analysis. Objective measurement of the elements of weakness or threat, or opportunity or strength, is often difficult to obtain and articulate. They are often elusive to identify and define. Once identified, it is not easy to achieve agreement and consensus among managers and decision-makers. This is particularly so if the weakness or threat reflects on a manager's shortcomings or if the imputed opportunity impinges on a manager's current activity and self-interest. How managers and decision-makers reconcile their differences is a part of the strategic planning process. That is why we emphasize that one of the key purposes of the strategic assessment process is to provide a forum for extensive discussion and exchange of reactions on specific strategic considerations. How the process of interaction is handled by key executives and their ability to respond to problems and opportunities give a good measure of the organization's ability to be successful. When top management can not identify, acknowledge, and respond to weaknesses, threats, or opportunities with a degree of clarity, precision, and dispatch, then it is not ready for significant change and success.

Presenting WOTS-UP Analysis Findings and Results

Findings of a strategic implications analysis can be presented very simply on a page or two. They can be developed in a simple format for an individual issue in which the issue statement contains four parts:

1. Characterization of the issue as either opportunity, weakness, strength, or threat.
2. Statement of the issue.
3. How you know the situation exists: basis of observation and evidence.
4. What remedial action is proposed.

Another simple format can be used to present a variety of findings in which multiple types of issues are included. In this situation, the finding is characterized as weakness, threat, opportunity, or strength and briefly described, often in short, succinct phrases. The strategic implication is then articulated for each finding, in terms of what action is proposed.

The brevity of the finding and results statements make them useful as agenda items for review and discussion by selected parties. They then become useful to record the discussion results and any decisions taken. Detailed documents of justification or investigation can be attached or distributed separately.

An example of each of the two formats, with some situational data included, is offered as Exhibits 9.1 and 9.2. The data included are placed on formats excerpted from Steiner's book, *Strategic Planning* (1979, 144–45).

Exhibit 9.1
Simple Format for Summary of Individual Issues Stemming from
WOTS-UP Analysis

Opportunity _____
Threat _____
Strength _____
Weakness _____

Statement of Issue: Poor Service Delivery

Two services, the conduct of internal intervention procedures (to be identified precisely) in two locations (to be specified), have long "wait times" of 6 to 8 weeks. Client complaints have increased substantially; cancellations are beginning to increase. The number of emergency situations, where clients cannot wait the necessary delay-time because of serious health problems, is severely increasing the cost for use of supplementary outside contract help, at costs higher than when performed in house.

Observation Based on:

Study data on Wait Times and Consequences conducted by Office of Budget and Management Review for three-month period, January through March 1996.

Proposed Action:

Establish small task force project to:

—Improve service delivery by 50% within six months.

—Recruit two more professional staff.

—Curtail use of outside contract staff by 25%.

—Explore use of new equipment to lower cost.

Exhibit 9.2
Simple Format for Summary of Multiple Issues Stemming from
WOTS-UP Analysis

ISSUE	STRATEGIC IMPLICATION
1. Weakness	
Poor service delivery:	Necessary to decrease wait time 50% within six months
Two services in two locations have wait time of 6–8 weeks.	
	—Authorize recruitment of two more staff.
	—Cut down substantial increase in contract services.

2. Strength

New equipment: (specify)   Equip one more location.

New equipment in location Z demonstrates greater productivity and quicker results at lower cost.

3. Threats

Competition: Cut wait time!

Competing organization offers similar services with minimal wait time at equivalent cost.

4. Opportunity

New technique and equipment available to initiate new service (label).   Explore market and feasibility.

10

Preparing the Strategic Plan

NEW VERSIONS APPEARING

Less than a decade ago, an examination of strategic plans in the public and nonprofit sector—the relative few that existed—displayed a commonality of components and content. With the experience gained in the wider use of strategic planning, strategic plans have begun to appear in several different versions. A Basic Version retains the traditional core of about five common components found in numbers of plans, labeled by some as a "Statement of Strategic Directions." The aim is to articulate the organization's strategic intentions to create a better future. Contained are statements of mission, goals and objectives, and values. The basic version sometimes defines the organization's "vision" and usually incorporates new strategic initiatives. Some minimal preparation for implementation is incorporated with assignment of "lead responsibility" for the new initiatives. An action plan denoting who is responsible for what, with a time schedule, is occasionally contained. Each of the above components is described below, and helpful ways to prepare them are offered.

A number of organizations now prepare an Expanded Version of the Strategic Plan that incorporates more features than has been done in the earlier years of strategic planning for public concerns. Some organizations, like the federal Internal Revenue Service of the United States Treasury Department in the mid-1980s, started with a basic version of a strategic plan and then began to add additional features as they gained experience with its implementation. The expanded features do not replace but add to the traditional core of components in the basic or simpler version. Some nonprofit organizations substitute longer-term strategic program plans or programs of work for the strategic plan.

DEVELOPING COMPONENTS OF THE BASIC STRATEGIC PLAN

The basic strategic plan can be found in many public and nonprofit organizations as different as the Office of Administrative Hearings in the Maryland state government or the National Association of Realtors. Usually contained are statements of mission, established goals and objectives, organizational values, setting of new strategic initiatives, minimal preparation for implementation, sometimes a statement of vision, and occasionally an action plan.

DEFINING STATEMENTS OF MISSION AND PURPOSE

As Peter Drucker put it, top management must decide: What is our primary business, and what should it be? This task is fundamental. Top management must identify and resolve these basic questions: Why are we in business? What are our major lines of activity (products and services)? Which are the markets we serve? Who are our customers? Where are we going?

Mission statements have emerged as the primary vehicle to identify the underlying aim and thrust of an organization, and to capture the essence of these questions. Although mission statements are expressed at various levels of abstraction, they are usually encapsulated and succinct. For example, in the business sector you can readily identify the AT&T slogan, "Our business is service," or Dupont's "Better things for better living." Although catchy and recognizable, they represent a serious declaration of an organization's basic purpose. In the nonprofit world, the American Heart Association prefaces its plan with the serious mission statement, "To reduce premature death and disability from cardiovascular disease." The American Red Cross presents a slightly longer version: "The aims of the American Red Cross are to improve the quality of human life and enhance individual self-reliance and concern for others." In effect, the statements express the philosophy and basic purpose of an organization. They also are valuable to effective public relations and positive image creation and are often used as fund-raising slogans or for advertising campaigns. When taken seriously by top management, they play an important role and justify serious consideration.

Why Are They Important?

Mission statements express to the public at large, and to your clientele in particular, the basic nature and purpose of the business you are in.

They act as a solid point of departure for formulating program strategy and directions and deciding on lines of activity to pursue and markets to serve. Their broad nature enables adjustment to change, in both technological and social terms, and allows shifts in direction and turnarounds as external conditions change significantly.

In effect, mission statements tell you the most fundamental things about an organization; they describe the ideal reason for the organization's existence:

—They state what the organization tries to accomplish in a broad sense.
—They define the basic philosophy and values of an organization.
—They provide an appealing and motivating inspiration.
—They are never completely attainable.

Thus the statement of mission is often known as the "ideal goal" of an organization.

Should They Be Written?

There is a wise saying, "What you have inside your head and don't communicate is worth the price of the paper it is written on." Some people debate and denigrate the merit of working with missions that are written down. To many of us, there is little room for debate. The basic value of a mission statement is to articulate and communicate to others the most fundamental purpose of an organization. This must be written down, approved, and sanctioned at the highest levels of the organization to achieve its full impact.

Criteria for Written Mission Statements: What They Do

There is no consensus about what a statement of mission should contain and tell you. But a review of many mission statements does reveal a consistency of criteria that suggests a "rule of thumb" formula. A mission statement indicates who your clients are or who you want your clients to be, tells in general terms what you do for them, tells why you are in business, and says the organization could go on forever and provides for a time far into the future.

What a Statement of Mission Does Not Do

A mission statement does not list all the specific activities performed (it may list some as illustrations), mention times or set deadlines, tell how much will be done, or serve as a goal or objective.

How Long Should They Be? Take the Sixty-Second Test!

Mission statements are always brief. They tend to conform to the "kiss concept": keep it short and simple. You can find a batch of mission statements, whether labeled as such or not, in the multitude of fund-raising appeals all of us get in the mail. In the literature of nonprofit organizations, the mission statement is often contained in the flyer or brochure asking for funds and telling you about the organization. For large corporations, check their billboard or television advertising. Underline or write down what they consider to be their mission statement. Accumulate five such statements and then take the sixty-second test. You must be able to say it out loud, or read it quietly, in less than sixty seconds. None takes longer than sixty seconds; most are shorter. In that limited time the statement should help you know very quickly what the organization does, for whom and why, and stimulate you to react positively. If it does, good! If not, it needs revision.

An impressive example of brevity is the mission of the American Heart Association: "To reduce premature death and disability from cardiovascular disease."

What to Do at Lower Than Organization-Wide Levels

At the level of individual programs or projects that are the province of particular organization units, rather than the organization as a whole, the term "purpose" rather than mission is more often used. Such statements are less idealized and abstract and more precisely functional. For example:

The Project for Students and Senior Citizens provides free manpower service designed to enable lower-income senior citizens and their families in the greater metropolitan area to maintain their own homes as long as possible.

The High School Involvement Program provides student volunteers with educationally valuable experience through service to the community.

ESTABLISHING STRATEGIC GOALS

What Are Strategic Goals?

Strategic goals are keys to future directions of change and may sometimes be called "strategic directions." They describe the desired future that is considered attainable within a specified time span of two to five years. These goals are based on and are compatible with the organization's mission or basic purpose. Their function is to provide definitive

direction for the entire organization or for a major component or program and to serve as the "planning umbrella" for integrating the efforts
of operating units and persons into a total, more cohesive, organization
effort. To do this, strategic goals are more specific than the mission statements, but they are still general enough to encourage creativity and innovation on the part of operating units.

The establishment of goals is a critical point of departure for an organization's program management system. They are formulated and
proclaimed by an organization's chief executive with the broad participation of the key executive staff. Their purpose is to set new directions,
which in turn guide the formulation of new strategic initiatives, determine program changes, and begin to mobilize the means of institutional
support to implement the new initiatives such as budget requirements,
staffing, and skill development. In effect, the strategic goals are the critical instruments for guiding the undertaking of desired change.

In organization settings it is never possible to have all the resources
available to do all the things you or your colleagues and staff want to
do to satisfy identified weaknesses and constraints or to exploit emerging
opportunities. Choices are necessary among an array of possible changes
you desire the organization to make. The findings of the previously discussed strategic assessments and the ensuing analysis of their strategic
implications should have identified a number of changes to be made.
These provide the basis for the formulation and choice of strategic goals.
In essence, the selection of particular strategic goals should reflect areas
of "key results," where needs or demands are greatest or the benefits
seem to be the highest.

What Do Goals Accomplish?

Strategic goals, when they work, are the keys to excellence and success.
They aim to assure the kinds of changes necessary to achieve the greatest
results within available resources. They help to create the conditions that
promote future growth and progress.

In pragmatic terms, strategic goals can be the key to survival. In times
of crisis or extreme deficiency, it is important to focus clearly, rapidly,
and aggressively on those areas of needed change to resolve the threatening conditions affecting financial stability or even survival. The setting
of new strategic goals by the chief executive, with widespread executive
participation and approval, gives you an approved platform from which
to launch an aggressive plan of attack. Goals are thus not only crucial
to the attainment of excellence and success but often necessary for survival.

The setting of goals seeks to accomplish several different things:
Select the Specific Situation to Change. Strategic change can focus on in-

novation, by doing something completely new; on expansion or contraction of current activity; on quality improvement, by doing things significantly better; on modernization of technology in ways of doing things with substantially different technique, process, or equipment; or on a new or different market segment.

Define the Direction and Emphasis of Change. To set goals helps define the direction you want to go and underscores the emphasis you place on it and what you expect to accomplish when you get there. It indicates the action desired. When a strategic goal is too broad and abstract and is thus capable of many diverse interpretations or is confusing to implementers, it is necessary to add clarification by indicating possible or illustrative outcomes.

Set Priorities. Priorities tell you where to concentrate your investment of time, talent, and resources. They emphasize the urgent and tend to eliminate the merely desirable and less important. This helps to focus on doing the most important things and not being distracted by the less consequential. In effect, the goals establish a clear-cut sense of direction rather than trying to do everything to please everybody and ending up pleasing nobody.

How to Write Goal Statements

Recognize that goals are always action-oriented, though they may sound like grandiose dreams. The first part of a goal statement is the action desired, that is, the specific change you wish to accomplish. That is why goal statements usually contain an action verb.

An example of a goal statement is the following excerpt from an approved corporate plan of the American Red Cross:

Service Goal 3

The American Red Cross will substantially increase its participation and leadership in a national voluntary blood system and will significantly strengthen Red Cross blood services to achieve effective delivery of blood products and related medical services. (1978, 19)

Goals usually are of two major types: those addressed to "program thrusts" such as the "Service Goals" of the American Red Cross and those addressed to institutional concerns that focus on developing a more effective organization through such management tasks as recruitment, training of people, and computerization.

In some organizations, goal statements provide a separate third category for all efforts to mobilize funding from the outside, and the category is called "Financial Goals." One organization broadens the third category of "Financial Goals" to include all basic resources of funding and personnel and calls this category "Resource Development Goals." The American Red Cross corporate plan uses three categories for its goals: service goals, resource development goals, and administrative goals.

Use of Goals to Express Strategic Change

Goal statements can specify different kinds of strategic action to accomplish change in an organization. Looking at various plans in organizations does reveal these kinds of change occurring in their goal statements:

Action	Verb	Intent
Expansion	expand	Do more by change in
	increase	product, place, people,
	broaden	technology or equipment.
Improvement	improve	Do it sooner, better,
	examine	cheaper, more effectively,
	eliminate	or with higher quality.
	achieve	
	decrease	
	strengthen	
	develop	
	implement	
Innovation	initiate	Do something new, different.
	establish	
	experiment	
	explore	
Adaptation/	adapt	Ensure that service and
Modernization	update	product reflect changing
	modernize	needs, events, and trends.
	examine	

Use of Subgoals and Statements of Possible Outcomes

Many goals are vague and overgeneralized. Thus in some systems of goal determination, a second dimension of "subgoal" is added; sometimes a third dimension of "illusions of expected outcome" is used. The use of subgoals and expected outcomes helps to render the stated goal more concrete and better understood. This enables the goal to be more easily achieved. It certainly avoids the frustrations and waste motion of trying to figure out what was meant by the vague or overgeneralized goal statement.

Subgoals actually are more specific subgroupings or categories of a general goal. The dimension of expected outcomes is used to indicate concretely the kinds of conditions that might exist when goals are successfully achieved. But expected outcomes are only illustrative; they are never considered as all-inclusive of the activities that might be undertaken to accomplish a stated goal. In some situations it is clear that goals are only suggestive and are not intended to be binding on those responsible for implementation. The use of illustrations of expected outcomes do provide a clearer understanding of what direction to go and can provide concrete options for policy decision by top management and board members. Frequent users of illustrations of expected outcomes are the nonprofit organizations that began to overuse the phrase "quality of life" in many goal statements.

An excellent example of subgoals that contain illustrations of expected outcomes follows.

1. Program Thrusts
Operational Goal: by 19___ the organization will be significantly influencing conditions which affect the quality of human life in this community by:

Subgoals	Illustrations of Expected Outcomes
1. Eliminating personal and institutional racism.	A. At least 30% of all boards, councils and committee membership will be filled with racial minorities, women and persons under 30.
	B. Programs will be in operation, of effective collaboration with ethnic and racial minorities to increase their power to make and implement decisions in institutions and the community which affect them.
2. Changing the conditions that foster alienation, delinquency, and crime.	A. Collaboration with city/county officials will have resulted in an improved juvenile justice system.
	B. These programs will be in operation for the rehabilitation of juvenile offenders which will serve as options to youth jails and reformatories.

                      C. Work with disadvantaged and
                          alienated youth will have tripled
                          in 5 years. (Hardy 1972, 56)

EXPRESSING ORGANIZATIONAL VALUES

The experts report that there has been an increase in publicized statements of organizational philosophy or creed. These statements usually express the beliefs of the chief executive. There is no uniformity in their content. Although many creeds or philosophies are designed to improve the public image of an organization, they often are, or can be, the cornerstone of an organization's overall direction or method of operation.

What Does a Typical Values Statement Contain?

What is included in a particular creed or philosophy statement depends on the values, aspirations, and commitment of the chief executive of an organization and is usually adapted to the nature of the business of an organization.

The value statement may contain any combination of these components:

a. key interests to be satisfied and balanced

—devotion to public interest and community

—devotion to board and donors

—devotion to employees, suppliers, and contractors

b. quality/excellence

—seeks high-quality product and service

—seeks high-quality employees at all levels

—seeks access to best technology available

c. efficiency

—seeks low cost, high productivity

—seeks to provide value for money received

d. atmosphere or climate

—good place for people to work

—good opportunity for advancement

—good organization to deal with

—emphasizes teamwork

—leadership supports staff

—develops employees

e. observance of codes of conduct   —integrity

                                       —fairness in all dealings

SETTING NEW STRATEGIC INITIATIVES

What Are They?

New strategic initiatives describe briefly the purpose and summary of action to be taken for carrying out an approved goal. They include the strategy to be pursued, that is, the specific approach that will achieve the desired results. To enable approval by decision-makers, a brief justification explains what results and benefits will accrue and establishes benchmarks for later monitoring and evaluation activity.

New initiatives are often, but not necessarily, the result of a series of strategic audits of performance and environment and the detection of strategic implications of weaknesses, opportunities, strengths, and threats. Or, initiatives could arise in a more informal way from the chief executive or any of the staff. Whatever the source, it is important that the idea of a new strategic initiative be systematically explored and subjected to intensive review before launching.

What Do They Accomplish?

Establishing new strategic initiatives starts the transition from planning—looking to the future—to the commencement of concrete action to be undertaken in the present. A new strategic initiative establishes the purpose or reason for the new initiative and requires a brief description of actions necessary for the best result.

Using a strategy compels a leader to think through the best possible way to achieve a superior result and a competitive advantage over others. The strategy may focus on a shift to another target clientele market, or it may employ new technology to provide a higher quality of product or service. If the new initiative is of large potential scope and cost, a pilot or demonstration project may be advisable. Whatever the strategy chosen, the strategic approach selected will determine and guide the dimensions of future action.

New initiatives should be justified in public. Decision-makers as well as implementers need to know why an initiative is proposed and what it will accomplish as well as its benefits. Strategic initiatives can be costly as they unfold, and it is important to reassure everyone that the benefits are cost-effective, that is, the expected benefits are appropriate to the cost and effort expended, with a safety margin thrown in. For example, where direct costs and returns are available, the job of justification is easier. When an HMO department head wants to increase productivity with new equipment or establish in-house capacity to cut costs of contracting out, it is fairly easy to calculate current workload and costs of contract consultant fees and compare them with the projected savings from new equipment. But in many nonprofit situations where the goal is to achieve "greater independence and quality of life for the elderly," it is of course more difficult, but nevertheless just as important, to justify new initiatives with supporting data that is expressed as objectively as possible.

Provision for Implementation

A major problem with strategic plans is that they often state well-intentioned wishes that organizations are often not prepared to implement. Critics are apt to call them "paper tigers." Even when new strategic initiatives are carefully formulated, a number of actions are essential to make sure the organization is ready and prepared to move toward implementation in ways that are timely and effective. It is imperative to realize that goals and initiatives are not self-executing; at best, they are statements of intent.

The statement of a new strategic initiative should activate the process of preparing for implementation and not chance the initiative's execution to the usual bureaucratic procedure. We therefore suggest that the strategic plan contain preparations for implementation with at least these three elements:

—Designation of initiative coordinator.

—Multi-year funding requirements (if needed).

—Program or project modification or development (if indicated).

—Progress indicators to keep the initiative on track.

In addition, though not included in the strategic plan, it is necessary to designate the persons essential for developing and carrying out the initiative and to develop the institutional support necessary for the successful execution of the initiative. Such institutional support could encompass structural arrangements, human resource staffing and development activities, and monitoring and progress reporting requirements.

THE IMPLEMENTATION MATRIX

In the Executive Summary of *Toward a Working Ohio: A Strategic Plan for the Eighties and Beyond: Investing in Ohio's People,"* Governor Richard F. Celeste tells us that the plan:

represents a new way of doing business in Ohio. It reports on Ohio's new strategic planning process, designed to identify long-range policy objectives, make effective short-term policy decisions, and see the implications and consequences of day-to-day management initiatives. It reflects a belief that government must target its limited resources at those objectives that make a significant difference in the lives of our citizens (State of Ohio, September 1984).

Initiated in 1983, the goal of strategic planning in Ohio focuses attention on where they want to go and how they can most effectively get there. A distinctive feature of the plan is its use of an implementation matrix that specifies key essentials for carrying out the plan: goal-oriented strategic initiatives, implementation time frame, funding level and mechanism, linkages to implementing and supporting institutions, and assignment of lead responsibility.

An example of Ohio's implementation matrix is contained in its section on human resource initiatives:

Initiative One: Establish higher academic standards, strengthen basic skills and prepare students to work and live in the future, one component of which is:

—Competency based education in English composition, mathematics and reading.

Implementation Time Frame: Autumn, 1979–83.

Funding Level and Mechanism: $76 Million—School Foundation and local tax revenue.

Linkages: public and private schools, colleges, and universities.

Lead Responsibility: Department of Education, Board of Regents. (State of Ohio, September 1984)

THE STORY OF THE STRATEGIC BUSINESS PLAN OF THE U.S. NAVY PUBLIC WORKS CENTER

An excellent example of a basic version of a strategic plan is the FY 1994 Strategic Business Plan of the Public Works Center, Yokosuka, Japan (U.S. Navy 1994).

The commanding officer of the Public Works Center in a forward to the eighteen-page strategic plan expressed strong support. He affirmed the center's dedication to providing high-quality services at a reasonable cost and to being responsive with continuing efforts to improve the value of services provided to customers. Customer satisfaction is the foundation for success, he stated.

The plan contains four major areas of focus: customer satisfaction, development and empowerment of personnel, innovative business practices, and community housing. He cited the application of Total Quality Leadership principles for working as a team in support of mission and vision.

Mission

The statement is brief:
"Our mission is to provide responsive, quality, cost-effective public works and housing services to our fleet and shore customers."

Command Vision

The statement makes six distinct points:
"The value of our products and services exceeds our customers expectations. We are an integral member of the mission team. We are proud of our accomplishments and committed to achieving even greater customer satisfaction in the future. We are recognized as a superior supplier of cost-effective, responsive, quality public works and housing services. Our employees are well trained, dedicated, quality oriented professionals who inspire confidence and receive praise from customers. We make continuous improvements by applying the principles of Total Quality Leadership."

Guiding Principles

The guiding principles echo the same themes mentioned before: customer satisfaction, quality products and services, sensitivity to people's concerns, application of Total Quality Leadership principles, professional reputation, and teamwork.

Strategic Actions

For each of the major lines of business, the strategic plan identifies succinctly the specific actions to be undertaken and designates an "assigned lead" or flags an action for future assignment. The action identifications are simple sentences starting with a verb, such as "develop a customer training and education program for environmental service" or "establish a hazardous material reutilization program."

INCORPORATING SPECIAL FEATURES IN AN EXPANDED VERSION

The additional features found in expanded strategic plans for public and nonprofit organizations move in four directions:

—One identifies the institution's "distinctiveness" that gives it unique character and creates competitive advantage;

—a second feature includes in the plan the presence of measurable goal progress indicators to enable better follow-up on what has been accomplished;

—a third feature specifies dimensions of "enabling support areas" to implement new initiatives such as added physical plant, library collections, or computerization; sometimes added are staffing and funding requirements for implementing new initiatives;

—a fourth feature provides the fiscal outlook that reflects the organization's increasing sense of the financial constraints it faces and expresses the need to prioritize and match programs and desired improvements to limited resources available. The fiscal outlook realistically explores promising areas of financial support.

The expansion of additional features are not necessarily all contained in each organization's strategic plan.

Expressing Distinctiveness; Creating Competitive Advantage

In an era of sharper competition for resources, nonprofit organizations more often seek to identify and develop their "distinctiveness." They strive to differentiate their unique characteristics and develop core competencies that make an organization stand out and be separate from many others.

Nonprofits create competitive advantage in ways that aim to generate and add value for targeted combinations of shareholders and clientele, whether they be students, patients, or "customers" or donors, board members, faculty, and employees. One thrust for creating value is the effort to develop a "center of excellence," either for the entire institution or, more usually, for a specified program or set of services that elevates the institution to community, regional, national, or international reputation.

The probe for distinctiveness and the quest to achieve parity with the successful few are becoming part of the searching examination of the strategic planning process and begins to occupy a prominent space in some strategic plans. Organizations find the process of developing strategic plans to be an effective vehicle for identifying and reflecting on which characteristics of distinctiveness and core competence an organization possesses and which they need to develop and why. Similar to what happens in the world of business, differentiating characteristics of distinction when achieved in the nonprofit world serve to generate new opportunities, attract resources, elevate quality, and garner a larger measure of "customer," donor, and employee pride and satisfaction. More often the distinguishing characteristics selected for development become the subject for an organization's strategic themes and initiatives. They build upon outstanding strengths; they forge greater competence.

Key questions that an organization can ask about their statement of distinctiveness and competitive advantage are these:

—Do the distinctive features really satisfy the needs, interests, and expectations of important stakeholders and clientele? Do they think so? How do you know?

—Are the distinctive features "bearable in cost" and sustainable over time?

—Are the distinctive competencies difficult to imitate by competitors and difficult to achieve by others?

THE STORY OF THE DUKE UNIVERSITY STRATEGIC PLAN

The Strategic Plan of Duke University expresses very well the university's distinctive characteristics in ways intended to create competitive advantage.

In a search for guidance in the next century, Duke University studied its young history since 1924 and examined the major goals and principles by which the university had grown into one of the nation's leading institutions. A central outcome of the study has been to amplify and expand Duke's original goals and principles to create a mission statement and expression of distinctiveness that will direct Duke University in the next century. Their report, not labeled a strategic plan but titled "Shaping Our Future: A Young University Faces a New Century," was produced by the strategic planning committee and approved by Duke's board of trustees (Duke University, 1994). It describes in detail the mission to provide a superior liberal education, articulates Duke's distinctiveness, spells out five strategic themes as institutional imperatives, explains the basis of its competitive advantage, and discusses the fiscal outlook.

Distinctiveness

The expression of Duke's distinctiveness forged by the "interplay of history, design and circumstance" explains Duke's unique character among American research universities. Mentioned is the "legacy of close collaboration between liberal education for undergraduates, graduate education, and career training in the learned professions, as well as strong emphasis in interdisciplinary study." Highlighted are Duke's commitment to excellence in undergraduate education, even as their faculty gains international prominence for the advancement of knowledge, and its long-term legacy of equal education for women. Duke takes pride in its "distinctive social and cultural ambience among leading private research universities—small town yet cosmopolitan, southern yet also increasingly international."

Core Commitments

Several core commitments shaped Duke's distinctive character since its founding in 1924 and are intended to guide them in the next century. The main ones are:

—Academic freedom that acknowledges the value of free expression to teacher and student in pursuit of a shared interest in learning and the free pursuit of research;

—Accessibility of a Duke education that admits students on the basis of academic ability and not their family's financial status; and

—Mutual respect between Duke and its faculty and employees that fosters the highest degree of quality, respect, and dedication to the people that work there; in return faculty and staff have a mutual obligation to dedicate their best effort to pursue Duke's mission and commitments for achieving excellence in education, research, and patient care.

Strategic Themes

Duke's institutional imperatives in the form of strategic themes identify key goals that set priorities. This enables limited resources to be allocated first to:

—Enhancing academic quality in each of its schools, particularly the School of Environment, with goals to attract and retain an outstanding faculty and to internationalize the university;

—Strengthening Duke's sense of community and its role as citizen that encourages constructive participation in community affairs by belonging and contributing to a collective university endeavor, as well as working in partnership with geographically proximate neighborhoods;

—Enhancing academic medicine with its continuing emphasis for world renown on quality of its education, research, and clinical programs;

—Increasing academic and administrative effectiveness by its wise use of both human and financial resources, particularly as the university reallocates existing resources to support promising new initiatives or to enhance the quality of key programs.

A Note on Competitive Advantage

Some may be surprised that one of the nation's leading educational institutions discusses openly and cogently its quest for competitive advantage. This is understandable and acceptable and may be necessary in these times of severe financial constraints, rapid and profound change, and increasing demand for value and quality.

The Duke report explains the source of competitive advantage in an excellent statement: "Competitive advantage in private higher education comes from several sources—from leadership and execution, from entrepreneurship and teamwork, and from careful planning and prudent risk-taking. When these qualities coalesce in an academic community of the best faculty and students as at Duke, a university of great distinction can result."

STATING MEASURABLE PROGRESS INDICATORS IN STRATEGIC PLANS

In the search for better results from strategic plans, many experts recommend a fundamental shift in managerial thinking. They suggest a performance-based management approach that emphasizes "outcomes" of results, rather than concentrate solely on "inputs" of resources. To do this, organizations use verifiable indicators of outcomes to enable measurement of progress toward planned goals and objectives. A number of strategic plans now contain statements of expected outcomes in measurable terms that indicate what is expected to be accomplished toward a specific objective, within a specified time period.

One example is selected from the Internal Revenue Service, Business Master Plan Strategic Extract, FY 1995–FY 2001: "In support of 2001 Performance Goals, reduce the burden taxpayers experience in fulfilling all their tax responsibilities, from record keeping to final account settlement. Reduce time by 7% and expense by 3%." (U.S. Treasury, Internal Revenue Service, 1994)

PROVIDING SUPPORT AREAS TO ENABLE PLAN IMPLEMENTATION

Organizations recognize that plans cannot be implemented without providing for such support areas as added physical plant and adequate space, sufficient library collections and reference services, and computerization. The University of Maryland Law School in its first strategic plan, 1984–1994, described the status of several support areas in need of development to undergird its strategic initiatives and then proceeded to identify the strategies and objectives of what they planned to do about them. They fully recognize the "impossibility of implementing any part of the Strategic Plan without adequate space, library support, and computers." The plan also specifies the additional staffing needed and estimates funding requirements for new buildings, renovations, and expansion of space, in addition to new or expanded programs. Including staffing and funding requirements is not common in strategic plans, since the specifics of staffing and funding are often specified as part of program budgets.

PROVIDING THE FISCAL OUTLOOK: PRIORITIES AND CONSTRAINTS

Strategic planning in nonprofit and public agencies is increasingly sensitive to the fiscal constraints they face and the necessity to match programs and improvements they seek to the limited resources available. There is greater awareness that not everything wanted can be done; activities may have to be curtailed and deleted. Organizations are being compelled to identify areas of highest priority to their mission and estimate what new resources are required to provide the degree of excellence sought. They are being forced to determine which areas offer better promise for support in an environment of sharp competition for limited resources.

The statement of fiscal outlook offers the best thinking and action planning for meeting financial dimensions of the strategic plan. Some organizations, such as Duke, for example, realize they will have to meet the new resource requirements to some extent through reallocation of current resources. Duke calls this "growth by substitution" or "exerting a form of entrepreneurship" by which they mean "growing in stature and quality derived from redirecting current activities to ones of greater priority and promise."

Thousands of organizations such as Duke find federal and state government support is contracting and that competition is becoming sharper. They increasingly look for financial support from those who support their ideals and purposes. They are compelled to probe their fiscal outlook in close linkage to the budget system. This is the area where key executives make choices about ongoing operations and new initiatives in the context of priorities and constraints. Expenses and revenues are scrutinized, constraints and opportunities are balanced, growth through substitution exercised, and some activities curtailed. "Bottom-line" results determine the major needs for which to seek funds. Top executives are challenged to meet aspirations, yet stay within financial limits and at the same time gain distinction and competitive advantage for their organization. This is a difficult task in the climate of an era of resource limits.

DEVISING ALTERNATIVE VERSIONS

Not all nonprofit organizations employ either the basic or expanded strategic plan. Some organizations substitute longer-term program plans or programs of work for the traditional strategic plan. Such program-oriented versions contain an overlap in content with the strategic plan but essentially focus on the organization's areas of program concentration in time perspectives that are either long-term (often up to five years) or annual.

Two considerations prompt and influence the program-oriented version and its planning process. The first is when a membership organization seeks to provide its members with a process and plan that achieves mutual agreement and consensual action on priority goals and objectives. This is particularly necessary when an organization serves in an informal federation that involves organizations of enormous diversity with a high degree of individual independence. A second consideration occurs in situations for which there are more urgent tasks than can be accommodated even in areas of common interest.

The longer-term program plan essentially includes a mission statement and longer-term program goals for each of the program concentrations identified by the membership and board. It contains detailed program objectives for each program goal with "examples" of activities to be selected. For example, the Independent Sector program plan sets forth five-year goals, objectives, and priority activities in each of its six areas of program concentration: public education, government relations, research, the "give-five" goal, and sector leadership and management, which includes values and ethics, communications, and "meeting grounds." Each year staff engage in an annual planning process to identify specific annual objectives and work plans consistent with the overall program plan. Annually the board reviews achievements for the past year and an overview of major activities for the coming year.

The Greater Delray Chamber of Commerce, Florida, in its Annual Report and Program of Work, simplifies the program version. It specifies the mission in a brief statement and succinctly answers the query: what are the chamber's basic and long-range objectives? It then details the annual program of work for each of the areas of program concentration: economic development, governmental affairs and education, marketing and promotion, membership, community image, and geographical area activities. Inserted in the chamber's program of work is an annual report for the previous year that provides a brief review of the previous year's major accomplishments, with a pie-chart that specifies by program concentration the proposed use of funds for the following year.

Part 5

CHOOSING STRATEGIES

11

Reinventing Government

The American movement to transform its public sector is creating a quiet but constructive revolution in the way the government does business. Not all agree; some high-level players and scholars cite particular concerns. Although outside assessments by academics and think-tank analysts cite contradictions, raise some negatives, and point to untidy processes, most generally concede that substantial progress is being made. The likelihood is that it will make a lasting contribution, although some, including its participants, question its sustainability.

FEDERAL NATIONAL PERFORMANCE REVIEW

The federal effort to "reinvent government," launched in 1993 with a six-month intensive National Performance Review, set out twin-linked missions: make government work better and cost less. President Clinton, in announcing the effort, said: "Our goal is to make the entire federal government both less expensive and more efficient, and to change the culture of national bureaucracy away from complacency and entitlement toward initiative and empowerment. We intend to redesign, to reinvent, to reinvigorate the entire national government."

Tremendous Involvement

The National Performance Review systematically and thoroughly solicited ideas from all segments of society: citizens, employees, private business leaders, management experts, academics, and innovative state and local governments; it culled the overseas government experience of countries like England and New Zealand. It organized a series of teams of federal employees from all over government to examine every department, ten agencies, and cross-cutting processes. The review focused primarily on how government should work, not what it should do. The job was to improve performance in areas where policy-makers have already decided government should play a role.

Commitment to Long-Term Effort

From the extensive effort, a report on the National Performance Review ensued (Gore 1993), announcing the beginning of a decade-long process of reinvention. The intent now actively being carried out is that the process will involve not only the thousands of federal employees on reinvention teams and in reinvention labs, but multitudes more not yet engaged. The aim is to transform—habits, culture, and performance— all federal organizations and to influence the behavior of state, local, and nonprofit sector organizations with whom they work in collaboration and contractual relationships.

Guiding Strategies

The report of the National Performance Review summarized the characteristics of success into four principles, around which the report is organized and upon which the program to reinvent government is proceeding:

1. "Cutting Red Tape." The strategy is to simplify and streamline stifling rules and regulations, processes, and structures that take too long, cost too much, use too much effort and personnel, and just get in the way of doing a better job of delivering quality services to a satisfied constituency.

2. "Putting Customers First." Vice President Gore, as leader of the reinvention effort, said it this way: "We are going to rationalize the way government relates to the American people, and we are going to make the federal government customer-friendly. A lot of people don't realize that the federal government has customers. The American people."

Perceptive Washington observers such as David Broder of the *Washington Post* tell us that this concern for "customers" will require that the government employee acknowledge that the public has things to teach, not just needs to fill. The intent is to bring bureaucrats closer to the people they serve and to open a real dialogue between government and its constituencies. Federal agencies are being required to ask their customers how they view government services, what problems they encounter, and how they would like to see services improved.

3. "Empowering Employees to Get Results." Federal employees will

be given the tools they need: training, supportive leadership and man-agement, and up-to-date information technology. Strategic planning is being utilized to move agencies and people in the right directions; per-formance measurement and stricter accountability will better enable all to know how well the government is doing and whether the government is doing the right things right. This strategy also seeks to decentralize more decision-making authority closer to the scene of operations and thus closer to the people.

4. "Cutting Back to Basics." Efforts are being taken to eliminate what is not needed: outmoded and unnecessary missions, offices, functions, field offices, forms, committees, and activities. Programs and processes are being reengineered to cut time, effort, and cost in supplying goods and services to gain better satisfied customers. Electronic transfer is being used to eliminate mass paperwork burdens for paying government ben-efits of all kinds: social security, welfare checks, and even food stamps.

Proposals of the National Performance Review

The National Performance Review report contained 384 major rec-ommendations for improving performance in the federal government. The recommendations covered twenty-seven agencies and fourteen gov-ernment systems. The report made its way to the *New York Times* best-seller list and was reprinted by several publishers. It received initially a favorable public reception and made newspaper headlines. The Govern-ment Accounting Office issued an analysis of the report's recommen-dations and officially agreed with 262 out of the 384, offered no comment on 121 for lack of information, and rejected only one (December 1993).

Who Operates and Sustains the National Performance Review?

Officially and visibly, Vice President Gore leads the reinvention effort under the sponsorship of President Clinton. In practice the National Per-formance Review (NPR) has been operated as a loosely organized, multi-pronged attack for reinventing government that has been described as a sometimes disorganized many-fronted war in the government's effort to make it work better for less.

Diverse groups of troops are engaged, each with different end goals and approaches:

—The administration's NPR top commanders and strategists, working out of the vice president's office, focus on broad, politically appealing issues and accom-plishments such as cost savings and personnel reductions.
—The NPR's independent small staff, supplemented by details of personnel from

the agencies and closely related to the vice president, spread the doctrine on reinvention. They initially designed and executed the performance review and developed its report and now follow through with status reviews and public relations and publicity.

—The army of reinventees throughout the executive branch who are in top management and also are on the front lines as program and project managers and their subordinates. They have primary responsibility and the big burden for reinvention efforts; they are engaged in day-to-day efforts to plan and improve government performance.

—The President's Management Council of representatives of the cabinet departments shares and coordinates department efforts to execute reinvention activities, chaired by the Office of Management and Budget.

—The Office of Management and Budget in the executive office of the president exerts leadership in the implementation of the Government Performance and Results Act, which establishes strategic planning and performance measurement in all federal agencies. These two approaches are scheduled to be key instruments for improving government performance.

Official First-Year Results of Reinvention

Toward the promise of a government that "works better and costs less," the NPR made a good start. Over 90 percent of the NPR proposals have moved forward—implemented by executive order or by agency action, or proposed in legislation.

Some other highlighted accomplishments are these:

—The president has signed twenty-two directives that implement NPR recommendations on such subjects as customer service, agency streamlining, procurement, labor-management relations, and intergovernmental cooperation.

—Over one hundred agencies have set customer service standards for the first time.

—Nine agencies have started major streamlining activities, cutting headquarters staff, reducing management layers, and moving workers to the "front-lines."

—Agencies are cutting red tape. Rules and regulations are being eliminated, as well as much paperwork, though some early congressional efforts to roll back federal environmental regulations were judged to go too far. We later learn that adversaries from both sides appear to have reached a consensus that, while the existing system can be improved, it must not be weakened according to a final report of the President's Council on Sustainable Development (*New York Times*, February 12, 1996).

—Procurement practices are being simplified to enable buying shelf items rather than "designer products" and to stock readily available commercial items. Although many agree that federal procurement regulations need greater flexibility and improvement, not all agree on the way to go. Some claim that National Performance Review's recommendations for rewriting federal acquisitions regulations go too far in the wrong direction. Criticism mounted from many quarters—industry, academia, the Federal Bar Association, and in a hearing generated by the Office of Federal Procurement Policy—about the effort to rewrite the federal procurement regulations from a set of rigid rules to a set of guiding principles.

—Agencies created 135 "reinvention labs" through which employees try new ways to conduct their business to improve customer service or cut costs.

—The federal government is changing the way it interacts with state and local governments, such as giving authority to waive certain statutory or regulatory requirements without seeking federal approval. By May 1996, the federal government had given sixty-one waivers to thirty-eight states in the field of welfare reform.

—Of the reduction of civilian personnel of 272,900 required by the president and Congress in statute, by fiscal year 1999, federal agencies were projected to reduce their staffing by 71,000 at the end of the first year. They actually achieved cutbacks of 200,000 by the time of the president's State of the Union message in January 1996.

Detailed discussion of progress is cited in separate chapters of the first official Status Report on the work of the National Performance Review (Gore, September 1994). Described are the accomplishments to date for each of the major categories of strategy: culture change, putting customers first, cutting red tape, cutting back to basics, and empowering employees. Appendices detail progress achieved in governmental systems like procurement, transforming structures, and financial management. Progress achieved in many agencies, such as the General Services Administration and the Departments of Transportation and Treasury, is described.

THE BROOKINGS INSTITUTION APPRAISAL

The Brookings Center for Public Management, a Washington think tank, produced a volume of commentaries that address the fundamentals of the National Performance Review (December 1995). Its title is explanatory: *Inside the Reinvention Machine: Appraising Government Reform* (Kettl and DiIulio 1995). It noted the NPR's aim to make "government work better and cost less." Brookings reviewed the NPR's official guiding objectives, examined in detail the successes and failures of the NPR, and probed whether the fundamental goals can be met.

The fullness of this comprehensive, balanced, and insightful analysis cannot be conveyed here; it deserves reading for a mature perspective on what is happening in efforts to reinvent government and previous attempts to do so. Some of its comments are reported below.

Balanced But Generally Positive Response

Within a year, the initial positive reaction to the report that was generally favorable on intent and direction began to yield to a number of diverse criticisms about its specifics. According to the Brookings commentary, these ranged from "journalistic quibbles and political nitpicks" to a more basic criticism for overstating potential cost savings, a difficulty inherent in a number of administrative reforms undertaken over the years. Concerns were expressed about the NPR's contradictions and inconsistencies, with serious doubt expressed whether downsizing with its destructive impact on employee morale and incentive was compatible with sustained quality performance improvement.

There was also extensive comment on the positive side. Public management expert Lawrence Lynn, Jr., felt that the Gore report has provided a positive stimulus to better public management and that the movement to reinvent government will prove to be a useful step forward in the history of administrative reform. When Vice President Gore was pushed for a report-card score for the first year status report of progress, he responded with a B+. The contributors to the Brookings volume of appraisal did not disagree with a B or B+, although they felt no single grade was an adequate appraisal. They preferred to focus their efforts on a set of standards and expectations by which administrative reform efforts can be judged.

Donald Kettl in his part of the Brookings study (1995) concludes that the NPR "has proven one of the most lively management reforms in American history. It has helped reorient the federal bureaucracy toward a far more effective attack on problems that it must learn to solve. Public support has been overwhelming. Indeed, a careful review of the NPR's first year shows impressive results that disprove the cynics."

Impressive Early Results

The first year demonstrated that the NPR was more than rhetoric. It began to take significant steps to transform the bureaucracy:

A Quick Start on Culture Change. Kettl concludes that the behavior of government workers can never be the same. The NPR's four guiding principles—cutting red tape, putting customers first, empowering employees to get results, and cutting back to basics—provide "new, if rough, guideposts by which to steer and judge the federal bureaucracy."

Simplification of Rules and Processes. The NPR has stimulated efforts to simplify and eliminate numerous rules and regulations that ranged from doing away with personnel manuals to making it easier to survey citizen satisfaction with public service. Some worry that simplification and elimination of rules and regulations may proceed too far.

Reform of Procurement Processes. Working with ongoing congressional efforts in procurement reform has resulted in important results in simplification of the procurement process with the Federal Acquisition Streamlining Act of 1994. One procurement expert suggests caution: Be careful that "if it ain't broke, don't break it and don't go back to where it was before someone fixed it."

Improved Coordination of the Government's Management Activities. Although cabinet departments have been frequent targets for better top management, the NPR further strengthened them. It enabled key officials in cabinet departments to be involved and work with a newly created President's Management Council. The Management Council has become a "valuable weapon" in the administration's efforts to garner agency support for the NPR and to enable top department officials to share experiences and approaches. It focused government-wide attention on key management issues and organized successful political support for NPR's legislative program.

Widespread Innovation by Federal Managers. More than a hundred Reinvention Labs started to find out what works and what does not and to produce ideas and information about how to do better jobs. The NPR is credited for generating tremendous activity, enthusiasm, and positive results in improving federal service and accelerating the pace of change.

In summary, Kettl considers the NPR to have the potential—with the New Deal and the Hoover Commission—to be "one of the three most important administrative initiatives of the Twentieth Century." The NPR demonstrated something not surprising to the insiders, but perhaps more than the reinventers themselves considered possible: Many public managers eagerly and quickly embraced the ideas and opportunities offered by the NPR and produced positive results in the form of lower costs and improved performance. The themes of the NPR also resonated well with the public and had great political appeal.

Concern About Sustainability

Despite the positive feeling of early progress, there is genuine concern about whether the reinvention effort is sustainable and whether it will solve critical problems. People worry that the " tensions" created by downsizing may undermine the culture, morale, and behavior of workers under stress and uncertainty. There is fear whether the negative environment against federal workers will enable them to pursue the reinvention effort aggressively and wholeheartedly. Others worry that indiscriminate downsizing will enable the best to leave or take early retirement.

Others fear that the efforts to empower workers and decentralize authority to make decisions closer to the people will not result in benefits to the ill-defined public interest. Rather, it will become easier to cater to special or personal interests.

A CRITICAL COMMENTARY ON THE NATIONAL PERFORMANCE REVIEW REPORT

As part of a "Mini-Forum on Reinventing Government" in 1994 in the *Public Administration Review*, Ronald C. Moe, of the Congressional Research Service and Center for American Government, Johns Hopkins University, commented critically on "The Reinventing Government Exercise." The article's subtitle expressed his viewpoint: "Misinterpreting the Problem; Misjudging the Consequences." The Moe article analyzes the Gore report, issued at the conclusion of six months of the National Performance Review, and addresses two main problems: (1) "Where does the Gore report fit in the history of reorganization efforts for the executive branch of government?" Moe queries whether the Gore report "constitutes a clear-cut break with traditional public administration values, and points the way toward a new paradigm in the management of the executive branch of government." (2) "What consequences are likely to follow if the philosophy of the Gore report and its specific recommendations are implemented?"

Criticism of the Report's Call for a New Management Paradigm

Moe traces the origins of the Gore report to the writers David Osborne and Ted Gaebler, who popularized the phrase "reinventing government" in a book by that title, and especially to Osborne, who participated in writing the Gore report. Reinvention is possible, according to Osborne and Gaebler, "if there is a cultural and behavioral shift in the management of government, away from what they call bureaucratic government toward an entrepreneurial government." This call for a new paradigm of entrepreneurial governance, Moe suggests, is answered by the Gore report.

The authors of "Reinventing Government," Moe suggests, "blended ideas of free market economics, and voluminous privatization literature of the 1970s and 80s," with the "most popular business motivational literature." The results, Moe concludes, is a "drink palatable to those liberals who believe government is best that uses its power to selectively intervene in the nation's economic life (e.g., national health care program, but who want this program to cost less, or at least to appear to cost less."

The Report's Deliberate Break in Management Philosophy

The Gore report, Moe concludes, represents an intentional break in management philosophy from earlier organization management studies. Earlier studies emphasized the need for democratic accountability of departmental and agency officers to the president and his central management agencies, and through these institutions to Congress. The Gore report, Moe claims, calls for a different management paradigm of "entrepreneurial government" that replaces the "bureaucratic paradigm," which Moe prefers to label the "administrative management paradigm."

The administrative management paradigm, Moe writes, accepts as its basic premise that "the Government of the United States is a government of law passed by the representatives of the people assembled in Congress. It is the Constitutional responsibility of the President and his duly appointed subordinates to see that the laws are implemented. For laws to be implemented, authority and accountability had to be centralized in the President." Within this structured system, considerable discretion in administrative practices was advocated and permitted.

A second premise of the administrative management paradigm is that there are two distinct sectors of society, government and private, governed by different sets of laws. Generally the sectors are kept distinctive in organizational management terms and seek their distinctive character in legal theory, not economic or social theories.

In contrast to the administrative management paradigm, Moe concludes, the Gore report seeks to achieve an entrepreneurial paradigm that rests on four premises:

1. The federal government and private sectors are similar in their essentials and respond similarly to management incentives and processes.
2. Federal government agencies should be viewed as entrepreneurial bodies which function best in a competitive market environment.
3. The size of the government is a function of the number of civil servants employed full-time, hence it follows that to decrease the number of civil servants is to decrease the size of government.
4. Federal agency management should be both tied and subordinated to budgetary priorities and processes.

Moe reasons that these are faulty premises that tend to lead to faulty conclusions about the state of government management.

Other Concerns with the Report

Moe then proceeds to question the four basic principles upon which the report is based: casting aside red tape, and shifting to systems accountable for achieving results; insisting on customer satisfaction; transforming cultures by decentralizing authority, and empowering employees to make more of their decisions and solve more of their own problems; constantly finding ways to make government work better and cost less by reengineering how they do their work and reexamining programs and processes. He questions whether these principles constitute a theory (that is, propositions subject to disproof) or whether they are simply hortatory declarations, and considers discussions of these basic principles relatively fruitless because the assertions are not presented in propositional form. He is concerned whether worthy recommendations can result from unworthy premises, and concludes that some are indeed worthy and others are unworthy.

Another concern he raises attacks the promise of savings made largely without recommending the elimination of any substantive programs. Other concerns he mentions with the report are the recommendation for biennial budgeting; the undermining of the rule of law; the diminishing of the institutional capacity of the central management agencies, particularly the downsizing of the managerial role of the Office of Management and Budget; the devolution of management authority to lowest levels possible from the president to agency "customers"; the desire to "melt the rigid boundaries between organizations"; the increasing role of interagency committees as management tools; and the way the report considers Congress as a "managerial nuisance" and does not consider Congress as co-manager of the executive branch. The Moe discussion summarily considers the Gore report to be "a major attack on the administrative management paradigm with its reliance on Public Law and the President as Chief Manager."

Moe recognizes that all studies of federal management are political to some degree and are slanted to further political priorities and fortunes, but he considers the Gore report to "break new ground in terms of its political salience if the recommendations are implemented." He fears it will bring about a government much less accountable to the citizens for its performance, as its institutional presidency and central management agencies are being intentionally weakened in their managerial role. His concerns reflect the worry that agencies and programs will be increasingly disaggregated by budgetary priorities that divert increasing amounts of government activities and services to quasi-public bodies, thereby avoiding salary and personnel ceilings and enabling contractors and consultants greater managerial responsibility for government programs.

The Moe discussion, it should be editorially noted, was written prior to any substantial experience with the report's implemented recommendations; the brief history will show that some of the concerns remain valid; others are off the mark. Many practitioners and serious students of government consider that the four basic principles of the Gore report reflect progressive management thinking and practice and will usher in significant progress in savings, customer satisfaction, and quality improvement (Kettl and DiIulio 1995); and others approve the increasing reliance on "outsourcing" with the private and nonprofit sector (Salamon et al. 1992) despite the fact that the principle originally stems from industrial experience. Other government observers do not believe that the Gore report and subsequent activities subvert the basic notion that the executive departments and agencies operate under the rule of law and report to Congress their accomplishments, despite their increasing attention to their "customers," the American people.

The Gore report makes clear that its focus is primarily on how government should work, not what it should do. The task was to improve performance in areas where policy-makers and laws have already decided government should play a role. No one seriously disputes that executive departments are fully subject to congressional laws and budgets.

THREE FUNDAMENTAL APPROACHES TO REINVENTION UNDERTAKEN

As the NPR implemented its principles and recommendations, several fundamental operating patterns emerged that also drive private-sector reforms. In concept and by political and public necessity, all three patterns are essential to pursuing a reinvention effort. But in practice the diverse approaches are somewhat in conflict and occasionally even counterproductive, as we learn from business experience where they have been applied.

The Pursuit to Deliver Savings

Although the overall mission and mandate was to make the government work better and cost less, political strategists within the White House emphasized quick efforts to "cost less." They reasoned that unless they could demonstrate in a period of huge deficits that they were shrinking and streamlining government with substantial savings, as the American public demanded, the longer-term effort to improve performance would not be taken seriously. It forced the reinvention effort to be a "money saver." Promised were major savings in three categories: a smaller bureaucracy ($40.4 billion), program and organization changes in individual agencies ($36.4 billion), and a reduction in procurement costs by streamlining the procurement process ($22.5 billion). Downsizing the bureaucracy turned out to be the backbone of cost savings. Of the promised cutback of 272,000 personnel, 72,000 were gone in the first year; over 200,000 were cut by 1996.

But "savings" is a limited and vulnerable strategy, however politically necessary. This is not only because tremendous savings by the elimination of waste and inefficiency and fraud are hard to amass in the large amount wanted and cannot be continued over time. In studies at the state level it was revealed that officials and voters think that government inefficiency is so great that expenditures could be cut without undermining the quality of public service. It was expected that spending limits would force government bureaucrats to eliminate the waste from the system. Although downsizing has in fact limited the growth in government spending, there is evidence that citizens still believe the public sector is fundamentally inefficient, even after downsizing and expenditure limitations.

Unfortunately downsizing has become largely a symbolic tactic, a way for elected officials to resonate with the concerns of the voters without directly attacking the problem of making government work better. Public officials, both elected and appointed, have turned to culture change, quality management, and reengineering for that purpose. In the real world we will need to do both cost savings and quality management improvement in some appropriate balance to make them work effectively, do the least harm, and gain the most beneficial results.

Quest for Continuous Quality Improvement

A second thrust of the agencies in their reinvention efforts has been the application of the concepts of Total Quality Management, in a movement of continuous, bottom-up, gradual, incremental improvement. The efforts build on the experience of industry that quality of product or service is what matters most; it leads to higher productivity and lower costs. TQM, as it has begun to be called, or TQL (Total Quality Leadership) in the Navy, seems to flourish and grow in many federal agencies. The advocates of Total Quality Management emphasize the importance of continuing effort to make changes and improvements in the way agencies go about their daily business.

TQM operates in the agencies on the front lines where programs and projects and their managers and subordinates provide services to the people. The success of reinvention will ultimately depend on the capability and skill of the frontline program practitioners who apply reinvention strategies to their efforts to serve the public. Yet, these are the people most vulnerable to actual and threatened downsizing and its uncertainty.

The TQM approach perceives quality in a broad, multidimensional "total" sense. Potentially it embraces almost all of the strategic themes of reinvention: the improvement of process, customer satisfaction improvement, culture change, and empowering the employee. In practice, total quality management is not so "total." Bureaucratic operating realities make it infeasible to be completely comprehensive. Rather the approach is often partial, incremental, and opportunistic to do whatever can be improved, fairly quickly and realistically. Small gains are acceptable provided you keep seeking continuous improvement and render greater value to the customer.

Introduction of Process Reengineering

Reengineering is often cited as a key instrument for reinvention. The concept and practice is borrowed from a much-heralded industrial approach extensively written about and widely practiced in the private sector. In concept, the design of reengineering differs sharply from the continuous, incremental, and gradual effort of total quality improvement. By definition reengineering is revolutionary. The book *Reengineering the Corporation* by Michael Hammer and James Champy (1993), which sold over 1.7 million copies in eighteen months, was subtitled "A Manifesto for Revolution." It defined reengineering as "the fundamental rethinking and radical redesign of business processes to bring about dramatic improvement in performance." Studies in 1994 by two of the big six accounting firms revealed that between 75 percent and 80 percent of America's largest companies had already begun reengineering and would be increasing their commitment to it over the next several years.

The authors, successful management consultants, are vehement in claiming that reengineering is not downsizing, nor is it driven to save money, though it often turns out that way. It is driven by the desire to improve performance in bold, different, ambitious ways. It is process-oriented. It differs from total quality improvement, which seeks to improve quality within existing processes and in more incremental and gradual ways. Reengineers seek to find breakthrough strategies that try to do the job drastically better, not just a bit better. The essence of the approach is to go beyond incremental improvements to a fundamental reexamination of processes, often with the incorporation of new information technology. The intent is to produce completely new processes and structures to achieve substantial improvements in performance. Reengineering, as does Total Quality Management, means managers build on what customers want and reengineer their processes to serve their customers' needs.

Public managers find the reengineering approach attractive; states like Massachusetts, Texas, and California have undertaken major successful initiatives with dramatic reductions in processing times and increased revenues. Success stories can also be found in federal agencies like the

Social Security Administration, where they are beginning to do electronic processing of government benefits that completely eliminate the paperwork burden. Although reengineering projects in industry are reported to have a high failure rate, public managers under severe pressure to cut costs and improve services are beginning to take the risks.

VARIETIES OF REINVENTION IN THE AGENCIES

What is known about reinvention and NPR activity came mostly from the vice president's office, the White House, or the small independent office established to implement the National Performance Review. Less is known about what was happening in the executive departments and agencies who had the responsibility to carry out NPR goals and recommendations; actually the management of the reinvention "details" were left to the departments and agencies. The Radin study of six NPR "Success Stories" in the Brookings volume offers a direct view of the agency role and response to the NPR thrust (Radin 1995).

Study of Six Works in Progress

Radin examined six agencies considered to be "success stories" by NPR officials and interviewed their staffs to determine how they went about implementing the process of reinvention. Examined were six types of activity judged to be relevant to the NPR: changing policies, reorganizing structure, reducing budgets, empowering line managers, improving customer service, and changing decision systems.

The study clearly illustrates that the six agencies displayed "significant variability in both the process and substantive response to the NPR within the bureaucracy." Only one agency developed substantial activities in all six areas. Others selected among activity types and displayed considerable variety in the way they did their reinvention efforts. Five of the six engaged in policy change; five changed decision systems; activities to improve customer service were found in three; budget reductions in three; reorganization in two, and all six engaged in activities to empower line managers. Agencies varied considerably in whether political and/or career staff were involved in each of the activities.

Other observations and conclusions emerged:

—All six agencies borrowed concepts, models, and expertise from private-sector management. In some instances the individuals who occupied the major strategy role came from the private sector; but where career officials played the leadership role, they too relied on private sector experience as their model.

—Agencies emphasized the relationships of their efforts with those of the NPR activity, but did not limit their improvement efforts to those solely derived from the NPR. Some felt the NPR provided a useful "cover" for their own initiatives and felt free to innovate.

—It was difficult to ascertain whether the new accountability approaches have been put in place, such as the measurement and assessment of performance as required by the Government Performance and Results Act of 1993. In the first year, it appears that GPRA was more promise than reality.

What is clear is that these organizations are engaged in serious improvement efforts, though not similar in pace, process, or substance. Not all the activity is attributable to the NPR, nor is there close guidance and supervision from the White House, the President's Management Council, or even the Office of Management and Budget, although OMB's leadership role is emerging as the implementing monitor for GPRA.

But for many, there is a nagging but understandable concern about whether the broadscale improvement effort will be sustained beyond political administrations. The unaddressed issue is how to institutionalize the continuing and constant improvement of public sector performance rather than be subject to the from-time-to-time frenzy of public-sector reform, which one of my cynical but wise colleagues has begun to label the "seven-year public itch."

THE AID STORY: A REMINDER; GOOD DEEDS ARE NOT ALWAYS REWARDED!

When the Clinton administration initiated the "reinvention" of government, the Agency for International Development turned guiding principles into hard reality. They created a "reinvention lab" suggested by the reinvention campaign to become more efficient, more effective, and less costly. The results were impressive:

AID has shed some 70 senior level positions, each paying about $100,000 a year. It has slimmed total staffing levels by 16%—from 10,800 people to 9,050. It has cut regulations by 55%, cut the time it takes to award competitive contracts from a year to 150 days, cut project design time by 75% and overhauled its program operations, procurement, accounting and budget procedures. (*The Sun* [Baltimore], February 18, 1996)

Although bureaucrats rarely expect thanks, the son of one brought Sara Engram's editorial page commentary in the *Sun* to our attention about AID's reinvention progress and "what thanks it received for doing more with less." The AID 1996 budget received "a whopping budget cut, along with potentially devastating restrictions on some programs" that made efficient administration less possible.

Engram understands the difficulty of defending aid for other countries to a Congress dedicated to slashing the budget when we have poor, homeless, and hungry people at home. Others in Congress may cut for ideological reasons, particularly cuts in family-planning assistance. The fact is that foreign aid is a tiny share of the budget—less than 3 percent of the budget—and AID gets only a sixth of that; yet the 1996 AID budget was cut 11 percent. The deepest slash targeted family-planning assistance, where cuts of 35 percent lost more than $200 million from 1995 funding; required were crippling restrictions aimed at interrupting U.S. aid "to some of the poorest families in the world," mostly administered by private nonprofit organizations in countries receiving the aid. A recent poll showed that an alarming number of Americans thought that the government spent more on foreign aid than on Medicare.

The small and diminishing foreign aid budget is considered to be "crucial to advancing U.S. interests around the globe and to make the world a safer place." It nurtures economic activity that raises living standards and slows the rate of illegal immigration, it helps emerging democracies set up a system of law, and it provides medical care and family-planning assistance with increasing birth rates and high rates of infant and maternal mortality. With numerous programs, the agency "plants seeds that eventually can help forestall political unrest or hostilities that spill over into wider wars."

The AID story is a defeat for efficient government; it illustrates how Congress can "talk one game and play another." AID reinvents to perform better for less. Its budget gets slashed; congressional restrictions are required to complicate its administration. Despite the clamor for performance and results in government by Congress, other reasons often motivate what it really does. Realistically, the bureaucrats get the message, and "reinvention" slips another notch. Engram wonders if the "ideologues" could care less (*The Sun*, February 18, 1996).

THE WIDESPREAD QUALITY MOVEMENT IN GOVERNMENT

Whatever the professional and public discourse, the reality is that extensive efforts are under way to engage in programs called Total Quality Management in the public sector, designed to improve the quality of public services. At the federal level, almost all agencies operate total quality management programs; many states and localities do so too. To meet the growing need for a central source of information, training, and consulting services in quality improvement efforts, the Federal Quality Institute was established in 1988. It serves as a clearinghouse and repository to provide a focus and stimulus to federal agencies for starting or maintaining Total Quality efforts. The institute offers quality awareness seminars to senior managers and maintains information on private-sector quality consultants.

In 1988 the institute began to administer the Federal Quality Improvement Prototype Award; a year later it created the President's Award for Quality and Productivity Improvement. These awards are given annually to an agency or major component of an agency that has implemented Total Quality Management "in an exemplary manner, and is providing high quality service to its customers."

An agency becomes eligible to apply for the President's Award only if one or more Quality Improvement Prototype Awards have been given to it or to one of its component agencies. The winning awards serve as case studies that the Federal Quality Institute says are widely read throughout federal agencies.

Recipients of the President's Award demonstrate proficiency in eight areas of organizational behavior that compare roughly with the categories of behavior required by the Baldridge Award given to private-sector organizations, but the standards have been adapted specifically to fit the public sector.

The categories and their relative weights are these:

1. Top Management Leadership and Support (20 points). This pertains to how senior management establishes and sustains a quality value system along with a supporting management system to guide all agency activities.

2. Strategic Planning (15 points). This demonstrates the extent to which quality considerations are included in the planning process.

3. Focus on the Customer (40 points). This focuses on the organization's overall customer service system, knowledge of the customer, responsiveness, and ability to meet requirements and expectations.

4. Employee Training and Recognition (15 points). This includes the organization's efforts to develop the workforce for quality improvement, as well as its efforts to use rewards and incentives for quality improvement purposes.

5. Employee Empowerment and Teamwork (15 points) This concerns the effectiveness of employee involvement in TQM.

6. Measurement and Analysis (15 points) This evaluates the use and management of information and data that underlie the TQM system and how the data are used to improve processes, products, and services.

7. Quality Assurance (30 points). This reviews the organization's approaches to assure total quality of products and services and the integration of quality control with continuous improvement.

8. Quality and Productivity Results (50 points). This asks for verifiable results of the organization's TQM practices.

A SERIOUS CONCERN: DOWNSIZING GOVERNMENT
MAY WEAKEN MONITORING OF LIABILITIES

Federal audits are finding rising risks in the curtailed oversight of the growth in federal loans and guarantees. People applauded when President Clinton declared in his State of the Union speech in 1996 that the "era of big government is over"; this meant to many the decline of a huge bureaucracy with its vast number of people and programs. But as the numbers of federal workers began to shrink substantially (by over two hundred thousand persons by early 1996), for a historic first, there has been enormous growth in a largely unnoticed side of the ledger: federal liabilities (*New York Times*, February 23, 1996). Federal loan programs for home buyers, farmers, students, and small business owners are expanding rapidly; they are expected to exceed one trillion dollars by 1998, up from 600 billion in 1992. In 1995 the government was compelled to set aside between 180 and 300 billion dollars to cover costs and estimated losses on these programs.

As government liabilities grew tremendously, major cuts occurred in the number of inspectors, auditors, and regulators to oversee federal loans and projects. With less capacity for oversight that provides supervision and monitoring of program liabilities, the Controller General in charge of the General Accounting Office, which is charged with auditing the federal government for Congress, claims that "the financial health of Federal Government loans and guarantees is at increased risk; the Federal Government now has insufficient financial accounting systems and managers to insure that liabilities are properly monitored." The head of the General Accounting Office is concerned that "when you don't have the management systems in place, and you are downsizing, especially when there are a lot of things in the liability side of the balance sheet that are going up, you have to extend oversight." Yet he claims that GAO, despite its savings on average of $15 billion a year and a new law that increases its oversight responsibilities, has been cut by Congress 30 percent in four years (*New York Times*, February 23, 1996).

What worries people is the history that in the 1980s government commitments grew but federal oversight weakened, with serious consequences in the move toward deregulation. Eventually, government insurance and credit programs lost hundreds of billions of dollars, as farm, student, and housing loan programs experienced many defaults and the savings and loan industry collapsed. Supporters claim that they are not overly concerned and point to the Federal Credit Reform Act of 1990 created to require that agencies set aside anticipated losses in credit programs. Experts in the Office of Management and Budget believe that government now has a better understanding of the cost of credit programs but concede that overseeing rising liabilities with dwindling resources presents "a risk if agencies don't have enough resources, if they cut willy-nilly."

The difficulty is that "people want the Government to go away, to be less intrusive, less bureaucratic, and more efficient," according to the deputy director of the Office of Management and Budget. They also "want all the guarantees, insurance, the promises."

The Small Business Administration Story

The administrator of the Small Business Administration is responsible for programs of loans to small business owners. He mentions how his agency "is a model for how the Administration has reinvented Government by slimming the agency down in partnership with the private sector, producing results by expanding credit opportunities, yet protecting the Government's assets." President Clinton was proud when he cited the SBA as an example of "all the work we've done to try and give the American people a Government that costs less and does more, of how the agency cut its budget by about 40 percent, and doubled its loan volume." The inspector general of the SBA, whose budget and positions were reduced, said that although they were making progress in improving some loans, he did express concern that "you cannot increase government's loan guarantees and cut the personnel for managing them, and reduce or hold steady the oversight, without increasing the risk," and then added, "It is a formula for disaster over time" (*New York Times*, February 23, 1996).

12

Strategic Competence in Nonprofit Organizations

A new capability for strategic response has emerged in the nonprofit world. Nonprofit agencies have been coping and groping for more than a decade with extensive financial cutbacks and with shifts in policies, programs, and sources of funds. Yet many demonstrate a high sense of resilience, the ability also found in nature to absorb, utilize, and benefit from shock and other changes.

The fortunate ones display a capacity for adapting—quickly, less formally, and often entrepreneurially—to hostile and rapidly changing environments. They use strategies that work, or they change. No single strategy, they recognize, is the final solution. Strategies blend and support other strategies, and they time-phase and shift over time. Hence, the new mind-set seeks not a single strategy but *strategy-competence*, the ability to handle sets of strategies as survival and success skills that enable an organization to select and execute a host of strategic choices from a wide variety of strategic options, the full menu they call it.

THE STRATEGIC RESPONSE TO FINANCIAL STRINGENCY

Serious Resource Constraints

In the decade of the 1980s and 1990s, the common complaint of nonprofit organizations was "resources are limited, yet demands from needy populations are growing, or at least more strongly articulated" (McMurtry et al. 1991). Most agencies reported declining or steady revenues, increased competition from other agencies, and rising demands for services from clients unable to pay. Yet most managed to survive. Studies of the period reveal that more than half of the agencies used specific strategies to cope with the impact of financial stringency and uncertainty (McMurtry et al. 1991, Liebshutz 1992, Bielefeld 1992). The strategies, studies show, aimed at survival, dire financial stringency, and rapid changes in policies and programs.

The nonprofit sector as a whole experienced extraordinary strains; cuts were dramatic for some agencies but negligible for others. For many board members and professional staff, survival of the agency was not enough; their commitment was to sustain its mission (Liebschutz 1992). In most cases, it appears that this was achieved.

During the period of financial stringency, privatization of public service delivery increased through purchase-of-service contracting. The disposition of federal, state, and local agencies to rely on third parties to carry out some of their responsibilities grew; nonprofit organizations became the major beneficiaries (Salamon 1984, 231).

Impact of Government Cutbacks

Although government resources continued to flow, they arrived at diminished levels. Well-established agencies were compelled to undergo considerable change. They were forced to eliminate services even in the face of increased demand and to make changes in their policies, programs, structure, and staffing.

The social and legal services subsector took the bulk of cutbacks in federal funding during the 1980s; it encountered the most substantial changes in trends of funding, employment, and current operating expenditures. Its percent of government support steadily declined from about 54 percent in 1977 to 42 percent in 1990. What is more disturbing, the Nonprofit Almanac reports, is that this subsector increased the share of its proportion of its annual funds used for operating expenditures from 73 percent to 97 percent. It was compelled to reduce its reserves to 1 percent, rather than the one-quarter of operating funds it had in 1977. This draining of reserves indicates the increasing fiscal restraint on the subsector. Although federal support remains steady since 1987, private funds are declining. The concern is that this subsector's lack of stable funding may limit its ability to meet increased demands.

Yet, contrary to expectations, relationships between government and the nonprofit sector remained substantial by the end of the decade, some say even "stronger than ever," certainly in New York State (McMurtry et al. 1991, Liebschutz 1992; Bielefeld 1992).

Extent of Reliance on Government Support

By 1989 government provided slightly less than 26 percent of total annual funds for the "independent sector," down from a high of 27 percent in 1982. In 1989, the percentage of total funds from government by subsector were 36.2 percent in health services (up from 32.4 percent in 1977); 17.2 percent in education and research (down from 18.2 percent in 1977); 42 percent in social and legal services (down from 54.3 percent in 1977); 40.9 percent in civic, social, and fraternal organizations (down from 50 percent in 1977); and 10.8 percent in arts and culture organizations (down from 14.3 percent in 1977) (Hodgkinson 1992).

Widespread Use of Specific Strategies

The hostile environment of limited resources in the decade of the 1980s compelled the use of a series of specific strategies to augment revenues and decrease expenses. Three studies conducted in the late 1980s clearly describe and discuss the specific strategic responses undertaken and provide some evaluation of the extent of success: The Arizona study (McMurtry et al. 1991); the New York study (Liebshutz 1992); and a study of organizations in the Minneapolis–St. Paul area (Bielefeld 1992). Although they pertain to organizations in different parts of the country, their conclusions contain many similarities. The Arizona study is selected for discussion.

THE ARIZONA STUDY

The Arizona study completed in 1989 sought to find out concretely how human service agencies were responding to their changing and uncertain environments. The aim was to determine the impact on an agency profile of clients, services, structure, and geographical location. They looked for answers to these questions:

—What are the main sources of revenue?
—What are the recent trends in availability of revenue, in service demand, and in competition from other organizations for both clients and revenue?
—What strategies are nonprofit managers using to respond to environmental change, and how successfully?
—Are these agencies maintaining service to needy clients?

The study was conducted by an eight-page questionnaire mailed to chief administrators of each of four hundred agencies from a sample of fourteen hundred in the state of Arizona that encompassed both urban and rural areas. Completed questionnaires numbered 198; some of the major findings follow.

Government as Important Source of Funds:

The most important source of revenue was purchase-of-service contracts with government agencies. They accounted on average for 34.1 percent of respondents' budgets, though for 53.6 percent of the agencies using this source it represented on average 61 percent of total budget.

The next source of revenue was charitable contributions, which on average totaled 32.7 percent; this included United Way moneys, private donations, and the agency's own money-raising efforts. Almost three-fourths of the agencies used funds from charitable contributions. Almost half of the agencies used client fees as a source of revenue and relied on them for about a fourth of their budget.

Increased Client Demand

Most agencies reported increased demand for service from all client groups: high-pay clients paid through insurance or personally; contract eligible clients whose service costs are paid under purchase-of-service contracts with public agencies; and low-pay or no-pay clients.

Predominantly Steady or Declining Revenue

Although almost 85 percent of responding agencies reported an increased demand from contract-eligible clients, fewer than 20 percent reported a corresponding increase in contract revenue. Significantly, although demand for low- or no-pay clients had increased in most agencies, most reported that revenues to pay for these services had dropped over the last three years prior to the study.

Steady or Rising Competition

For all client types, about half of the agencies experienced increased competition for funds; slightly fewer reported steady levels of competition. The source of competition is largely intrasectoral; other nonprofit agencies were the principal competitors. Of the 48.1 percent who reported competition from for-profits, the greatest competition was for high-pay clients, as would be anticipated. But for reimbursement for contract-eligible clients, 73.1 percent reported increased competition from other nonprofits.

Strategies Used by Service Providers to Augment Revenues

The Arizona study surveyed the strategies used to increase revenues and reported their relative success. A list of twenty strategies was provided to each respondent, divided among three categories of clients; agencies serving high-pay clients, agencies serving contract-eligible clients, and agencies serving low-pay clients. The query was this: Which strategy—if any—did you use to augment revenues, and what is your estimate of success, in terms that it exceeded expectations, fell below expectations, or was unsuccessful?

Although the strategies differed by category of clients served, the most commonly used with greatest success for high-pay clients were marketing initiatives to increase numbers of clients and to expand services to maximize revenues. Significantly, very few strategies met expectations for more than two-thirds of the agencies using them. The highest rating of effectiveness for any strategy used was 74 percent for increased staff attention to fee collection for agencies serving high-pay clients.

For contract-eligible clients, the most effective strategies were those designed to gain new contracts, those for increasing time and effort to keeping existing contracts, and those to expand contract opportunities through increased networking with other contracting agencies. The most success came from efforts devoted to keeping existing contracts, reported by 85.4 percent.

The most commonly used strategies to serve low-pay clients were appeals for new funding sources, special fund-raising efforts, increased efforts to gain media attention, and involvement of board members in fund-raising activities. But overall these strategies were less successful than strategies with high-pay or contract-eligible clients.

Generally, agencies employ a wide range of strategies to attract clients and funds with a fair degree of success. The full list of specific strategies used to augment revenues, with the number responding, percentage using strategy, and percentage reporting success, is contained in the Arizona study (McMurtry et al. 1991).

Strategies Used to Adapt to Revenue Shortfalls or Excess Demand

These strategies are designed to cut expenses and respond to trends in such conditions as increased demand from all client groups, particularly those unable to pay; steady or declining revenues; and increased competition from other agencies.

Although respondents were asked to indicate their use of the strategy in the last three years, they were not asked to indicate their level of success. The strategies selected for study were grouped into five categories adapted to fit nonprofit service providers in the voluntary sector (McMurtry et al. 1991).

The five categories are these:

—strategies to increase productivity, such as increase employee participation in decision-making, initiate staff training efforts, and grant employee recognition and inducements;

—strategies utilizing "organizational slack," such as increase work loads, obtain more volunteers, and computerize record-keeping;

—strategies involving service cutbacks, such as eliminate or shrink programs, reduce outreach, and increase waiting time;

—strategies to acquire power over task environment, such as network with other agencies, restructure board, and increase time making legislative contacts; and

—strategies to alter the organizational domain, such as conduct mergers, franchise one or more programs, or become an affiliate of a larger organization.

Most Commonly Used Strategies

The vast majority of organizations attempted to enhance productivity in at least one way, although eight out of ten attempted four or more increased productivity actions. Also common was the organization's efforts to network with other organizations and adjust board membership to enhance its influence. Another popular effort was to take up "organizational slack" that increases output to meet greater demand with no increased cost. Staff workloads were increased, volunteers were recruited, and resources were freed through computerization of record-keeping.

Implications

The authors indicate that even the long-established nonprofit service agencies, which include some of the best known, are forced to reexamine traditional assumptions about how it goes about its goals and operations. They suggest that the agencies may be forced to undergo considerable change if they are to survive into the twenty-first century.

Although the agencies, as 501(c)(3) tax-exempt organizations, are defined by their charitable and educational missions, more than a fourth of the agencies in the study received no charitable contributions. Client fees constitute a comparatively small proportion of provider budgets. Most significant is a growing reliance on government tax dollars. The traditional view of the nonprofit sector is that agencies are primarily guided by donated funds. The reality now is that a major source of revenue is government monies. This calls into question the presumed independence of the "independent sector" and raises the question: Who makes the decisions whether and what kinds of services will be financed and delivered to whom, and at what cost, if any. The government assumes tremendous control through its determination of the services it is willing to contract for and under what terms and conditions.

The study authors conclude that without an infusion of new dollars, some nonprofit human service agencies may be forced to eliminate services and programs, even in the face of increased demand; others may choose to go out of business entirely.

The study authors suggest two policy implications:

1. Although the greater use of contract services "has improved the range and quality of services available to contract eligible and full-pay clients, it has reduced the capacity of the system to serve the working poor—people not poor enough to be eligible for public assistance but not affluent enough to pay for services." In a period of limited resources, this issue is a difficult one.

2. The other implication suggested is that it may be necessary to restructure the number of agencies and the competition among them through mergers, franchising, and the greater use of cooperative or federated organizations in ways that seek quality at distinctly lower cost and with greater stability. Such strategies are increasingly used now, and continuing pressure from limited resources will increase the willingness to experiment and "cope and grope" with different ways of doing business.

In perspective, nonprofit organizations have more than a decade of experience in dealing with an era of limits; most have survived, perhaps stronger and certainly more strategy-competent than ever.

EXPERIENCE WITH MERGERS

A Review of the Literature

A study of the literature of eighteen nonprofit mergers, acquisitions, and consolidations (Singer and Yankey 1991) reveals that when they occur, they frequently are last-resort efforts to survive in response to environmental pressures rather than well-planned and well-executed growth strategies. Nonprofits often merge or consolidate, more so than do industry and business, when they face limited resources, pressure from funders and third-party payers, and increased competition.

Technically, mergers and consolidations are viewed as permanent relationships between two or more organizations that combine staff, boards, and facilities. The merger completely absorbs one organization that loses its corporate existence by another organization that preserves its existence. The consolidation dissolves each involved organization and a new single entity emerges.

Reasons for Merger Identified

The study identified a number of reasons from the literature:

—greater organizational efficiency through economies of scale, such as combined management functions and physical facilities, reduced staffing levels, and increased purchasing power;

—increased effectiveness of client services, such as providing a more comprehensive array of services in a single setting;

—greater financial stability through increased or more reliable base of funding;

—greater organizational stability through a partner that has strong leadership and management;

—increased market power by gaining control over pricing of services;

—enhanced community image by absorbing an agency with a bad reputation into an agency with a good reputation;

—increased power and prestige for executives and board members; and

—reduced competitive fund-raising by combining resources.

Mergers As a Process

Mergers are a process with a beginning, a middle, and an end. Four phases have been identified: making the decision, planning, implementing, and evaluating.

Decision Making. Organizations need to consider a number of issues when considering a decision to merge. It is advisable to develop a comparison budget that details each organization's finances separately and then combines them to determine potential cost savings. Markets need to be analyzed; resources need to satisfy goals and objectives, and avenues to maximize returns on resources must be considered.

Planning Phase. Required for a successful merger are five elements: a willingness to change, people who are self-starters, a clear sense of the organization's mission, an understanding of the organization's clients and community, and consideration of whether their needs are consistent with the mission.

Written Merger Plan. A written plan is essential that spells out tasks to be accomplished with detailed goals and objectives. The written merger plan, whether prepared by committee, task forces, or combined board, may take four to six months to write; it assigns tasks and completion dates. Key issues include:

—program items in terms of geographical focus, program philosophy, staffing patterns, staff training, and orientation;

—financial policies, practices and trends, real estate, accounting systems, and selection of accountant;

—legal matters such as corporate structure and charter, licenses and approvals, and selection of law firm;

—governance such as board composition and organization, and selection of top leadership;

—administrative items such as selection of a director, structure, and staff changes;

—personnel such as staff pay scale, morale, and benefits;

—public relations such as naming the agency and effect of merger on clients and funders.

Implementing. One of the issues often neglected is how employees will be affected by the merger. To remedy this, two merging hospitals set up an employee transition committee to consider how employees would be affected by the merger and what could be done to improve the situation. A plan was developed and executed; employees were surveyed to gain their input and response to the merger. This visible display of employee concern and attention to their interests smoothed the transition.

Evaluation. The study review produced little information on evaluation because little attention has been given to evaluating whether organizations have been satisfied with completed mergers and consolidations. But studies of corporate profit-seeking mergers reveals that most companies surveyed considered the merger outcome to have been either disappointing or a total failure. One study of forty for-profit merger transactions revealed that 65 percent of the companies surveyed estimated poor outcomes; other surveys estimated negative results between 50 and 80 percent.

TRANSACTION SURVEY OF CLEVELAND MERGERS AND CONSOLIDATIONS

Purpose and Methods

Using information obtained from the Council on Agency Executives and United Way Services of Greater Cleveland, the study identified thirty-nine local area nonprofit agencies that represented eighteen distinct transactions. The programs ranged in size from several employees to more than twelve hundred. The study was conducted by structured interviews of two to three hours duration with open-ended questions to allow maximum latitude in response. (Singer and Yankey 1991).

Survey Results

The Deciding Phase. In seventeen of the eighteen transactions, executive directors and board members identified financial reasons as a major determinant for exploring a merger or consolidation. They cited ongoing financial or funding difficulties by the "acquired" agency or program; the transaction was considered to be an alternative to closing the agency or program. Two-thirds of those surveyed felt that external funders were a major influence in the decision to explore a merger, consolidation, or acquisition.

Financial stability was considered by all to be the criteria most used to determine the feasibility of a merger. Other criteria used are: compatibility of mission (72 percent), benefit to the community (39 percent), effect on employees or volunteers (22 percent), and enhancement of services (17 percent).

When asked whether they could recommend to others a few important guidelines, they gave a variety of advice. Almost half of the participants in the transactions under study felt it was important to keep staff informed. They were explicit in saying, "Don't keep secrets, and if downsizing is involved, say so." Keeping board members informed was frequently cited, by 39 percent.

The Planning Phase. Who provides the vision and leadership in planning the merger? Individual agency executives were cited as the leaders in ten of the eighteen transactions; committees of board members and agency executives were cited in eight of the eighteen. Less credit was given to individual board members or to outside organizations such as funding or planning entities.

Morale was high in 73 percent of the acquiring agencies, while only 43 percent of the acquired agencies reported high morale. An interesting correlation reveals that 75 percent of the acquired agencies that were judged to have low morale did not report the effect of the merger on employees to be an important criterion for the feasibility of the merger.

The Implementation Phase. Forty-six percent reported that leadership and direction on implementation came from an implementation committee. In one-third of the transactions, productivity turned down during the implementation phase. The comments on low productivity reflected lowered morale and often concerned job security and role confusion. People did not know if they would be employed by the acquiring agency or what their job would be. Suggested guidelines were good communications, good planning, and good leadership. A joint retreat was credited as being the pivotal factor in enhancing morale and increasing productivity.

Evaluation Phase. No formal evaluations were undertaken for any of the transactions. In the absence of formal evaluative data, participants were asked to list the most positive and negative results of the merger, acquisition, or consolidation. On the negative side, 80 percent cited lay-offs and low morale as the result and offered emotional comments about loss of jobs. Hurt feelings were expressed by volunteers and staff that they "were sold out"; others felt a loss of identity in not being a force in the community.

Cited as positive results, financial stability and/or enhanced fund-raising were claimed by 93 percent. Other positive results cited were continuation of programs and services that might otherwise have ceased, enhanced community image, and improved staffing. Participants in the transactions generally considered the mergers beneficial. But in most cases the merger was considered to be a necessary survival strategy or a means to provide better services to the community.

The study concluded that financial reasons prompted mergers or consolidations. Financial stability emerges as a prime incentive and reward. Honest and clear communications are necessary to smooth the transition. Staff morale proved to be a thorny issue; mergers are very unsettling to employees, and human concerns need to be seriously addressed. Almost all respondents in the nonprofit transactions considered the outcomes to have been beneficial, in contrast with studies of for-profit mergers and consolidations where the majority estimated poor outcomes.

GROWING INFRASTRUCTURE OF PROFESSIONAL AND TECHNICAL SUPPORT

The contemporary strategic management movement is now supported by an extensive and growing infrastructure of knowledge, experience, statistical data, and assistance focused directly on the public and nonprofit organization. Numerous opportunities for academic, graduate, and nondegree education and training are now available; this was not so a decade ago. The rapid development of undergraduate and graduate education and training in strategic management for social, nonprofit, and public concerns is reaching for the universality achieved for strategic management courses in business schools. In fact, one university (Case Western Reserve) uses the practicum in strategic planning to enable students to consult (for free) with community nonprofits on their strategic planning processes.

There now exists extensive research, consulting organizations, journal articles, books and bibliographies, and friendly publishers. Institutional grants are available from national foundations such as Ford, Kellogg, Drucker, and Lilly; scholarships are awarded by centers such as the Mandel Center for Nonprofit Organizations located at Case Western Reserve in Cleveland.

Emergence of Pathfinders to Extensive Literature

The journal articles on strategic management that directly relate to nonprofit agencies are now so numerous in various journals it is becoming time-consuming and expensive for academics and practitioners to keep up-to-date. The growth of literature is astonishing; the Foundation Center has published a six-volume bibliography of nonprofit literature.

Selective, analytical summaries and guides that exceed the traditional bibliographic essay are emerging. Published in 1993 was a "Guide to Journal Articles on Strategic Management in Nonprofit Organizations, 1977 to 1992" covering articles that appeared in nineteen leading journals (Stone and Crittenden 1993). The guide utilized categories that closely parallel work on strategic management in for-profit firms and reflect the primary parts of this revised edition of our book: strategic process and formulation, performance, strategy-content, implementation, and governance.

The useful guide indicates to academics where substantial foundations of knowledge exist or do not exist. It cites articles useful for teaching and curriculum development and presents future research questions. Significantly, the Guide concludes that three-quarters of the articles were of "practical relevance" and judged meaningful to practicing managers. But they observed with great insight that fewer than half presented results in a way that clearly indicated their implications for action or translated research results into specific ideas for action.

In 1996, a research report surveyed strategic planning literature about research in nonprofit organizations in four broad categories: exhortations from advocates of strategic planning promoting its alleged benefits to just do it; normative frameworks and analytical tools for how to do it; anecdotes and case studies of successful applications to follow the leader; and an emerging but small body of empirical research starting to explore fundamental questions about what prompts strategic planning, the types of planning processes used, and what factors affect planning outcomes. The useful survey of strategic planning research highlights serious gaps in the research in strategic planning in nonprofit organizations. Though the survey authors are advocates of strategic planning, they confess to being uncomfortable at the meager supply of rigorous empirical research to guide strategic planning and the proliferation of "scholarly" literature that "smacks of boosterism" (Kearns and Scarpino 1996).

Growth of Authoritative Statistical Data

Authoritative statistical data is now periodically available. Regularly published and revised is the *Nonprofit Almanac* (Jossey-Bass) that presents a valuable series of statistical profiles and trends of the size, scope, and dimensions of the nonprofit independent sector. The *Almanac* uses the National Taxonomy of Exempt Entities, a classification system for more than one million nonprofit organizations. It covers national trends on wages, financial conditions, employment, and sources and uses of support. Profiles of nonprofit organizations are classified by their major sector of activities; profiles by states are also included.

Growth of Associations

Flourishing are advocacy and professional associations such as the Independent Sector, the Society for Nonprofit Organizations, the National Council of Nonprofit Organizations that represents the statewide nonprofit associations of twenty-eight states, and the Association for Research on Nonprofit Organization and Voluntary Action. The movement is internationalizing as evidenced by the International Society for Third Sector Research, formed in 1993 to promote research and teaching about the voluntary or nonprofit sector.

As one looks back and thinks ahead, what is happening in the nonprofit sector in the decades of the 1980s and 1990s is reminiscent of the surge in research, education, and consulting in business management after World War I and in government management in the late 1940s and 1950s after World War II.

13

Emerging Interdependence of Government and Nonprofit Sectors

A MASKED REALITY

The rhetoric of assault on the "Welfare State" in the decade of the 1980s and 1990s masked the reality of what actually happened. The negative dialogue assumed a basic conflict between government and the private nonprofit sector. Implicit was the strong feeling that government had not lived up to its promise when it took over many of the social services that really belonged to the voluntary charitable sector. Some claimed it actually made things worse by undermining initiative and threatening economic prosperity as well. The political dialogue was more than talk. It achieved significant reductions in government expenditures on social programs and stressed "privatization"—divestment of social service functions and their return to the private sector (Salamon et al. 1992).

The facts make clear that the dominant pattern is not one of conflict. Rather, it is a state of increasing interdependence and collaboration between a decentralizing government and a more professional private nonprofit sector. In our pluralistic society, public and private institutions work together in a mixed economy. Evidence indicates that a maturing private nonprofit sector is highly utilized by government; it provides an alternative and complementary set of mechanisms to deliver public financed services and in some instances to share in the financing and delivery of services.

The changing pattern of government–nonprofit sector relationships establishes a new environment for undertaking social change. The new pattern substantially affects management, strategizing, and policy-making in both the public and the nonprofit organization. No longer is

it sufficient to discuss strategic change without considering the implications of the new relationship and being prepared to cope with the
consequences. This places a special responsibility—and opportunity—
upon the academic community to continue to reveal the "actual realities"
underlying popular rhetoric, to provide intellectual guidance, and to
work in a mode of relevance to the working world. This is increasingly
being done, as evidenced in the writing of Salamon, Hodgkinson, Rivlin,
Weisbrod, Kearns, and others.

RISE AND DECLINE OF AMERICA'S WELFARE STATE

A Half-Century of Government Growth

Triggered by the serious depression of the 1930s and continuing on
for half a century to the early 1980s—through the New Deal and the
Great Society—the federal government substantially increased its social
programs, benefits, structure, and staff. Put in place were a number of
social innovations that spelled out government's responsibility to do for
the people what they could not do for themselves and for which the
market mechanism did not, or could not, provide. The rise in government programs reflected a lack of faith in the capacities of the voluntary
sector as ineffective or insufficient to cope with public needs. The pressure was for public systems of care available to all as a matter of right;
the age of entitlements was born. Many social services were introduced,
such as Social Security, Medicare, Medicaid, unemployment insurance,
Head Start for preschool children, and welfare. They were often adapted
from longer European experience and have become thoroughly ingrained in the American expectation. Costs of social programs rose drastically in response to vast needs and their indexation to officially
calculated rising costs of living. At one point, social programs and so-
called entitlements amounted to half of the federal budget. The decade
of the 1960s to 1970s showed contributions to social welfare increased
by 600 percent (Heath 1986).

Retrenchment in the Reagan Years and Beyond

In the 1980s the situation changed. Criticism focused on the welfare
state and "big government," high social costs, government meddling,
and overregulation. President Reagan, known as the "great communi-
cator," called for "government to get off our backs" and often stated
"government is the problem—not the solution." The rhetoric continued
with calls to cut the bureaucracy, decentralize to the people through the
states, and privatize to put government back into the private sector
where it belonged. As the president said in 1981: "We have let govern-

ment take away those things that were once ours to do voluntarily" (quoted in Salamon et al. 1992).

The arguments were these: Social programs hurt people; they undermine individual self-initiative and hamper grassroots organization; they transform indigenous voluntary organizations into extensions of the state apparatus; large social program costs weaken our economy. Moreover, government took over those functions that properly belonged in the private voluntary sector. Critics complained that the growth of the welfare state saw the manning of social programs by middle-class persons who lost touch with the needs of the disadvantaged in the community and "sapped poor communities of whatever dignity and strength they retained" (quoted in Salamon et al. 1992).

During the period of the Reagan years, the policies were clear: retrenchment, decentralization, debureaucratization, deregulation, and de-institutionalization. And much was done to achieve them. In fact, the cuts made in President Reagan's first year amounted to a 7 percent decline in federal aid to state and local governments. This was a historic first-time decline in thirty years (Rivlin 1992).

Shift from Centralization to Decentralization; Historic Transfer to State Responsibility

For the first 150 years of this country, all levels of government were small, with states going about their business and the federal government operating in its own orbit, in an arrangement some called "dual federalism." This strikingly changed when the depression in the 1930s prompted a shift of power to the federal government. New responsibilities and "bold experimentation" were undertaken to resolve the multitude of economic and social crises of depression times. Rivlin (1992) tells us that during this period the distinctions between federal and state roles blurred, and scholars talked about "cooperative federalism."

In response to the problems of the depression the federal government developed more than five hundred categorical programs of aid granted to the states. They contained detailed rules and formulas for matching and distributing the money and necessitated bureaucracies for carrying out and overseeing the programs. As the complexity of the categorical grant arrangements increased and complaints arose, there emerged a revenue-sharing plan with the states and some cities that channeled funds without the onerous administrative rules and restrictions. States enjoyed the revenue sharing because it granted financial support and made small demands. But some say Congress preferred to control the funds because it gave them power over people and jurisdictions, and categorical grants continued to grow. This growth in grants-in-aid to states continued until the Reagan years of the 1980s, when they were reduced and restructured into block grants that gave states more latitude in how they spent the funds. The cuts fell heavily on the poor and hit cities more drastically than states (Rivlin 1992).

Starting in the 1980s, the trend toward centralization stopped, and more power and responsibility devolved to the states, often in the form of transferred responsibility through mandates and too often without compensating resources. Although uncompensated Congressional mandates are now prohibited, states still fear that they will not have sufficient resources to fulfill Washington requirements.

A common complaint that grew stronger in the 1990s is that the federal government is too big and undertakes too much. Many suggest the federal government should give more responsibility to the states. State governors are in general agreement that the federal government should grant money in blocks with less detailed conditions and give them greater latitude for flexibility, experimentation, and problem-solving.

Political developments in Congress (1995–96) accelerated the transfer of responsibilities to the states. Legislated were historic measures of devolution and cutback of programs that Washington observers claim reverse the "fundamental thrust of sixty years of social policy" (David Broder, *Washington Post*, December 12, 1995). The Congressional initiatives were influenced by efforts to balance budgets and shifting ideology about big government. Congress substantially changed policies and curtailed funds that Broder says they seek to "hobble or eliminate scores of programs enacted from FDR's time through Nixon's."

Central responsibility but with diminished resources was transferred to the states in block grants in large policy areas such as welfare and Medicaid that generally can be spent as states see fit, rather than conform to Washington's conditions. But some governors worry that savings in efficiency and flexibility may not be sufficient to compensate for the lesser amounts of money to be available, and important social and environmental programs may be hurt. People most in need may not be able to be helped. Provision is being sought in some instances for federal guarantees to provide a safety net so that impoverished children and women are protected and ensure that states will be given larger amounts of money as their numbers of needy increase.

In a political epilogue that concedes the end of an era and matches the rhetoric and deeds of the 104th Congress, President Clinton proclaimed in his State of the Union address in January 1996 that the "era of big government is over."

NEW PERSPECTIVE: TRILATERAL INTERDEPENDENCE OF FEDERAL, STATE, AND NONPROFIT ORGANIZATIONS

Growing Reliance on Nonprofit Sector

As the federal government and the states clarify their responsibilities amid the continuing federal devolution to state and local efforts, a third dimension has emerged. A professionally maturing nonprofit sector is actively working with strengthened state and local entities in carrying out their responsibilities for delivering social services. They work together in ways that seek to provide services of quality at least cost. No longer can we rethink federalism and its devolution without considering the role and cost-effectiveness of the nonprofit sector contracting with governmental systems in the delivery of social services.

Scholarly examination of the nonprofit sector and its changing relationship with government reveals a greater reliance of government on the nonprofit sector than normally expected, and reciprocally so (Salamon et al. 1992). For example, government provided about one-fourth (almost 26 percent) of the total annual funds for the so-called independent nonprofit sector in 1989. One study by the Urban Institute found voluntary agencies at twelve sites around the country depended on government funds for an average of 38 percent of their resources. Fees accounted for about 30 percent, and private giving for only about 21 percent (McMurtry et al. 1992).

The threat and reality of government cutbacks worry officials of nonprofit organizations. When political rhetoric in 1996 demanded that "Washington welfare be replaced by neighborhood charity," officers of some major charities were disturbed and called the idea alarming and unfeasible (*New York Times*, February 26, 1996). The concern is that their organizations cannot replace government programs that are being eliminated or curtailed, but can only afford to supplement them. They claim that poor people would be left without aid. The deputy director of Catholic Charities, USA, which is one of the nation's largest network of private social service agencies asserts that "private charity is built on the foundation of Government welfare; . . . we can do what we do because the Government provides the basic safety net, money for food, shelter, and clothing; we could not help many people if we were paying for their rent and food." The fear is that little children, old people, and the sick and disabled would be left without the help they need to survive.

In perspective, private social service agencies provide only a small proportion of the aid the federal government expects to spend in 1996 such as twenty-six billion dollars on food stamps and eighteen billion dollars in welfare, child care, and child support. In contrast to the large sums of aid by the federal government, the fourteen hundred local agencies operating with the Catholic Charities, USA, spend two billion dollars a year, with more than half that amount coming from government agencies for foster child care and other such services. Similarly, the fourteen hundred United Way organizations raise a total of $3.1 billion a year, which goes to forty-five thousand agencies such as the American Red Cross, Boy Scouts, Girl Scouts, soup kitchens, job training centers, and day care centers.

Greater Use of States As Problem-Solving Laboratories for Change

Only three decades ago in the 1960s, state and local governments were perceived as incapable of providing service in a modern society. Weak state governments had governors with few powers and small staffs of limited professional qualifications. Their executive departments were likewise poorly staffed and badly organized. Legislators met infrequently for only a few weeks a year with few staff and less clerical support.

But states responded to the challenge of receiving and administering grants-in-aid and revenue sharing in the 1960s and 1970s. They reformed and organized to meet expanded and often federally mandated responsibilities. When the Reagan retrenchment occurred, the unexpected happened. With less help forthcoming from the federal government, states and to some extent cities and counties strengthened their own capacities and resources to resolve social and economic problems of the 1980s and 1990s.

States reformed their governor's offices and the executive departments. One initiative strengthened the governor's leadership to formulate and carry out strategies for action. This was done with longer-range strategic planning. A number of states—Ohio, Illinois, Florida, Wyoming, and South Carolina and others—developed formal strategic planning processes and written plans. States created fundamental management capacities such as professional staffs, executive budget systems, and analytical staff work.

Strengthened capacities have enabled many states to become laboratories for experimental change and centers for improvement. State experiments in welfare reform undertaken by seventy waivers from the federal government to forty states (as of June 1996) provide an outstanding example. Another area of significant experimentation concerns the health care experiments by thirteen states to place millions of poor people on Medicaid into managed care programs or risk losing their medical coverage, a plan that New York State alone estimates could ultimately save the state, New York City, and other localities hundreds of millions of dollars (*New York Times*, June 28, 1996).

Despite the increased capacity and innovative spirit of states, concerns are expressed about proposals to replace the federal government's social services or its standards with state assistance and neighborhood charity. Bob Smucker, vice president of Independent Sector, which is a coalition of foundations and nonprofit agencies, comments that there was no guarantee and no evidence that states would maintain current levels of social services if federal assistance were severely curtailed. He reminds us that federal standards were originally set because states did not or were not able to meet basic human need (*New York Times*, June 28, 1996).

Promise of Synergy for Trilateral Collaboration

Despite the strongly expressed concerns among the parties, there is evidence of greater collaboration among a decentralizing federal government, state governments, and a growing nonprofit sector. This trend toward trilateral cooperation offers the potential of significant advantage for all parties.

Collaboration promises greater service satisfaction, increased flexibility for change and experimentation, systematic problem-solving and innovation, and high levels of quality and cost-effective savings. Opening up are opportunities for resource and experience sharing, benefits of scale, joint use of capital-intensive new technology, less fragmentation and greater consolidation, strengthening and empowerment of communities, and the elimination of overlap and waste. The advantages of collaboration appear compelling, but results can be accomplished only to the extent that modes of partnership are pragmatic and problem-solving and that professionalism prevails over partisan and parochial struggle and rhetoric.

As further argument for collaborative partnership of federal/state/nonprofit agencies, Lester Salamon, director of the Institute of Policy Studies at Johns Hopkins University, notes that the United States has different levels of resources and needs. The greatest needs, he says, are likely to correspond to the areas of most limited resources. He suggests that the advantage of the federal government lies in its ability to "move resources from places that are doing well to places that are not doing well." He considers positive any effort that would reinforce the long-standing partnership between government and nonprofit organizations (*New York Times*, February 26, 1996).

Departure from One Size Fits All

The trend of continuing decentralization with trilateral collaboration offers another advantage; it enables a necessary departure from the old dictum "one size fits all," as seen from the perspective of Washington.

States in collaboration with cities and nonprofits and in flexible partnership with the "feds" can better probe, experiment, fine-tune, and respond to the growing complexity and diversity of local needs and circumstances. Pilot projects can be tried with less risk to scarce resources, to gain experience and determine what really works. Many experimental pilots are already under way in a number of states, as in social welfare reform, with dramatic results.

Throughout the decade of the 1980s the rhetoric and much of the policy and financial action presumed conflict—in simplistic one-dimensional terms—among government, its geographic levels, and the nonprofit sector. The relationship was perceived as a competitive one in what economists call a zero-sum game, in which one party's loss is the other's gain. Not conceded was that both government and the nonprofit sector have diverse strengths and limitations as well. Each could operate in a complementary and collaborative mode, to provide what each could do better and shore up the other's limitations.

For example, governments do not often recognize that differences in behavior of culturally diverse groups from Asian, African, or Latin American nations require culturally sensitive delivery mechanisms that are closer to the people in the community. Not appreciated sufficiently is the "community strengthening approach" in which small community groups enlist in partnership with government moneys and committed volunteers and prove to be more cost-effective in delivering services than governments located further away—geographically and culturally— from the community.

An Institutional Approach to Trilateral Collaboration

Seeking intergovernmental partnership has a long history with disparate results. An Accompanying Report of the National Performance Review of 1993, *Strengthening the Partnership in Intergovernmental Service Delivery* (1993f), has revived the topic. It made cogent suggestions to improve and simplify service delivery through an intergovernmental partnership of federal, state, and local government entities. It proposed that the United States Advisory Commission on Intergovernmental Relations (ACIR), "a once-proud, federally funded institution that has fallen on hard times," be reinvented. The ACIR had the function of convening officials of federal, state, and local governments to discuss common problems of intergovernmental cooperation and to make recommendations to best allocate governmental functions, responsibilities, and revenues. It sought to achieve less-competitive fiscal and other relationships among levels of government.

The general response was less than universal acclaim, not because of any lack of technical merit. Rather, the indifference to the recommendations stemmed more from a political environment of intense, emotionally charged resentment of "big, central, inefficient, wasteful, one-size-fits-all government" in conflict with states "rights."

New realities—financial stringency, profound and rapid change, and popular dissatisfaction with public services—compel a serious reexamination of intergovernmental service delivery. One approach worth serious examination is to broaden the charter of the Advisory Commission, which now includes representatives of federal, state, and local governments, to also include representatives of nonprofit entities. This mechanism would provide a policy level and technical forum away from the glare of political spotlights to guide and achieve a constantly improving set of relationships among diverse geographic locations and levels of jurisdiction. In no way would it operate in competition and conflict with existing professional associations or regional and other government councils, but rather it would be supportive of their endeavors.

THE EMERGING COLLABORATIVE MODEL

In widespread efforts all over the nation, a common thrust reaches out to marshal and interweave public and private and nonprofit resources in new ways of collaboration. Governments at the several levels and nonprofit agencies work together without the traditional walls of separation; they seek to stretch scarce resources to accomplish more for the citizenry with less. Government entities increasingly use nonprofits to get done what was often considered government work that extends in some jurisdictions to schools and prisons, though not with universal success, as evident in the negative experience of Hartford, Connecticut, and Baltimore with their education experiments.

More often government employs purchase contracts with outside agencies to deliver public services of high quality at competitive cost. They inject competition into their service contracts to ensure the best price. Unfortunately, contracts once given are sometimes inadequately supervised, with many dollars of unallowed funds being permitted (*New York Times*, December 2, 1992). But the trend is positive as more effective monitoring is achieved.

Collaboration is particularly evident at the state and local level, most often in the delivery of human services and sometimes with shared financing. Typical of the growing trend is the comment made by the executive director of the Drug Abuse Foundation in southern Florida in discussing their five-year plan to better address substance abuse treatment in the community:

The . . . development was a part of the Public-Private Sector Partnership. That means it's a partnership where the Drug Abuse Foundation works with the pri-

vate sector to assist us in building the needed facilities. We then go to the public
sector and ask them to assist us in operating it. In that way government is not
asked to pick up the total cost of operations, so it's a shared relationship. . . . We
think that the Public-Private Sector Partnership is the way public services should
be provided in the future. . . . We still need the public support through governmental funding (*Sun Sentinel* [Ft. Lauderdale, Florida], June 15, 1992).

A Global Trend

The emerging phenomenon of a changing government and nonprofit
sector relationship is not just "made in America" but reflects a trend of
the global community—in societies such as England, Sweden, France,
and Germany; in Eastern Europe, as in Poland, Bulgaria, or Russia; and
in Asia's Japan.

One typology distinguishes four "possible" models to represent the
realistic relationship between government and the nonprofit sector in the
modern state (Salamon et al. 1992). These models enable international
and cross-cultural comparisons. The essential feature is to distinguish
between two sets of functions that are involved in making human services available: first, the financing and authorizing of service and, second,
the actual delivery of the service.

The four patterns are as follows:

Government Dominant Model. This is where government performs the
"dominant role" in both financing and actually delivering human services. It involves government as both principal financier and the principal
provider of welfare services, using the tax system to raise funds and
government employees to deliver needed services.

Nonprofit Sector Dominant Model. This is where nonprofit organizations
are dominant in both financing and delivering services. This pattern occurs where opposition to government involvement in social welfare provision is strong for ideological or sectarian reasons or where the need
for service has not yet been widely accepted.

Dual-Track Model. This is where both government and the nonprofit
sector are extensively involved in both financing and delivering human
services, but by "each in its separately defined sphere." In this dual
pattern, nonprofits complement offerings by government by filling needs
not met by government effort. The distinguishing feature is the existence
of two sizable but generally independent systems of service finance and
delivery.

Collaborative Model. This is where government and the nonprofit sector
are both active in making human services available, and they often work
together rather than separately. This model characterizes the widespread
system in the United States.

Of course, variations on the collaborative theme exist. In fact, some depict the system in terms of "bargaining behavior" rather than pure cooperation. Actually, nonprofits often exist merely as agents of government program executives performing under contract as "collaborative vendors." But they can—although less often—participate more fully to plan, design, and evaluate programs as collaborative partners. Or nonprofits can be the recipients of technical or economic institution-building assistance or enabling grants in a new spirit of empowerment by government, as is done traditionally by governments in their foreign-assistance capacity-building efforts to developing nations and by some foundations with their operating grants.

The use of the term "collaboration" does not intend to convey full cooperation all the time. Rather, it connotes a serious relationship that may indeed be cooperative but may also be alternately characterized as one of bargaining, interdependence, contract, or subservience. Experience indicates that collaboration does not automatically occur; it is not a spontaneous, instinctive process. Rather, it is deliberately prompted by needs, people, and events and then purposefully designed and nurtured. In effect, collaboration must be "managed" to achieve effective results.

The Emerging American Model

A wealth of new data from statistical sources (like *Nonprofit Almanac*) and scholarly literature (like Salamon et al 1992; Weisbrod 1991; Hodgkinson et al. 1992) depict a disaggregated and decentralized mode of collaboration within and between the government and the nonprofit sector. Data in a model of collaboration indicates what is happening in several dimensions:

At Multiple Levels. The model reveals that collaboration occurs at all levels of national, regional, state, county, city and/or community. Since the 1980s, the government has placed greater reliance on the nonprofit sector at the state and local rather than the national level.

Several Types of Function. The model tells us that collaboration entails different kinds of functions. Data can distinguish between the provision of service that establishes an obligation or authorization to provide service and/or its financing, with its actual delivery. In practice, the functions can be separate or combined or shared. But most often government provides financing for service delivery under the terms of contractual agreement, increasingly arrived at in competitive bidding.

Multiple Kinds of Activity or Subactivity. Data indicates the nature of the activities performed by the collaborating organizations within a designated classification schema, the National Taxonomy of Exempt Entities (NTEE). The activities of tax-exempt organizations are classified into twenty-six major groups ranging from arts, culture, and humanities to mutual/membership benefit organizations. For example, in 1989, the proportion of total funds from government by subsector were as follows: 36.2 percent in health; 17.2 percent in education and research; 42 percent in social and legal services (down from 54.3 percent in 1977); 40.9 percent in civic, social, and fraternal organizations; and 10.8 percent in arts and culture organizations (down from 14.3 percent in 1977) (Hodgkinson et al. 1992).

COLLABORATION WITHIN SECTORS

Many Kinds of Collaboration Exist within the Public Sector

A series of expert papers and pamphlets by professional associations, designed primarily for operating public officials, document widespread examples of cooperative arrangements that exist between and among governmental jurisdictions and nonprofit entities. In systematic fashion, published materials identify and encourage the kinds of opportunities for cooperation that can provide better facilities and services at less cost. One excellent example is *Improving Local Services Through Intergovernmental and Intersectoral Cooperation*, published by the Coalition (of twenty-one organizations) for the Improvement of State and Local Government (Donald Stone 1992). The document indicates that collaborative efforts exist in various combinations among cities and counties, governments in the region, nonprofit service agencies, and business organizations.

The cooperative types of relationships most prevalent are:

—dealing with mandated regulations in areas such as criminal justice ordinances across local barriers, cooperating with other jurisdictions in maintaining a strong gun-control law, enforcing building safety and housing occupancy codes, or cooperating with planning and zoning regulations to produce a fair playing field among contiguous jurisdictions;

—service-delivery cooperation in areas where technology and required scale of investment in things like waste treatment or urban mass transit are so costly that sharing among neighboring units is required;

—special financing and delivery of services where local governments cooperate with private nonprofit agencies by utilizing them under contract, subsidy, or just encouragement. The Coalition suggests, "This is a partial if not principal way to provide child care, mental health, drug treatment, and many other human services. . . . These are vital to any jurisdiction's quality of life." Vast sums of money are at stake. Dr. Bernard Arons, leader of a mental health team working for the White House, estimates that local and state government agencies spend sixteen billion dollars just on mental health and drug abuse services (*New York Times*, June 10, 1993).

—state and local cooperation. Much effort focuses on lessening the often difficult and burdensome impact of state government on local jurisdictions. All too often, detailed prescriptions and mandates incorporated in state laws and codes impair local government capability and accountability.

—regional councils. Other areas of cooperative effort pertain to the services of a council of governments (COG) or regional planning commission (RPC). Councils exist in all but four states and total more than five hundred nationally, served by the National Association of Regional Councils. The councils provide regular communications among the member governments, provide a variety of administrative services for members, and carry out many cooperative initiatives where larger-scale operations are more cost-effective. Examples are mass transportation, water supply, and solid and liquid waste disposal.

Areas of Collaboration within the Nonprofit Sector

Although the nonprofit-sector movement has not focused systematically on collaboration within the sector to the same extent as the public sector, much cooperative effort has been undertaken in the form of mergers, affiliations, and other strategic alliances and the start of "branch offices" for getting closer to the people.

One form of collaboration is the expanding use of local affiliates of a national organization in varying forms of relationship from loose confederation to organizational integration. Some local affiliates of national organizations conform to the franchising concept of the business world, wherein national units supply services, name, and standards to local nonprofits with their agreement in exchange for a periodic fee.

The Health Industry

In the changing health industry, academic institutions of national reputation are affiliating with community or regional medical centers. The hospital at Duke University has signed an affiliation agreement with the Good Samaritan Medical Center in West Palm Beach, Florida. Administrators claim it makes available the resources of a nationally renowned university medical center not available at a community hospital. For example, the drug research capacity at Duke enables faster access to experimental drugs as well as newly approved ones in medical areas where life and survival are at stake. The affiliation is designed to upgrade capacity in ways that update and expand medical care in specialized heart and cancer services. This is the first comprehensive agreement between any of the Palm Beach county's community hospitals and a major national university (*Sun Sentinel*, June 4, 1993).

Another trend is the passion for outreach of prestigious nonprofit institutions to imitate the new private-sector doctrine of "any place, any time" by establishing branch offices closer to where the people are, with schedules of service that accommodate clients' needs. A national center like the Cleveland Clinic from Ohio discovered that one-fourth of its patients originated in southern Florida and decided to open a branch in Ft. Lauderdale, while the famous Mayo Clinic from Minnesota opened a branch office in Jacksonville in northern Florida.

Of course affiliation with a national organization can have its downside. When the leaders of the national United Way received negative publicity about excessive salaries and expenditures amid allegations of unwise organizational ventures and criminality, affiliates all over the country were affected. The affiliates suffered decreased contributions from the public, which took much effort to replace.

The Art World

Among art museums there also is occurring the organizational freedom of moving and extending to where the action is and yet maintaining a collaborative relationship with its central base. The Guggenheim Museum in New York opened a branch in the Soho district of downtown Manhattan; it plans to open three sites in Venice, with the Italian city covering most of the costs. The Whitney Museum of American Art in New York already operates several branches around the United States.

The outreach movement is also active abroad; the Tate Gallery in London, which conducts a growing number of satellite operations, operates a branch museum in Liverpool and opened a second one, a $4.95 million branch museum in a small fishing village in Cornwall. The Arthur M. Sackler Gallery in Washington, D.C., opened China's first Western-style museum, in Beijing. These efforts will not be without their cross-cultural and financial complications.

The next decade will see numerous affiliations between art museums and strong academic art centers as the traditional educational dimension of the museum grows stronger, often in response to the need for more patrons and resources, but not infrequently born of a passion for reaching the people.

Learning What Makes Collaboration Work

Collaboration—working together rather than alone—is not new. But it appeals to an increasing number of persons and institutions who must confront a shrunken base of resources and seek ways to decrease costs and increase effective outcomes. Executives are pressed by funders and boards to ferret out less expensive but better ways to deliver service; they are encouraged to work with others in sharing costs of planning, research, training, and overhead costs.

The collaborative movement proceeds far beyond the boundaries of cost control; it seeks to improve the quality and greater certainty of outcomes. When a problem is addressed through an interagency collaboration, jointly working organizations tend to do broader, more comprehensive analysis of issues and opportunities; they also have complementary resources that diversify their capability to accomplish tasks.

The rise in collaborative efforts has compelled foundations and experts to review the experience of collaboration, and the evidence does suggest that managed collaborative effort can produce beneficial and sometimes dramatic results. The McKnight Foundation reports on one initiative to reduce the number of families in poverty: "Collaboration results in easier, faster and more coherent access to services and benefits and in greater effects on systems. Working together is not a substitute for adequate funding, although the synergistic efforts of the collaborating partners often result in creative ways to overcome obstacles" (Mattesich and Monsey 1992).

Key questions on collaboration are being addressed, such as: What are the ingredients of successful collaboration? What makes the difference between success and failure in joint projects? In effect, what makes collaboration work? These questions were answered by the Amherst H. Wilder Foundation in a special study on collaboration (1992) that reviews a large amount of literature, case studies, and research; summarizes the major findings; and presents some critical conclusions (Mattesich and Monsey 1992).

14

Applying Popular Private Sector Strategies to Managing Public Concerns

NEW WAYS FOR MANAGING IN THE PUBLIC AND NONPROFIT WORLD

Strategies for total quality management and improved customer satisfaction, accompanied by streamlining and reengineering—all so popular in the private sector—have begun to penetrate the web of public and nonprofit organizational culture. These strategies are being embraced in new strategic planning processes that are adapted from the traditional business planning model. Actively engaged with the complexities of working in a new arena of strategy design and implementation, public and nonprofit officials are going back to school to learn how to operate the new strategies.

A Quiet Revolution—But No One Believes It

No one proclaims the end of bureaucracy as we know it. But a number of public and nonprofit organizations demonstrate a capability for applying a private sector model of strategic planning that promises to change drastically their ways of doing business. These organizations are better able to cope, despite dire resource constraints or perhaps because of them, with the serious problems engendered by a fast-changing and often hostile environment. Most surprising, many organizations are able to manifest a human behavior of courtesy and attention rather than arrogance and rudeness. And when things do go wrong, as they do, they are more ready to redress the wrong as do most progressive private firms, good restaurants, and smart airlines. Of course, the new pattern is not universally present; rather, it appears to grow like quilting—"a patch here and a patch there"—with the quilt emerging as a work in progress. But significant progress and change in culture takes time. It is excessive to assert that a managerial revolution is under way, as some do. But evidence supports the view that fundamental change is occurring in the way things are done in public organizations and nonprofit agencies. Certainly, a reorientation in thinking and behavior is taking place.

But the general public does not believe it, for negative stereotypes about public and nonprofit bureaucracy and tales of incompetence die hard. For some, the epithets against those "do-gooders" in the nonprofits and "faceless, mindless bureaucrats" in the public agencies are too convenient and satisfying to be abandoned.

Fundamental Change Under Way

Strategic efforts to reinvent government and collateral efforts to transform nonprofit management are extensive. The pressure is great to make smaller government and a collaborative nonprofit sector work better and cost less. A prime focus revolves around the imperative to raise quality of product and service and seek ways to improve customer satisfaction. Serious efforts are under way to stamp out bureaucratic arrogance and apathy. "Customers are being given voice and choice" and are being asked their needs and expectations in organized focus groups. Waiting times are decreasing with application of reengineering technique. Adaptation of private sector thinking more often grants the customer conditions of convenience, courtesy, and accessibility in a mode of "anyplace and anytime." Hospital emergency rooms and drugstores are no longer the only places that deliver off-time night service and come right into your community and home to serve you. Ask anyone who has been in a Florida nonprofit hospital that practices TQM (Total Quality Management), or observe the dedicated staff of a hospice organization that provides home care services, who insist that patients are human beings with rights and deserve treatment accordingly. Check with someone who had an auto license renewed after dinner promptly and courteously in the decentralized, small, but attractively designed outreach office of the Maryland Motor Vehicle Bureau in a nearby merchandise mall. They can only be impressed, pleased, and proud. Or learn about someone who has had a social security disability claim processed with dispatch, after the reengineering teams shortened the decision-time drastically. When they learn how long it took previously, clients can only be amazed.

The new computer revolution under way with new information technology enables new efficiencies in government and nonprofit agencies not previously imagined. Millions who receive government benefit checks now are apt to enjoy safely an electronic bookkeeping transaction that completely eliminates the paperwork burden. Growing numbers of citizens tap out their ideas, request information and forms, and register complaints to the Internal Revenue Service on computers that record on electronic bulletin boards in cities far away, and bureaucrats respond— almost promptly.

The Beginning of a Continuing Impact

The new strategies adapted from industrial practice but still fluid are changing resistant bureaucratic cultures. They will continue to do so because they derive from an intersection of three basic compelling forces:

Economic Necessity. This is evidenced by widespread financial and human resource shortages that impair the capability to satisfy strongly articulated needs and demands for services, which continue to rise in cost.

Strong Pressure from the Citizenry to Do Things Differently and Better. This is reflected in an often-angry dissatisfaction with what exists now; the demand is great for better quality, more service satisfaction, lower costs, and less taxes.

A Network of Federal Government Entities Working Together with State and Local Agencies and Nonprofit Organizations. They are learning to experiment, change, and grow. Emerging is an increasing trilateral interdependence of federal, state, and local and nonprofit organizations, born and nurtured of economic necessity. They are working together in complementary ways that strive to respond fairly and effectively to the fundamental needs of the people, despite serious fiscal restraints.

WORKING WITH TOTAL QUALITY MANAGEMENT

What Does TQM Really Try to Do? What Are Its Fundamental Concepts?

Total Quality Management is both a philosophy and a set of guiding concepts that are dedicated to construct a continuously improving organization. In essence, the TQM movement is designed to get management involved with their frontline workers—the program managers who develop and deliver product and service—to learn how to work together in analyzing work processes to achieve continuous improvement.

To achieve quality results TQM addresses these action areas:

Work Processes. It conducts continuous employee analysis of work processes to improve their performance.

Customer Requirements and Standards. It maintains close communication with customers to understand their quality needs and requirements.

Customer Interface for Service Delivery. It improves direct server interaction with customer at points of transaction for goods or service.

Management Support. It collaborates with management on obtaining resources, expertise, and data and gains the approval authority to implement improvements.

Employee Competence and Training. It develops employees to be competent and confident in using the tools of total quality management.

Fundamental Concepts of Total Quality

There exists a tremendous body of literature about the basic principles, concepts, and philosophy of total quality management. Most experts today tend to agree with the fundamental concepts of total quality management. But as you would expect from such a burgeoning field, there are hosts of variations and nuances. The following points selected from several respected works in quality management offer a general core of concepts that are appropriate for government and the nonprofit agency.

1. *A New Paradigm Forges a New Role for Managers.* TQM is not a quick fix or only a set of tools and techniques. Rather it represents a profoundly new way of managerial thinking. It offers a new management mind-set that challenges managers to focus on ways to secure continuous quality improvement.

TQM does not take hold overnight; it struggles, shifts, matures, and endures in time, but only if nurtured with constancy of purpose. Some small or even large improvements can be immediately made. But the potential for major change of total quality management demands substantial, continuing effort over time. This is necessary to establish the habit and capacity to translate intent for improvement into better product and service as a routine way of doing business.

2. *Commitment to Quality.* Commitment is the core of TQM. To be effective and creditable, it must include two key dimensions, measurability and the customer's perceptions of quality. This means management must identify its customers, understand customer needs, and direct resources toward continuously improving product and service with respect to customer-relevant attributes. And it must be done with measurable specification of performance, cost, schedule, and access.

3. *Customer Focus and Involvement.* Efforts to improve quality must keep in mind the need to increase customer satisfaction within the organization as well as the satisfaction of those on the outside. But customer needs and the kinds of customers continue to change; therefore, the need is for continuous reassessment.

4. *Decentralizing Decision-Making Power.* Too often there exists a communications gap between the front offices of "headquarters" and employees on the front lines where operations are under way. Officials up the hierarchy are frequently unaware of what happens down in the organization and out in the field. The reverse is also true. The field fails

to understand and fully appreciate front-office thinking behind its strategic plans and policies that govern program operations. But efforts to close the gap are happening. The corrective trend is a dual one. The first is to decentralize power to make decisions by the employees closest to the problems, who know most about solving them. At the same time, operating employees are being more fully involved in the setting of an organization's strategic directions and plans that guide their efforts.

5. *Worker Participation in Work Analysis.* An important distinction between traditional concepts of work analysis and that of TQM is the issue of who does the analysis. Traditionally, work analysis was performed by "experts," either time-and-motion-study "efficiency" persons or by the procedures or management analyst. Under TQM thinking the experts are the workers who do the work; they are the ones who analyze their own work processes and try to improve them. The mode will vary; they may work alone or, increasingly, operate in teams with other workers or in concert with selected experts in aspects of the work. Employees are trained to do work analysis and simplification, although consultants and facilitators are often brought in to help.

6. *Benchmarking.* Benchmarking is the process for determining a standard of excellence against which other similar things can be measured or judged. Then results and outputs are compared in a systematic way. The task is to decide how the benchmark can be achieved and how to make changes in the organization's performance to meet or exceed the benchmark, or revise it.

7. *Process Orientation.* TQM organizations focus improvement efforts on its processes rather than only on finished product or service. This involves looking at definable stages and steps or activities of a process in sequence. Each step portrays a producer of activity that serves a customer. How well it performs depends on the purpose, the supplier inputs, the total process, and the needs and satisfaction of the customer.

8. *Continuous Quality Improvement.* Experts claim that the central and unifying concept around which quality centers is continuous quality improvement. This assumes that no process, product, or service ever attains perfection or that expectations remain static. Deliberate changes for improvement are therefore constantly necessary.

9. *Investment in Knowledge and People.* TQM depends on a knowledgeable work force personally involved in the improvement effort. It assumes that expanding knowledge is a responsibility of both the individual and the organization. The aim is to grow and maximize human potential in ways that contribute to greater organizational effectiveness.

10. *Total Involvement.* The ultimate aim of TQM is for every person in the organization to participate and play in the total quality game. No one sits on the bench. Although certain areas of activity will receive

greater emphasis because of their strategic value to the organization, it is expected that all persons will be empowered to participate in the total quality program.

TQM Changes the Program Manager's Management Behavior

As the TQM movement takes hold in agencies, management behavior transforms. The commitment to create continuous improvement begins to be part of ideology, culture, value, and belief. This moves the program manager beyond the next deadline or specific performance standards. Rather, the mind-set becomes one of continually making improvements, not just doing better in this one next case. This quality commitment reorients and changes management to a positive and dynamic force that continuously supports employees in their improvement efforts. It does this with training, knowledge of basic concepts, analytical tools, information technology and data access, and team efforts to work together. The cumulative momentum of quality improvement is a potent instrument for constructive change.

Most significant is the reliance on worker analysis of their own work rather than constant monitoring and heavy-handed checking by others, or use of outside experts or staff from headquarters. In this way management and the workers learn to work together, with the total quality–oriented manager geared to empower and enable their employees rather than control them. They encourage independence and self-reliance, yet collaboration and teamwork; they train and coach rather than direct and supervise. They learn to use objective benchmarks, or standards of excellence, against which similar things are to be measured or judged. And they give priority attention to customers and their needs. In all this they realize that to improve the organization effectively, they must focus improvement efforts on its work processes.

New TQM Responsibilities for the Program Manager

Program managers are increasingly being trained and held accountable for the improvement of quality of product and service, particularly in federal departments and agencies that are actively engaged in Total Quality Management as an integral effort for reinventing government. Journal articles claim that nonprofits are "ripe" for TQM (Kearns et al. 1994); a number of hospitals have already made dramatic strides with Total Quality Management.

Agencies have undertaken to increase responsibilities for the program manager to make quality improvement of product and service an important part of the job. They are being urged to:

1. *Integrate TQM into Each Job.* Each program manager has the obligation to search for ways to improve the performance of work for which responsibility is assigned. The focus is on what to do and how to be most effective in improving quality by making changes that add measurable and recognizable value to customers and thus enhancing customer satisfaction. This may involve use of focus groups and other techniques to find out what customers expect and how satisfied they are with current service and product. A collateral concern is how to be realistic and effective in dealing with an environment resistant to change and innovation.

2. *Perform Analyses of One's Own Work Processes.* Work analysis consists of analyses of customer, supplier, and process. A starting point is to first do customer analysis to clarify who the customer is. Then you can determine customer needs, expectations, and wants. A next step is to determine who the suppliers and contractors are and how they perform in supplying inputs. Then you are ready to examine the work processes whereby inputs are supplied and outputs produced to meet the needs of customers.

In describing and analyzing one's own work, activities are bunched into various categories that characterize the value of the work to the organization. One classification categorizes work as follows:

—value-added work that adds a benefit for the customer;

—necessary but not value-added work that must be done but is supportive or maintaining, such as preparing budgets or ordering office supplies or desks;

—unnecessary work that seems to be done with no recent justification, such as unneeded reports or forms and outmoded committees; and

—waiting or dead time where you are being held up by waiting for some data, a delayed meeting, a non-available conference room, late supplies from contractor, or a delay from the previous person in the process.

You make your own classification depending on the kind of work and the patterns of occurring problems and opportunities that impact on quality performance.

3. *Apply Tools of Analysis.* A number of tools are available for analyzing work; five are described in the book *Total Quality Management in Government* (Cohen and Brand, 1993, 95–116). The tools are designed to help you and your team visualize a process, pinpoint problems, find their causes, and determine solutions. They can be modified, combined, and adapted to the individual circumstances of the task.

Some tools are available for work analysis :

—The fishbone or cause-and-effect diagram is used to ferret out causes of an undesired effect before undertaking a solution.

—The pareto diagram and bar chart is a graphic technique that ranks events in order of frequency, duration, or importance. By ranking frequency of events, the pareto chart pinpoints the factors or problems that require primary attention.

—The flowchart or process chart has a fifty-year history of use in the federal government and industry; preparing flowcharts is now assisted by commercially available computer software. The flowchart is a step-by-step graphic presentation of a sequence of events involved in a particular process. It is used to accelerate processing times, eliminate redundancy, and curtail unnecessary effort and wait times. It is utilized in reengineering efforts to improve customer satisfaction.

—The run chart takes measurements at regular intervals of time. It enables you to monitor performance or identify trends and learn whether important changes occurred and at what point in time.

—The control chart is essentially a run chart with upper and lower limits set from a process average or other form of benchmark standard. It identifies variations in performance, a key fundamental of quality analysis where precise measurement is feasible.

IMPROVING "CUSTOMER" SATISFACTION

Many organizations in government follow a trend in the private sector to provide better service to their customers. They do not experiment with bold new theory. Rather, they apply important lessons distilled from the experience of a number of American organizations that have begun to master ways to create superior and distinctive customer service. We know that what industry does to satisfy customers is largely applicable to government and to the nonprofit agencies as well, of course with adaptive modification.

No longer can conventional wisdom and customary cynicism maintain that service in America is impossibly bad. It often is mediocre, substandard, or downright poor. But to counter any blanket indictment, the experts with evidence at their command tell us this: not always, not everywhere, and not necessarily. Positive change is on the rise in business, government, and the nonprofit sector, often with dramatic results.

Organizations now better know what good service is and how to deliver it. Knowledge is available of operating principles that guide the running of successful service-focused organizations. Many role models exist to teach us how to make substantial improvement in customer service, when management is willing, able, and committed to it.

Creating Superior Service Is a Deliberate Act

Creating high-quality service on a reliable basis does not happen automatically; it is a willful act of management. When quality service is found lacking, the primary reasons are no mystery. They usually are lack of skill and knowledge about how organizations manage quality service. And second, there is the absence of a commitment by management to quality as a serious organization goal.

We have access to highly transferable, learnable principles that the experts tell us are portable and can be applied beyond the specific industry in which they are practiced. They are appropriate for adaptation to government provided you are aware of government's special conditions of equity and nondiscrimination and such other constraints as qualifications and limits of authorized legalities and entitlements.

The Server-Customer Interface Is the Significant Moment

Creating service is a people event; it takes place between the service provider and the customer. The service interaction does not occur unless the provider and the recipient come together at a transaction point; they meet or have contact whether it be face-to-face, electronically, or through the written word. This has been called "the moment of truth" that creates the single most important impact on customer satisfaction, even though it may only be a part of the service process.

When service is delivered, the recipient's prior expectations may determine the sense of satisfaction. Yet what customers expect can be vague, ill-informed, or beyond the ability or authority to respond. Or specific needs may not be communicated well to the provider. The net result is that expectations are often not met; misunderstandings ensue.

To create superior service you must know, anticipate, and even shape the reality of customer expectations so that you can meet and exceed them. That is why private-sector organizations often seek to shape the service at the moment of contact. They seek to create a favorable impression and thus influence the level of satisfaction. The private sector with the encouragement of the tax laws may often use food and drink to sweeten the moment of contact. Public-sector constraints compel the use of other ways that provide a satisfying contact; they can offer better access, convenient hours of doing business, empathy, caring and respect, and other positive attitudes. Of course, the basic component of customer satisfaction is skillfully delivered competent service.

Recipients Play a Special Role in the Service Transaction:

When the service interaction does happen, the recipient plays an active role, often telling what is wanted or needed. But there are many situations where the customer does not know exactly what is needed or wanted, or allowable. They may have to be informed about what is possible and feasible.

Some government and nonprofit services are necessarily complicated; they depend on legal and administrative eligibilities and entitlements. When the conditions that surround a service are complex and technical, more education is required. But how education is performed is crucial to the transaction. It cannot be arrogant, judgmental, harsh, or mean. The manner and attitude of education must be professionally restrained and considerate. This is doable with motivation and skillful training.

How Arrogant Are You?

Survey studies by organizations such as IBM to gauge the organization's image among customers often make clear they have been viewed as "arrogant." They have been perceived as possessing a "don't care" or "take it or leave it" attitude; they were considered "bureaucratic" in that they were viewed as "inflexible and slow to respond." Efforts today at IBM are different; they work hard to respond to customer expectations and they succeed. Executives are compelled to interview clients and report on efforts to be responsive to clientele expectations.

Government agencies too often project images of arrogance and inflexible bureaucracy. As you know, citizen perception of government service is decidedly negative. But government agencies are beginning to follow private sector principles of progressive organizations and are making strenuous efforts to increase customer satisfaction and offer quality service. Many nonprofits do the same.

When Service Fails—As It Can Do—Follow-up Actions Must Be Taken

When a service fails or does not live up to expectation, it is a personal affront that often is blamed on the service provider. Emotions can erupt, personalities can collide, prior prejudice and bias can surface. Yet the service provider must remain in control and attempt to make the human contact turn out well for the organization and the individual.

All too often, organizations fail to anticipate what can go wrong in its service and therefore are ill-prepared to recover from the failure. Superior quality organizations seem to know what to do when something goes wrong, as it can periodically; they are prepared.

Recovery or remedial actions can take a multitude of forms, depending on the nature of the wrong. Some wrongs or failures may be simple annoyances; others cause serious delay or loss. Remedial actions therefore can range from sincere apology to urgent, substantial redress and correction. In effect, remedies convey a sense of empathy and understanding and some form of what has been called "symbolic atonement." This is a form of partial justice to compensate somewhat for the annoyance or deprivation sustained. Or it could involve a follow-up that takes some time to offer additional solace. This could be a promise of repeat or future service.

Complimentary meals, lodging, or drinks so often used by airlines and hotels are not an acceptable device in government. What is intended in all recovery actions, and government and nonprofit agencies can do this, is to convince the recipient to say: Things did go wrong but they really did something to make it up to me. I feel better about them and about the problem "they" created. And I feel they will do better next time.

Five Guiding Principles

In their book *The Service Edge*, Zemke and Schaaf (1989) describe five major operating principles that occur in over a hundred companies that perform high quality service on a regular and reliable basis. These organizations practice a pattern of behavior that builds extraordinary levels of customer satisfaction. Serious students of government claim the patterns are advantageous for government service and the nonprofit organization as well; each reader can be the judge. The operating principles that high-quality service organizations have in common in varying degrees, somewhat modified by government and nonprofit experience, are briefly described below:

Operating Principle 1. Listen, Understand and Respond to Customers. The Gore report on the National Performance Review makes clear that federal organizations must listen to, understand, and respond to evolving needs and constantly shifting customer expectations. But listening has to have purpose:

—Identify the customers' transaction point, and you can plan and shape the impact and outcome of such moments.

—Be informed of customers' changing needs, wants, and expectations, but be aware of the possibility of their conflict and inconsistency.

—Really listen to unexpected ideas and suggestions.

—Involve customers in ways that mean they feel they can be frank and honest in their complaints and suggestions.

But to start, you must identify who are your real customers. If you know who are your customers, then you can decide the best ways to listen to them. It can be face-to-face or formal survey research. Or it can be customer toll-free telephone and fax numbers, with systematic comment and complaint analysis to nip problems in the bud stage. Or it can be special treatment to disgruntled customers by showing concern and responsiveness. Sometimes there can be customer advisory panels and sessions for mutual education for discussing technical processes and getting reaction on best ways to serve. A popular technique is the convening of focus groups to probe a topic in terms of what the participants think and feel. It is very important to use what you hear and let the customers know you are doing so.

Operating Principle 2. Define Superior Service; Establish a Service Strategy. Setting and stating a service strategy gives focus to what specific attributes of service you intend to deliver that meets real customer priorities. But how strategy is stated varies in form. It may take the form of a simple, concrete pledge to respond to a customer letter within forty-eight hours, complete service within seventy-two hours, or have no wait time beyond thirty minutes.

The Maryland National Bank states its commitment to customers in this strategy statement:

MNBA is a company committed to . . .

—providing the customer with the finest products backed by consistently top quality service;

—delivering these products and services efficiently;

—treating the customer as we expect to be treated by putting the customer first and meaning it.

Whatever the form of the stated strategy, it is simply a statement of what you intend to do and must do for the customer to be distinctive in providing service quality.

Anatomy of a Service Strategy

No precise formula exists for stating service strategy but experts observe that an effective strategy possesses four characteristics: It is a serious statement of intent to satisfy customer needs and wants, describes ways that noticeably distinguishes you as superior in service, has value in your customer's eyes, and is deliverable by the organization.

All elements are essential, but the fourth characteristic has special importance because it is so often violated in a campaign to provide superior service. If pledges to superior service are not carried out, they are more harmful than having no statement to begin with.

Other experts suggest that to communicate service strategies effectively, you answer three questions: What is our unique contribution? To whom do we provide this service? What key value do we want them to perceive about us? And by value they mean an attribute of the service that appeals to and satisfies customer's needs, wants or expectations.

Thus a Service Strategy Framework, suggested by Chip Bell (Zemke and Schaaf 1989), can be depicted like this:

1. To Provide: (Our Unique Service Contribution)
2. To Whom: (Your Customer)
3. So That We Are Perceived by Them As: (Key Value)

Whatever strategy is used and communicated, it is important to communicate it with frequent repetition. Ensure that the message reaches down into the operating units where the direct transaction contact with the customer takes place.

Operating Principle 3. Set Standards and Measure Performance. Organizations that are recognized for distinctive service consistently meet their customer's expectations. What they do is establish clear, customer-oriented performance standards and then carefully measure performance against those standards. Experience at Internal Revenue Service and Social Security confirms that without a commitment to measurable standards service quality is only rhetoric. With standards you can achieve a managed service delivery system in which constant improvements can be made and fine-tuned to changing customer expectations.

There is understandable conflict in many organizations about how to set standards. One point of view stresses that standards must reflect the customer's perception of what is really desired or wanted. Another point of view starts with asking the professionals on the job to determine in a technical sense what the customer really needs. This apparent conflict is clearly defined in medicine and hospitals; doctors often wonder how the patients can tell them what to do. Arguments frequently take place in technical organizations where professionals complain that the customers are not qualified, or informed, or sufficiently clear, or able to articulate what they really need, want, or expect. And if you follow their mandates too closely you will do them a disservice. But the customer-oriented expert retorts that if you ignore the recipient, you only enhance customer dissatisfaction and distrust.

The solution to the expert-customer dilemma rests with a delicate balance between the use of an organization's technical expertise and knowing and meeting the customer's ever-changing definition and expectation of good service. In the face-to-face encounter between the technical expert service provider and the customer, there can be sensitive and tense situations. Often the technical expert focuses on the quality of the service itself; but the recipient is oriented to how it is delivered: where, when, and under what conditions. The customer may be more concerned with courtesy or compassion, or threatened and disturbed by arrogance and harshness, even if the technical quality of service is high.

To resolve the dilemma, often agencies solicit and use the input of service recipients, who are periodically canvassed about their desires and satisfaction. And changes are made to accommodate their suggestions and comments.

General Factors of Customer Service Quality

The experts have been looking for some generally applicable systems for measuring service quality and customer satisfaction in the private sector. Some feel this has value in the public sector as well, certainly as a starting point for discussion and adaptation to greater precision and specificity. One set of general criteria for service quality offered by Texas A & M's Len Berry (Zemke and Schaaf 1989) is:

—reliability. The ability to provide what was promised, dependably and accurately;

—assurance. The knowledge and courtesy of employees and their ability to convey trust and confidence;

—empathy. The degree of caring and individual attention provided;

—responsiveness. The willingness to provide prompt service; and

—tangibles. The physical facilities and equipment and appearance of personnel.

But when this list of criteria was shown to frontline workers and managers, they were not always impressed because it gave them little or no clue about what to correct. They said it may be good for management, but they needed more specific suggestions about what was bad so they could correct it. They preferred a more specific checklist that could concretely guide them. That may explain the presence of very specific evaluation sheets used by management for guests in fine hotels, asking about the quality of concrete items of service.

Operating Principle 4. Train and Empower Employees to Work with the Customer. Training has long been recognized as essential to any improvement effort. People are considered a strategic resource that should be developed to increase their ultimate value. But the nature of in-service training is changing; four trends are noted:

—No longer does training consist of any kind of training that management suggests or that workers want. Rather the training emphasized is strategically focused; it contains the skills, knowledge, and tools to do things that are the important things the agency is trying to accomplish; it focuses on essential strategic directions and ensuing initiatives.

—Second, training more often customizes its design to a clear definition of who are its customers and their real needs.

—Third, in-service training is more than delivering knowledge; it is more often action- and application-oriented. It builds upon the best practice and experience of organizations where results have been established. It deliberately empowers and enables students to apply newly acquired skills to their responsibilities in the real world.

—Fourth, training has begun to assume a dual dimension of mutuality between the student and the organization. Not only is the employee's training shaped to contribute to the organization's improvement, it does this in ways that nurture the employee's capacity to grow and develop and realize his or her fullest potential. Newly acquired skills, values, and decision-making capacity that prove to be of value to the student's personal and career advancement certainly will contribute to the organization's effectiveness.

Operating Principle 5. Recognize and Reward Accomplishment. High-quality service organizations understand the motivation of recognition and reward. They recognize it satisfies a basic human need and want; they use it as confirmation of accomplishment and reinforcement of commitment.

Although government and nonprofits have inherent constraints on financial rewards, they do have other ways that need to be exploited. Effective incentive and reward programs primarily of a nonfinancial nature can be created to recognize individual or group achievements. One way extensively used in government and in nonprofit agencies with volunteers is recognition rewards given in public forums with written confirmation. These serve as rituals of celebration that loudly proclaim to the organization in very human terms the importance of selected individuals who have performed with distinction. This basic human need for feeling important in the workplace has been confirmed in management research all the way back to 1924, when the Hawthorn experiments were conducted at Western Electric with telephone assembly workers. More than seventy years later this is again confirmed. A survey conducted by the Hay Group confirmed that employees in some companies rated their job satisfaction higher than workers in other companies that may have paid higher salaries and benefits. When asked why, they responded that they believed themselves to be important in their organization.

STREAMLINING AND REENGINEERING

Efforts to streamline and reengineer organizations are widely applied in private-sector organizations and now are being employed in government and nonprofit organizations.

Eliminating the Unnecessary

The federal government in its effort to reinvent government undertakes systematic efforts to cut out unnecessary programs and activities, eliminate duplication, and consolidate offices. The federal National Performance Review (Gore 1993) identified a number of obsolete agency programs that no longer had a justifiable purpose or benefit and other situations that were duplicative. They recommended cutbacks and consolidations of field offices that were considered compatible with better service to customers. Although a number of recommendations are beyond the jurisdiction and authority of any individual program manager, individuals may be invited to participate in an organization's survey team's effort to streamline and cut back the unnecessary. If so, the search is for the obsolete, the duplicative, and unnecessary forms, committees, or boards.

Reengineering Work Processes

Reengineering—rethinking and redesigning work processes—has become a major improvement tool in the private business sector and now is being performed in government and somewhat in the nonprofit sector. Process improvement has long been a management tool; more recently, the practice of process reengineering has become bolder and more ambitious in design. Many organizations were forced to recognize that they were not doing their business in the right ways. They spent too much time and money doing things that did not give the customer top-quality service. They began to examine their work processes and found they could cut processing and wait times, lower costs, gain higher customer satisfaction, and even balance workload among too-busy employees and those not busy enough.

Government is on the same track with a systematic approach to reengineering work processes. The National Performance Review focused on several government-wide processes such as procurement and budgeting. Federal agencies are following through on internal agency processes, particularly those that affect the customer directly. Electronic conversion of repetitive paper transactions that eliminates paperwork is one dramatic example in such areas as service payments and form or report filing and processing.

The results of reengineering are often dramatic. Its systematic approach to managing work emphasizes the work process; it adapts work processes to constant change that meets customer needs and expectations. It improves performance by satisfying several objectives: quality, cost, schedule, customer service, access, convenience, and eliminating the unnecessary and obsolete.

One commonly used technique for work process analysis is the traditional flowchart, which has been used in government in various versions for the last fifty years and is now computerized with several versions of commercial software.

Using New Ways to Calculate and Manage Costs

As we reengineer and improve work processes, we are trying to measure added benefits in terms of decreased wait time, faster processing, or enhanced customer satisfaction. But we often can not calculate the money value of our efforts to cut costs. We therefore cannot provide reliable cost savings; our claims of savings often lack credibility. The reason is our traditional cost-accounting and budgetary systems do not provide costs according to services or processes. They traditionally identify costs by categories of expense such as salaries, supplies, fixed costs, and fringe benefits, all by programs. We do not identify and calculate costs by process or service.

A new way that is rapidly developing in business is called "ABC," Activity Based Costing (*Fortune*, June 1993). As you find ways to trim waste, improve service, or enhance quality, you can identify the activities involved and ascertain their true costs on the basis of a comparison of the activities before and after the reengineering.

Discovering True Service or Process Costs

What ABC does to discover true costs is identify the disparate activities of a specific process and determine their separate costs. It does these things:

1. First each employee lists what he or she did each day on a particular service or process. This is similar to what was done in traditional work measurement in government in the early 1950s.

2. Then the employee estimates how much time, by percentage of total work time, he or she spent on each activity of a particular process or service.

3. Based on that information, it is easy to take the traditional budget of salaries and calculate the percentage cost of time taken in listed activities of particular processes. In this way you can know what each of the activities performed, on a particular process or service, truly costs, as well as the composite cost of the entire process. Then any improvement made to decrease costs, decrease time, or add value to a particular activity can be calculated in terms of its contributing impact on the total cost of the process or service.

For example, if the aim is to improve the process of receiving, reviewing, and adjudicating benefit claims, whether it be Social Security or veterans, you can flowchart and calculate the costs of the separate steps involved prior to the improved changes. Then you can calculate the costs of the process after the new system of electronic conversion is developed. The savings where this has been done are proving to be dramatic, although the investment in new technology and employee training must be considered.

As was discovered in the days of work measurement, you may not need to redo cost-accounting and budgetary systems on a continuing basis. It may be appropriate to do a one-time study of the facts before the conversion and after, to determine the value added or true savings by the improved process. This will help to assure credibility when cost savings are proclaimed; they will have a sound accounting basis.

The ABC costing tool can provide measured costs of improved results in a particular process or service. Or the tool can be used to determine which processes are the most strategically valuable to examine, reengineer, and achieve the greatest results. It will be increasingly important for program managers who are in charge of providing total services or important components thereof to know what their costs are and how valuable are the changes made. This enables program managers to be more cost conscious and cost-effective and becomes crucial as the quest for constant quality improvement at less cost is further institutionalized into the regular way of doing business.

Efforts to Increase Productivity

Efforts to boost productivity have long been present in American industry, but strategies to increase productivity in government and nonprofit organizations are more often being used. One study (McMurtry et al. 1991) explored which strategies were used in the nonprofit world to boost productivity. The highest number of organizations in the study indicated that to raise productivity they initiated efforts to increase staff participation in decision-making. These efforts were joined by starting or increasing staff training and by increasing staff recognition for higher productivity. The study revealed that many organizations accommodate the stress of limited resources by "drawing on organization slack." They often increased staff workloads or rebalanced workloads with the assumption that more output could be achieved by existing staff. But such efforts at overloading work need to be carefully monitored to prevent serious deterioration of morale of overworked staff.

Increasing Employee Involvement; New Ways to Tap Employee Ideas

More organizations are rediscovering that their employees close to the work know most about how to be more productive, improve quality, and cut costs. That is why most large organizations in the private sector operate employee suggestion systems; the federal government does too.

But the way to solicit and utilize employee ideas is changing; the era of the box with a slit on top near the water cooler is over. Today organizations perceive suggestions from employees as part of programs of employee involvement with continuous improvement and teamwork. To reflect the change to a broader emphasis for unleashing employee ideas, the National Association for Suggestion Systems, founded in 1942, became the Employment Involvement Association. Employee involvement is now the target; organizations are looking for better ways to do it.

Two noteworthy trends for tapping employee brainpower are evident; one is the extensive use of multidisciplinary "self-directed teams" in a variety of tasks that range from problem-solving to quality improvement, process redesign, or cutting costs. The other trend in employee involvement is the increasing use of electronic communications such as computers, faxes, modems, telephone lines, or access to electronic bulletin boards.

The unleashing of employee ideas has been broadened to include customers that use the organization's services. One division of the Internal Revenue Service in the Department of the Treasury designated special telephone lines for "Reinventing Government Ideas" for use by customers and employees and also provided a fax number for the purpose. Electronic channels have additionally been used to conduct surveys for employee and customer ideas.

Concurrent with the increased emphasis on soliciting ideas from the workplace, there is greater effort to recognize and reward employees for valuable ideas. One division newsletter formed panels to review suggestions, honor the best ones, and report the results.

ADAPTING THE ENABLING ROLE OF INFORMATION TECHNOLOGY

The government and gradually the nonprofit sector have begun to acquire and use state-of-the-art information technology that is beginning to change the way they do business. A new era of electronic management offers tremendous potential for breaking time barriers in processing and transaction time and promises to generate large savings.

Electronic Conversion of Repetitive Paper Transactions

In areas as diverse as food stamps are from Social Security payments, repetitive paperwork transactions are being undertaken electronically, and public benefits are transferred directly and quickly to recipients. The opportunities for electronic processing are huge because only a percentage of repetitive paper transactions are as yet so transferred. Much is being done to apply electronic processing to the many places where huge volumes of repetitive paper transactions occur. Such applications have begun to remove the necessity for paperwork and generate large savings in time, effort, and money.

Easier Access to Internal Financial and Performance Data

Information technology is enabling easier development of and access to computerized data banks that contain valuable information for improved programming, budgeting, decision-making, and evaluation. Performance data banks are beginning to contain data on supply and demand of services and costs of inputs and expenditures; data reveal outcomes in trend lines and even include response patterns of wait-times and backlogs. Such performance data enable more precise cost and performance comparisons as a basis for improvement efforts.

Use of Electronic Bulletin Boards

Government agencies follow the experience of industry in developing systems of electronic bulletin boards in which suborganization units may have a separate directory for their own bulletin board. These bulletin board systems enable government units and their employees to communicate interactively about their services with other employees in the organization, with employees in different organizations or departments, or with other echelons of government and a plethora of external users. The electronic bulletin board enables direct access between and among them for two-way interactive communication or multiple-party teleconferencing. The Internal Revenue Service, for example, enables its Statistics of Income division to operate its own SOI electronic bulletin board system to communicate interactively with its employees and a variety of users about the data it produces. The bulletin board is used largely by IRS employees, but also by other parts of the federal government, state governments, the banking industry, universities, corporations, private individuals, and the media.

Traveling the Information Superhighway: Access to the Internet

A new world of global electronic access now exists. Available in words or images of a computer screen are data, people, institutions, and networks. Hard to comprehend is the fact that there exists an infinite conceptual realm called cyberspace where millions of people exchange information using computer-based tools. With emerging computer software, at the "click of a mouse" you can summon text and image, and also sound and video, from around the agency, the government, and the country and increasingly from around the world. You can achieve an unimaginable variety of interactive contacts. All you need is a computer, modem, and telephone line and of course the enabling know-how and software, and you can tap into tremendous amounts of information and communicate interactively with other computer links.

Access to the information superhighway works through the "Internet," a link of millions of people, networks, institutions, and computers in a loose confederation of linked networks with no one actually in charge, but with rules and regulations beginning to emerge. Estimates on the rapidly growing numbers of people using the Internet claim that the number will reach a hundred million by 1998. New technology can access and transmit a whole library of books across the country in seconds. New networks are uniting the human voice, data, video image, and interactive media for the entire nation and beyond. To access an organization to the Internet is costly, but if you are a member of an affiliated network or organization, you have ready access. For others, a series of commercial services provide limited or unlimited access for monthly charges.

Training in Making Information Technology User-Friendly

Working with information technology is a large investment in time and money, even though it has tremendous power to reshape how one does a job. But it can be effective only if workers are comfortable with computers and competent in their use. Experts tell us that you get minimal impact if you install new technology and then train the people. You must deal with employee needs at the same time as you introduce technology. Recognize that computers and information technology do not come naturally to many people. It is not the world they were brought up in, as it is for many youngsters who work with computer games. Most of us lived in a precomputer age and struggle to adjust to new times. But the payoffs are worth it.

Part 6

IMPLEMENTING STRATEGIC THRUSTS: USING MODERN PROGRAM MANAGEMENT METHODS

15

What Is Modern Program Management?

In this everyday world where consumers so often receive shoddy product service, some organizations and certain people stand out in contrast for their consistent excellence. No one knows for sure which ways will guarantee continuing excellence despite the promises of a barrage of well-publicized literature. What is known is that some very important lessons and methods have been identified from the vast experience of managing successful programs over the last three decades. Much of this experience is screened, organized, and offered under the label of "modern program management" for application in both public and private sectors. The material is oriented to the small and medium-size organization.

Program management focuses on ways to provide high-quality service and product within the defined bounds of distinctly separate programs and projects. This is called the "bite-sized" approach to management. The qualifying adjective "modern" is added to emphasize the dynamic of continuous change in managerial thinking. In no way is the importance of time-tested fundamentals in management experience diminished; they are incorporated in our approach. In fact, the fundamentals of program management are the prime focus of this book, whether they are new or tested by time.

Excellence in organizations does not last forever. Management excellence is not, and can never be, an automatic and permanent condition. Organizations earlier cited as outstanding in well-publicized surveys and popular literature and then found to be in serious trouble convince us that excellence can wax and wane. Doing an outstanding job requires constant hard work; it can never be an easy one-time effort.

SOURCE

Historically, as a term and label, modern program management stems from the space-age experience of the late 1950s and 1960s. At that time, the undertaking of manned space probes and development of large weapon systems were managed with precisely planned programs and projects. This management approach, dividing up large areas of work into smaller pieces of action, produced a significant reorientation in managerial thinking. It moved away from overreliance on managing by a hierarchical pyramid structure in which centralized organizations are run from the top down, commanded and controlled by a few key individuals. In this centralization, decisions were made at the top and then were handed down as orders through layers of organization. In a significant change in direction, the newer program management approach emphasized less centralized structures, with greater decision-making at lower levels.

Much of the work was thus carried on within the boundaries of individually planned and operated programs and projects. This allowed for greater responsibility and involvement in decision-making for many program or project managers, at levels well below top management. Yet overall direction and control could be reserved by officials at higher echelons.

The highly visible success of the early space ventures attracted many imitators of its program management approaches. It led many nonspace and nonmilitary organizations to restructure themselves so that they also could carry all or part of their work through precisely planned programs and projects. Many organizations began to design and manage each program and project as a separate but carefully defined system of action. Program or project managers were designated for each program segment. What this did was reduce the total work program—or special portions of it—into smaller-scale, independent, but highly accountable pieces of organized activity. Each piece relates people, money, and other resources to a defined purpose and activity and is labeled "program or project." Some persons call the approach "bite-sized management"; others label the approach "modular management," or simply "managing by chunks or bundles of activity." But whatever the label, a smaller unit of managerial action is the essence of the program management approach, where responsibility is clear and focused.

Today it is commonplace for organizations to use greatly simplified program management methods and designated program managers. They provide simultaneously a great variety of quality services and products at consistently high levels of performance to targeted (but different) clientele groups. You can find applications of the program management approach in both the private and public sectors and the independent nonprofit sector.

EARLY OPERATIONAL CONCEPTS

An important by-product of the highly successful space age experience was the development and use of the program management approach. To accomplish bold military and space goals, managerial concepts and techniques were adapted to the requirements of programs for weapon systems or space probes; in some instances, original techniques were developed, such as the use of Pert for the Polaris missile. A series of management concepts emerged, largely derived from systems thinking and practice. We can identify some key ones that are widely accepted and practiced today, such as:

—reduction of program scale into smaller units of action;

—use of written, precise program or project plans and budgets with clear objectives and purpose;

—designation of program-focused managerial responsibility and accountability;

—direct application of combination of management techniques to specific programs and projects; and

—striving for total team effectiveness.

Despite differences in method, scope, complexity, and the extent of formality, most of the above emphases still exist in a large number of private and public organizations; they constitute the core concepts that define and guide the application and practice of the program management approach in today's organizations.

Reduction of Program Scale

Organizations that used the program management approach divided up the totality, or a special portion of its work program, into precisely defined pieces of program action called programs or projects. There usually existed a predetermined classification of program categories called "program classification structure." The effort to establish program structure reconciles the designation of organizational accountability with program responsibility.

Use of Precise but Flexible Program/Project Plans

Programs or projects were precisely defined and planned in terms of their managerial components: objectives, budgeted resources, planned operational activity in an estimated time and cost framework, end product, and end results desired. It was readily understood that components can and will change over time; the flexibility to change continuously over the life of the program was built into the system. The setting of objectives set the framework toward which all other components were related. In other words, if you did not know where you were going, there was no way to decide what it takes to get there.

Efforts were taken to interrelate and tie together all essential components of a particular program that was managed as a separate system of action and, in effect, constituted a complete micromanagement system. Thus, finite amounts of personnel and other budgeted resources were mobilized to be used within boundaries of particular programs and were designed to accomplish specified end results. The resources were used to generate a set of operational activities that were intended to satisfy a set of clearly expressed objectives. An important focus of the system was the need to achieve quality output of goods and services without costly, significant time delays.

Program-Focused Managerial Accountability

To provide a focal point of accountability for programs and progress, program managers were designated to guide and direct each individual program or project. Usually the program managers were responsible for managing the total framework of integrated functions: planning and strategizing, organization, activation, implementation, budgeting, monitoring and control, and evaluation.

Directly Applied Combination of Management Techniques

Each program manager could directly apply a combination of appropriately selected managerial techniques and working methods that were orchestrated specifically for use in each program situation. Thus each program or project was subjected directly to management scrutiny and control. This could be referred to as the "spotlight" approach, whereby the right combination of management techniques could be beamed and finely focused on the precise conditions of a particular program or project. One significant feature of this flexibility was that it enabled program management systems to be flexible and simpler in the use of less complicated managerial requirements, when smaller scale and less costly conditions permit. Thus management information and evaluation systems could be as simple or complex as the program warranted.

Total Team Effectiveness

Program management-oriented organizations contained a number of program situations that demanded that each member of the program or project group or team must perform effectively or the desired end result will not occur. In such situations, members of the group or team were designated separate but related tasks that were to be performed in coordinated fashion. Serious shortcomings in performance may result in negative or even disastrous consequences for the group—or for the client, if there was one. Sports teams and medical surgical teams are dramatic examples of situations requiring total team effectiveness.

WIDESPREAD APPLICATION

In the 1970s, the working methods of program management diffused and spread widely throughout government, industry, and the private nonprofit sector, in both the United States and abroad. Originally derived from large-scale space-age systems experience, the methods were transformed in two distinct ways: they fragmented and they tended to simplify.

Fragmentation

In fragmented fashion, the working methods of program management were creatively embodied in a series of distinctly separate management minimovements labeled variously as management by objective, strategic planning and management, program or performance budgeting, project planning and management, project organization, or program evaluation.

Each of the several movements seem to pose singularly different emphases of the systems experience. Accompanied by extensive training activity, these managerial movements were diffused throughout the government at federal, state, and local levels. They also spread to many institutions of business and industry. At the same time, many of the large private voluntary organizations and their local affiliates adapted many aspects of the systems-oriented program management approach.

The reasons for fragmentation into separate management minimovements are not clear, but it is interesting to speculate. Perhaps it was merely a deliberate response of managerial entrepreneurs who were able to seize a grand opportunity and capitalize on the existence of a gold mine of systems knowledge created by the military and space efforts. If so, they succeeded in meeting the big market potential of America's vast working society. Or, perhaps the process of fragmentation into diverse movements may actually have been an adaptation response to moving from a complex, large-scale situation, with highly trained and educated program and project managers, to less complex situations in public and private sectors that did not have available highly trained program managers. Or, as one wise colleague succinctly expressed it, "It merely is the pragmatic way Americans get the mattress through the keyhole when the door is locked: they cut it into pieces." Perhaps one management expert said it well when he asked, "How does an American eat an elephant?" and answered, "Bite by bite."

Whatever the causes for fragmentation, the implication for the contemporary program or project manager is clear. To do the job of program management effectively, it is necessary "to put the pieces together" and blend several emphases of the various system-oriented mini-management movements. The accepted challenge for this part of the book is to provide a comprehensive set of fundamentals and working methods for the modern program and project managers in which they can be confident, comfortable, and competent.

Greater Simplification

Too many people think that program management deals only with large-scale and complex efforts, particularly in the military establishment, and employs only sophisticated analytic technique. That gross misconception stems from the early association of program management with large-scale, costly and technologically complex military and space efforts, such as the moon shot and the Polaris submarine program. That complex approach to program management was largely characteristic of the space-age efforts of the 1950s and 1960s and in some large-scale and costly military and space programs today. But the popular conception of complexity and sophistication is obsolete and misleading for much of program management as it is widely practiced today, in both the public and private sector and also in nonprofit organizations.

Actually, many of the working methods of contemporary program management have been simplified. As the methods were adapted for use in less complex and less costly program situations, they became less complex managerially and began to emerge in a somewhat simplified form and format. This is clearly evident in a number of nonprofit voluntary organizations. The simpler methods of program management are in wide usage today, and their application is growing. Most often the users of modern program management methods are unaware of their space-age derivation.

Though it is true that program management methods have adapted to less complex and smaller-scale applications with corresponding simplification, it is also true that, even under the best of conditions, program management approaches do impose time-consuming methods that are often resented by busy managers and employees. It is therefore extremely important for the modern program manager to accept the challenge of achieving further simplification through the vigorous pursuit of certain activities:

—Get the job done with the "lean approach" of fewer participants in the arena of action or staff support despite the clamor from many experts for more participation.
—Minimize the paperwork burden by striving for less complicated paperwork requirements and simpler work flow.
—Reduce the multiple levels and points of control, review, and clearance.
—Reduce the need for managerial oversight and support by undertaking individual job enlargement and enrichment to enable people to do more on their own initiative.

This last point—seeking to achieve a higher level of managerial self-reliance and independent responsibility—is proving to be a popular and desirable working condition. It particularly appeals to a better educated work force accustomed to a freer lifestyle. Reducing externally imposed managerial requirements diminishes the amount of stress imposed deliberately or inadvertently by other managers. Self-sufficient program managers who know what to do, and how, and can pursue tasks largely without close supervision are certain to be considered at a premium in the job market.

INCREASING STRATEGIC ROLE OF PROGRAM MANAGERS

In a recent trend, program managers are increasingly being asked to participate in the setting and review of strategic directions and plans. Federal agency program managers, out in the field and at headquarters, are being trained to prepare, review, and comment on strategic plans and their impact on operating programs. This is a recent development because strategic planning tended to be a high level, front-office endeavor. As program managers work more closely with senior executives, they become the connecting link between the formal strategic plan and the operating programs and budgets; this enables strategic plans to be better implemented.

The advantage for top management is that they will be working with a more responsive bureaucracy that better understands, participates in, and supports front-office top level strategic thinking. Field operating officials report that they have a better sense of "knowing what is going on" at headquarters. Program management officials who participate in agency strategic planning efforts indicate the experience to be a valuable one for the agency and for them as individuals. As agency directions change rapidly and frequently, the need for program managers to participate in strategic planning efforts becomes a necessity.

BENEFITS AND PITFALLS

Benefits

The experts' claims for program management are often excessive. But when it works, experience demonstrates that the program management approach provides substantial and extensive benefits.

Clear-Cut Directional Goals. Program management sets or changes the direction for an organization for each of its programs. Those employees who are directly involved participate in the process of setting directions so they know where they are going.

Focus on Results. Program management defines specific results in measurable, time-limited terms, the specific results that the organization and the individuals wish to achieve. It focuses on the end result, not only on the process or activities employed to achieve them.

Stricter Accountability. Program management encourages clear and strict accountability for program performance within structural boundaries. It asks, "How does the use of defined resources contribute to specific intended results of a particular program activity or service?" It does this in three ways:

—clarifies program responsibility by breaking the organization's program down into smaller pieces, that is a structure of individual program modules, and by designating a responsible program manager to act as a focal point for each program;

—creates a cogent statement of what to accomplish by individuals and organization units and clarifies what is expected from each; and

—enables senior management, boards, donors, and legislative bodies to know exactly what is being accomplished for the money spent.

Continuous Evaluation. Program management provides the basis for objective evaluation of how well individuals and organizations are doing. This includes three different modes of evaluation: self-evaluation, supervisory evaluation, and evaluation by use of externally hired consultants.

Measurable Effectiveness. Since program management is geared to achieve measurable and verifiable results, it helps to reveal the effectiveness of an organization and pinpoints its weaknesses or deficiencies in specific programs, thus providing a clear focus for remedial or rewarding action.

Foresight or Creative Management. Program management increases foresight in meeting future needs and operational requirements by requiring that organizations plan ahead in realistic program terms and be prepared for the future rather than just react to it. This reduces crisis management, popularly referred to as "fire fighting," where unexpected contingencies and crises keep occurring and demand immediate attention and solution. This constant need to "put out fires" in a state of turmoil and turbulence drains staff energy and curtails the capacity to think about and shape the future. There is no future if every day is full of turmoil and crisis.

Focus on Potential. Program management helps an organization get beyond or above its current difficulties and discomforts, whatever they might be, by helping to focus on its potential. Potential is what an organization or a particular program could be at its best if the best possible outcome in the future could be achieved. This focus often reduces the amount of petty quibbling, bickering, and excessive concern with operational detail by concentrating attention on the positive image of future success.

Greater Credibility. Program management places an organization in a desirable position with funding and oversight agencies because it demonstrates the capacity to go beyond rhetoric and promises, plans, and data gathering. Rather, it imposes an integrated management system that ranges from planning and preparation for action through controlled implementation, evaluation, and readjustment. This provides a better possibility for achieving quality results.

Team Building. Program management creates working conditions whereby persons can work well together in the pursuit of quality results, participate in the major decisions affecting them, and resolve the normally expected amounts of stress, strain, and conflict.

Facilitates Motivation. Program management provides clearly perceived goals and objectives, which are fundamental to human effort and motivation, especially when individuals participate in their formulation and review.

Easier Public Relations and Fund-raising. Program management makes the public relations and funding jobs both easier and more effective by providing a concrete package of goals, objectives, resources, and results with which to work.

Continuity. Program management addresses the problem of having to "reinvent the wheel" whenever key personnel change, by providing continuity into the future through a framework of goals and objectives.

Pitfalls

Systematic program management admittedly does entail a series of general pitfalls that can render the work situation more complex and time-consuming. It is important to understand and anticipate difficulties and reduce the burden to the minimum consistent with doing an effective job.

Paperwork: Too Much or Too Little. The process of managing programs systematically does require a certain amount of paperwork for its design, documentation, and control. Paperwork, if kept simple and brief, can be an effective and efficient instrument of the program management process. The absence of adequate documentation of the program management process will defeat the purpose of systematic program management and deny clear-cut accountability for performance and results.

The Abuse of Participation: Too Much, Too Little, or Too Late. All experts agree that it is important to promote the participation and involvement of persons in the decisions and conditions of work that affects them. But sometimes program management is accompanied by an excessive number of meetings and committees in an effort to keep everyone involved and informed. The cost in time and money of communication can be high. Though sometimes it may be necessary to err on the side of keeping people informed, it is more often necessary to restrict the number involved to carefully calculated minimums.

The other extreme is unfortunate: All key matters are decided by a tight small group with minimum participation or communication with the persons concerned and affected until after decisions have been taken and put into effect. It is prudent to select carefully the parties that must be involved and informed, but keep them to a minimum.

Too Much Data Collection. There is no end to the need for data in a systematic program management system. Data collection can be time-consuming, costly, occasionally wasteful, and sometimes may not be directly relevant. Data, when collected, may not always be analyzed in time to determine its meaning and correct use. Know how to use the data before it is collected. It is wise to perform a use assessment before time and money are invested in data collection.

Start and Stop Syndrome. Viewing the functions of planning, control, and evaluation as one-time events will result in killing them. To start the process and do it once is not effective. It requires a continuity of effort to gain the necessary experience and competence to do it well. Expect two to three years of step-by-step effort to produce a competent program management process.

Excessive Rigidity and Inflexibility. One key danger of any management system is the tendency to cast the future into blocks of concrete, where the planned components of goals, objectives, defined resources, and intended results are considered inflexible and incapable of change. This can generate a series of missed opportunities, broken promises, and outdated and unrealistic goals and assumptions. There is a pressing need to build in a pragmatic review and feedback process to keep the system flexible and easy to change as experience indicates.

Analytic Overkill. The program management process attracts the excessive use of advanced analytic techniques. This may generate "analytic overkill," where sophisticated analysis is undertaken that is time-consuming and costly but may not be justified by the simple type of decision to be made or by the lack of availability of reliable data.

Dislike of Discipline. Many people are uncomfortable with imposed discipline that tells them what to do and how and when. Others openly resist systematic and time-consuming thought processes. They prefer to be quick and impulsive and often seek speedy decisions and rapid action. By resisting the extremes of systematic and thoughtful processes, program management staff can ensure that the design and review of all the major processes are understood, acceptable, and manageable within the available time and resources. The trick is to transform excessively imposed discipline into a greater measure of self-reliance and self-discipline, where employees are not subjected to someone always looking over their shoulder and telling them what to do or what not to do. This is not an easy task for many managers.

Excessive Autonomy and Independence. The program management approach, by its use of smaller-scale units of action, has many managerial advantages to the program at hand. But it does create the potential problem of excessive autonomy and independence from the parent organization. Large individual programs can fragment an organization and create separate feudal baronies cut off from the larger organization. In some instances, this can be a positive condition; but in many other situations the excessive independence can remove essential oversight, guidance, and control that can prevent major disasters or mistakes. Decisions by either the program executive or the parent organization may not be sufficiently well-coordinated to ensure soundness.

16

What Program Executives and Managers Actually Do

WHO ARE PROGRAM EXECUTIVES AND MANAGERS?

The most fundamental resource in organizations, and usually the most expensive, is the cadre of program executives and managers—those who manage the development and delivery of service and product. The reason is clearly evident. Program management is what organizations do and program managers are the ones who do it.

Let us clearly identify who are the participants in program management before we describe their role and basic responsibilities. Program or project managers may exist at all levels. They usually are in charge of a program, project, service, or product. Most often they do not perceive themselves to be managers. In fact, they usually regard management and the title of manager as a lesser interest, if not one that is actually resisted and resented. This is so, even though their job responsibility probably includes many managerial functions and their job success may depend on their mastery of strategic and managerial insights and skills. This is, of course, in addition to and complementary to their technical competence.

In hospitals or health maintenance organizations, doctors title themselves as "heads," "chiefs," or "directors," not managers or executives. Only at the very top of the structure in a hospital is the term "administrator" used. In the same mode, educators are labeled as "deans" or "heads" of departments. But whatever the label, two features distinguish program managers, (1) their involvement in some substantive aspect of an organization's functional activity and (2) their involvement in developing, planning, operating, or managing a program, project, or service.

Not all persons involved in program management are managers designated to head a program; they may be staff working in a specific program or project activity under the supervision of, and working with, a designated program manager. These staff persons participate in various phases of the managerial work done in support of their program, often for or with the designated program manager in charge.

Program managers are not the sum total of an organization's managerial talent, nor is program management the entire management process in an organization. There are also the resource managers who perform the resource management process that creates and supports an organization's basic administrative tools and support systems, such as budgeting, financing, procurement, accounting, and personnel administration. The purpose of resource managers is to develop and maintain a human, material, and financial resource base that is maximally responsive to the demands of the program component of an organization.

Potential conflict may, and often does, exist between program managers and resource managers, stemming from differences in their roles. The resource manager attempts to make available necessary resources and to facilitate their effective utilization. Usually this is done with only one of the several resources needed, like money, people, or material. On the other hand, the program manager seeks to use multiple resources working together to maximally promote the quality delivery of service. In practice, the program managers often tend to downplay or belittle the role of the resource managers who, in effect, try to tell them how to do the job.

BASIC RESPONSIBILITIES

The program manager's major role is to serve as a focal point of central guidance and accountability for the quality delivery of a particular service and product to targeted clients. The program manager may serve in all or some phases of action, that range widely from an initial perception of need to the design, approval, execution, and assessment of results for a particular program or project. The program manager is crucial to setting levels of quality, cost, and timing. Program managers may not be the actual providers of service, but they are always responsible for how well the programs or "packages of activities and services" are provided.

At the top, managers are held responsible for the total number of programs in their jurisdiction, but they are very much at the mercy of the skill and effectiveness of individual program managers beneath them. It is not excessive to state that how well the various individual program managers do their jobs determines whether an organization is ultimately successful or not. In effect, the cadre of program managers are the essential elite on whom depend the level of quality and the extent of client satisfaction, the only sound and lasting basis for organizational success.

It is easy to understand why progressive organizations take much time and effort to attract, support, reward, and develop a trained cadre of program managers, when one begins to realize the significant role they play. Conversely, it is very shortsighted, if not foolish, for top management to ignore the needs of their program managers or fail to achieve their participation in essential decisions affecting their program. The replacement of effective program managers is an expensive and time-consuming process.

To practice with competence and confidence in an organizational setting, the modern program manager must define and master a set of basic responsibilities and ensure that a minimum of essential conditions are established and fulfilled.

Basic responsibilities

a. Apply the key managerial functions to participating programs, projects, or services. These are strategizing, structuring, program budgeting, program planning, monitoring and control, scheduling, and evaluating.

b. Design, demonstrate, and execute appropriate working management methods to carry out operating tasks.

c. Clarify the criteria by which performance will be judged.

d. Introduce and guide ways to encourage constructive managerial and employee behavior.

e. Undertake guided but self-paced staff self-development of each employee and oneself.

Essential conditions

a. Clear statement that defines operationally the full scope of managerial functions and operating tasks to be performed.

b. An available body of knowledge and experience that is accessible and affordable.

c. Clear statement of performance criteria.

d. Practice of leadership style that maximizes teamwork, high motivation, change, sound decision-making, positive organization climate, and values.

e. Individual self-development plan for each employee and oneself.

KEY MANAGERIAL FUNCTIONS

Six key managerial functions make up what we call program management work: strategizing, structuring, program budgeting, program/project planning, monitoring and control, and evaluation. These managerial functions constitute the core basis for the program manager's job and are defined in the following glossary.

Glossary of Key Managerial Functions

Strategizing (and Strategic Planning). A systematic process for setting organizational goals, performing an array of strategic situation analyses regarding performance and environment, making strategic decisions, and developing the plans necessary to carry out the goals and the implications of strategic analyses.

Structuring. The process of determining, dividing, and establishing the program and organizational subdivisions of an organization into lines of authority, responsibility, and relationships.

Program Budgeting. A management approach to budgeting that presents the purpose and objectives for which funds are requested, estimates the costs of the programs proposed for accomplishing these objectives, and specifies the indicators for measuring the accomplishments and work performed under each program.

Program/Project Planning. A management tool for establishing a program/project and ensuring that it is clearly designed to guide a manager to accomplish these managerial tasks:

—identifying early the problem to be resolved;

—establishing purpose and objective;

—specifying and mobilizing required resources;

—obtaining necessary reviews and approvals; and

—providing objective basis for evaluation of progress.

Monitoring and Control. A series of measures designed to alert us when we are about to get into trouble in sufficient time to take constructive action. Control measures (1) provide timely feedback on what is happening or not happening in order to keep on track the actions we plan and to know what problems are occurring or likely to occur and (2) establish contingency plans, or just plain alternatives, for handling the unexpected or expected matters that do go wrong.

Evaluating. A systematic means for finding out how well you are doing the things you set out to do and the probable reasons for their success or failure. Evaluation methods are designed to obtain reasonably objective data to learn about what you have done in the past, or are doing now, in order to improve your performance in the future.

A fundamental point underlying program management is that key managerial functions are integral and interdependent and thereby constitute an integrated management system. When the managerial functions combine to form an integrated system, they provide the framework for telling program managers what to do in sequence as they guide their program through strategizing, structuring, funding, approval, activation, execution, and evaluation.

In the smaller organization, the program manager may perform all the managerial functions. In larger organizations, the program manager remains responsible for all the functions but may draw upon expertise located organizationally in other parts of the agency or may contract for services from the outside community for some of the management functions. For example, outside consultants are often used for program evaluation to establish greater credibility for the evaluation findings.

PERFORMANCE CRITERIA

How do program managers know when they are doing a job that is judged to be outstanding? The simple and quick answer may be "when the boss or board thinks so." But rigorous thinking rejects any simplistic one-dimensional response as being inadequate. We prefer to identify several essential conditions for professional or successful performance. This appears to make the situation more complex than necessary, but experience indicates that multiple conditions are necessary for sustaining a truly outstanding performance. Actually, six types of performance criteria can be identified whose importance in any given situation may vary in priority of significance. It is important for an organization's top management to make clear its performance priorities and value preferences so that program managers know clearly what is expected.

The criteria discussed provide a solid starting point for the program manager to decide what must be done for a real situation to be judged successful, outstanding, professional, excellent, or whatever favorable label you prefer.

Another criterion, not included here but certainly urgent, is the observance of legal, regulatory, and moral codes.

Providing Quality Output of Product and Service

Furnishing quality output is paramount to achieving excellence. Output criteria may be expressed in terms of the quality and quantity of the services and products that are supplied to the program's clientele. Standards can be set and specified, though quality standards for human services may be difficult to measure. In some situations, precisely scheduled timing may be important to meet critical end product deadlines; the consequences of failure may be serious and costly.

Some output related questions are essential for the program manager to consider.

—Are the services and products of professional quality?

—Are the users or consumers of service and product of sufficient number? Is there a deficiency in demand for the product or service?

—Are the services and products adequate in number and type to expressed need/demand? Is there a deficiency in available supply?

—Are the services affordable and conveniently accessible? Are they priced properly and located conveniently?

—Are the services rendered in a timely fashion?

Making Efficient Use of Inputs

It is imperative that program managers be cost-conscious and make efficient use of inputs (resources) relative to outputs. That is what is meant by "input/output ratio." Resources are usually scarce and growing more costly—a condition that compels program managers to be efficient. But whether they are scarce or not, the program manager should be committed to cost efficiency, avoid waste and fraud in the use of resources, and be held accountable accordingly.

It must be made patently clear that the most generally applicable efficiency criterion is attaining the lowest possible cost for a given unit of output, product, or service. In human-service nonprofit organizations, the identification of units of service may be difficult and costs may be distorted by grants or subsidies. In the business world identification is easier because profitability is necessarily the generally used input/output relationship and price must clearly exceed cost. "Bottom-line profit" is used as a clear-cut indicator of efficiency. The absence of the profit criterion in the public and the nonprofit sectors makes it critical that program managers be sensitive to efficiency and cost effectiveness.

There are key efficiency questions for the program manager to consider.

—Is current capacity fully or partially utilized for producing product or service? Are people busy and productive, overly harassed, or often idle?

—Which elements of the product or service are proportionately the most time-consuming and costly?

—Have less costly alternatives been explored?

—Are the costs of doing business in line with fees, contracts, or pricing policy?

Providing Customer Focus and Satisfaction

New emphases on creating and sustaining an organizational focus on customer satisfaction places additional demands on manager performance. Managers are expected to identify external customer requirements, establish and maintain positive customer relationships, and continuously improve customer satisfaction. It is increasingly expected that managers be able to participate in agency programs for enhanced customer satisfaction. The IBM corporation has asked its executives with direct client relationships to interview several of their clients to determine the extent of customer satisfaction and to submit the written record to be part of their performance rating.

Acquiring Sufficient Resources

Quality output results are not possible without sufficient resources that can be used to acquire and mobilize inputs of people and material. The resources must be obtained from within the organization or from the community and environment. Under conditions of scarcity and competition, this requires considerable skill and in most organizations merits high priority. Some organizations have special personnel doing the specialized function of resource acquisition and development. But the program manager is ultimately responsible for the program's success and must be actively involved in resource acquisition, whether or not there are special people in the organization to do these things.

Resource requirements are generally of four types:

Monetary. To finance the program and thereby satisfy budget allocations and to pay staff and program expenses for at least the budgetary period of twelve months.

Personnel. To plan, execute, and evaluate the program.

Material. To enable the use of new, progressive technology.

Volunteers. To be recruited to help operate or evaluate the program; mostly used in nonprofit situations, but increasingly used in government activity.

Key resource acquisition questions to consider include:

—Does the program attract sufficient resources (money, staff, and volunteers) to be financially stable and of professional quality for at least twelve months?

—In cases of deficit, have efforts been effectively planned and taken? With what results? What do top management say and do about resource efforts? Are they cooperative, resistant, or apathetic?

—Is the budgeting process (and skills) adequate?

—Is the program to attract and use volunteers effectively managed?

—Does top management appreciate the need for new technology?

—Can the new equipment be justified?

—Is workload excessive for staff in any location, creating high staff discontent and separation?

Administrative Rationality

Most organizations aim to do things rationally. It just does not turn out that way. To be perfectly rational is impossible because the ingredients for rational calculation—that is, information, knowledge, and skill—are always imperfect or limited. Yet rationality—the considered selection of the most effective and efficient means to achieve a given set of goals, objectives, and methods—is an important criterion for performance.

Administrative rationality is a special form of rationality that involves the best ways for managing organizations. The core point is the need to use an integrated management framework that applies to programs, the interrelated functions of strategizing with structuring, budgeting, program design, control, and evaluation. Also essential is a constructive managerial climate in which employees can do their best work. The use of progressive managerial method aims directly at the development of sound decision-making based on solid fact-finding rather than off-the-cuff expediency.

Management concept, system, and technique are by no means perfectly rational. But they do help to mobilize and develop the essential instruments of rational calculation: information, knowledge, and skill. Management systems can and should be designed and installed to make it easier for the program manager to do the management job with the least effort and hassle.

The program manager should consider these key questions:

—Is a deliberate effort being taken by staff to know and master progressive, time-tested managerial methods, or are staff resistant or apathetic to management methods?

—Does the leadership style provide a constructive climate of teamwork, motivation, and morale where one can do top-notch work in pursuit of excellence; or do tensions and frustrations reduce the employee's capacity and confidence to do a good job?

—Are decisions based upon adequate and objective facts, knowledge of the situation, and environmental impact or short-term expediency and personal whimsy? Does top management invite, in timely fashion, the participation of program managers in decisions affecting them?

Satisfying Powerful Interests

A key item for judging a program manager's effectiveness is the manager's capacity to satisfy the interests of powerful parties. These are the persons who have the power to hurt or help you and your program. But often interest satisfaction is difficult to formulate and articulate for these reasons:

There Is a Multiplicity of Interested Parties in Every Program. They may be board members or chairpersons, a chief executive officer, one's staff or clientele, big donors, or one's boss. And sometimes, if not often, these interests diverge or are in sharp conflict. For an individual professional, the client or patient is primary, but in organizations, it is not so simple.

The Interests of Key Parties May Be Hard to Identify and Describe Because the Manner in Which Interests Are Expressed Seems to Vary. Sometimes interests are expressed in broad and abstract psychological terms like the human need for security, status, prestige, or power. Other times, interests are expressed in physical production terms of goods and services (and their adequacy) that are designed to meet levels of expectation by a specific interested party: client, boss, or board. Or, interests may be expressed in terms of dollars and cents.

It is Very Difficult to Specify the Extent and Depth of Satisfaction Desired or Attained. Dissatisfaction may be expressed in emotional or negative terms as frustration or discontent. It is hard to gauge how strongly a person may feel about an issue from the words used. Some persons use language excessive to a situation's reality when under stress or in anger.

Helpful Hints

Nevertheless, despite the difficulties in coping with interest satisfaction, there are some helpful hints and practical steps to consider.

Identify, List, and Rank the Interested Parties Most Important to You and Your Program. In practical terms, importance may be indicated by the power of particular interested parties to hurt or help you or by the possibility that they can make a manager's job more difficult, easier, or more rewarding. Key parties of interest have the potential power to change one's job, tenure, program, or salary. In stark terms, they determine survival or success. In most situations they can start, stop, or modify program activity. But a manager should keep perspective and realize that power of all key parties are not of equal importance and consequences and that their priority of importance may change from time to time. A manager cannot satisfy everybody all the time. Do what is significant and important.

Here are two examples of the importance of key parties of interest. First, all executive directors of private nonprofit organizations know they depend for job tenure and job conditions on a board of directors, particularly the chairperson or a strong committee chair. Some board members can have a strong impact on program authorization and financing. Second, program directors or department heads in a hospital or university setting soon realize that a major donor of public or private funds directly to their program stands out as the major party to be pleased and satisfied. Unfortunately, the presence of substantial donated funds or program subsidy makes the donor or grantor more important than clients or others in the chain of command. Once the major donor is satisfied, the program head gains a degree of independence from other interested parties.

Know What Their Interests Are as Specifically as Possible. Attempt to know what interested people want and their expectations. One never fully knows in advance the exact nature of demands. But the importance of satisfying the interests of key parties suggests that you spend sufficient time and effort to know what it takes.

Since it is difficult to judge how deep or strongly parties feel about specific issues, wants, or demands, it is useful to look for indirect indications of intensity in what is said or written and to observe what they do and decide.

It is helpful to know the answers to these questions:

—Who are the major parties of interest that have the power to help or hurt your program?
—Are strong, clearly visible, and overt pressures and demands being extended? Or, are the pressures subtle, and the messages of unclear and uncertain intent?
—Are the interests in conflict? Will that mean that satisfying the interests of one group will lessen the ability to satisfy other interests?
—Is it possible and feasible to satisfy the expressed interests or frustrations? Can they be negotiated?
—If the key interests are not satisfied, what is at stake? What are the likely consequences?

Devise Strategies (Goals and Objectives) and List Action Steps to Ensure that Key Interests Are Satisfied and Rendered Helpful. If it is not possible to satisfy the key parties, know what to do to neutralize the impact of dissatisfaction. Try to practice the art of damage control, which is similar to how firefighters (and politicians) try to contain the path of fire, and its impact, in forest fires and large conflagrations.

A New Role for Senior Executives

To be effective, improvement efforts in the campaign to reinvent government and transform the nonprofit organization must do more than apply a series of managerial techniques; they require a shift in cultural attitudes and behavior. They demand a new role for senior executives. Vice President Gore in a speech on March 29, 1994, underscored that federal executives were always accountable to Congress, the president, and the public for implementing the law. But tomorrow's federal managers must do more to innovate in ways that yesterday's managers could not have comprehended. The vice president underscored seven key points that make up what he called the "new job of the federal executive (Gore 1994)." According to the status report (September 1994) of the National Performance Review, the new executive role revolves around seven differences in the way that federal executives used to operate and how they now must act to be effective:

1. In the old way, federal executives were expected to know best, and they created special offices at the top of their organizational charts—e.g. The Office of Strategic Planning— to manage change and create innovation in an isolated manner. In the new way, federal executives need to involve all employees in developing a clear vision and a shared sense of mission.

2. In the old way, federal executives were expected to keep staff working within organizational boundaries. In the new way, federal executives will need to help staff cross boundaries to work effectively with other organizations.

3. In the old way, federal executives were expected to use rules to circumscribe discretion, because employees were not to be trusted. In the new way, federal executives must empower their employees to achieve the goals of the organization, within statutory constraints and the organization's agreed upon vision.

4. In the old way, federal executives were expected to protect and enlarge their operations and to satisfy higher levels of management. In the new way, federal executives will need to satisfy their customers.

5. In the old way, federal executives were expected to communicate one level up and one level down. In the new way, federal executives will need to communicate through every level of their agencies.

6. In the old way, federal executives were expected to tell their subordinates what the executives needed. In the new way, federal executives will need to ask subordinates what they need to do their jobs.

7. In the old way, federal executives were expected to use hierarchical arrangements with checks and controls over every input, elaborate reporting mechanisms and extensive rules and regulations. In the new way, federal executives will be expected to concentrate on performance and carefully measured results—output, not input (Gore 1994).

Though drastically oversimplified to fit the requirements of a speech and the limits of one page in a status report, the vice president's comments capture some core concepts that underline the managerial patterns of progressive firms in the private sector and are being introduced into government and gradually into many agencies of the nonprofit sector.

TEN IMPORTANT LEARNING AREAS FOR THE MODERN PROGRAM MANAGER

The management scene is changing fast. The expanding role of program managers to strategize and innovate, work more closely in team efforts, and be constant in improving themselves and their organizations compel a new set of learning needs. New courses are emerging with new content to assist agencies to reinvent and transform themselves to adapt to profoundly changing public and nonprofit sectors. Though many of the courses derive in content from the experience of the private sector, they are steadily being adapted to the unique conditions of public and nonprofit agencies.

For program managers to be skilled, comfortable, and competent to participate in or lead their organization's reinvention or transformation efforts, ten enabling areas are described and discussed in many parts of this book. They are:

—Learn the fundamentals of strategic planning, in the context of strategic management derived from the experience of the private sector but adapted for use in government and nonprofit agencies.

—Be competent in ways to practice total quality management.

—Be able to redesign and simplify work processes and participate with others in reengineering activities.

—Effectively engage in efforts to improve customer service and set customer service standards and strategy.

—Learn the enabling role of information technology and be skilled in ways to access valuable resource data.

—Work well with or lead self-directed teams.

—Know how to assess program performance and be able to identify critical issues.

—Understand how to apply the program management approach, framework, and structure. Be able to design manageable program plans with verifiable progress indicators that better enable the measurement of results, and be familiar with efforts to use program performance budgets for better accountability and cost control.

—Learn how to streamline organizations by cutting back to basics, take steps to increase productivity, and learn how to cut red tape.

—Know how to determine strategies of competition such as achieving distinctiveness and core competencies that can be employed in gaining contracts and garnering new clients and funds.

17

Setting Objectives and Devising Action Plans

THE RISE AND DECLINE OF THE MBO MOVEMENT

Management by objectives, or "MBO" as it was called, was a very popular and widely accepted technique and system. But managers and employees began to criticize objectives setting as too burdensome and time-consuming. Resentment mounted; other managerial techniques and systems such as strategic planning and total quality management emerged to absorb the setting of objectives. Management by objectives lost popularity and limited its approaches.

Early Success of MBO

MBO originated in the private sector, moved into government, and was adapted to the larger nonprofit organizations like the American Red Cross and the YWCA. MBO training and literature were widely prevalent.

Back in 1954, Peter Drucker proposed that objectives then used as a managerial technique should serve as a main vehicle for a systemic management approach to directing an organization. Others then developed the concept into a system and made it operative. Three decades later, the MBO system was practiced in thousands of different organizations throughout the world, in many settings ranging from industrial organizations to churches, management institutes, hospitals, government agencies, and other nonprofit organizations.

The early efforts of the MBO pioneers stemmed largely from an unhappiness with the techniques then popular for appraising managerial performance. The appraisal techniques of the late 1950s measured the degree to which managers were thought to possess highly subjective traits, such as initiative, innovation, judgment, cooperation, or punctuality. The traits certainly did not reveal actual results achieved. Thus two appraisals of the same manager could be sharply different because of the subjective nature of the traits or the orientation or bias of the appraiser. Gradually, measurable objectives that embodied concrete results replaced or supplemented the subjective evaluation of traits. The development of objectives for use in evaluating performance opened up the use of objectives to serve as a focal point for other functions of the management process.

MBO Defined As a System

MBO was designed to help program managers achieve significant results on their jobs. It had been defined by George Odiorne as a management process whereby the supervisor and subordinate, operating under a clear definition of common goals and priorities established by top management, jointly identify the individual's major area of responsibility in terms of the results expected and use these measures as guides for operating the unit and assessing the contribution of each of its members (Odiorne 1965, 55–56).

Widespread Resentment

Managers and employees have long objected to the process of setting objectives. Some considered it burdensome and time-consuming. Managers disliked setting objectives and devising action plans and then having to monitor constantly the individuals to see that they were "on track." Employees also resented the objectives they perceived as "meddlesome micromanagement" and had the "feeling" that someone was always looking over their shoulder and keeping score on them.

The criticism pertains less to the broad concept of setting objectives than to the ways it is administered. The original intent was to give focus to work and to establish reasonable boundaries of expectation and accountability for worker and superior. The dissatisfaction stems from MBO's burdensome, mechanical process that created manager and employee resentment, with too little compensating humaneness and fairness. Too often, the setting of objectives resulted in the targeting of numerical quotas that have been severely criticized by experts like Deming, the grandfather of quality control, and those promoting total quality management. They considered quotas counterproductive in quality work. Employees resented the heavy-handed interference by some supervisors.

New Doctrine for Setting Objectives

But setting objectives can be an effective management tool for the program manager provided it is administered with sensitivity for employees and managers. Successful approaches to setting objectives embody new leadership doctrine that shifts away from the command-and-control way of barking orders at employees, demeaning them, and asking them to park their brains in the parking lot. Rather, leadership thinking now seeks to avoid confrontation and to provide a favorable, supportive environment for setting objectives that emphasizes four tasks:

—develop and articulate what you want to accomplish; strategic planning practice helps to do this;

—create environment and method where employees can figure out what needs to get done and how to get it done well; program design can contribute to this;

—empower and enable people to work, grow, and learn together; the use of enabling training and team efforts will help;

—support, recognize, and reward employees; recognition programs are found necessary and useful.

These tasks, properly executed, provide a positive environment for setting objectives and lessen the burden and resentment of their use.

THE OBJECTIVE-ORIENTED MANAGER

Though systems for management by objectives have declined and been modified in use, many managers still find the technique of setting objectives useful. Managers who use objectives in their management approach begin to look at their job differently. For example, they can develop a strong orientation to the future. They want to know where they are going and thus will approach the job in terms of looking ahead, planning ahead, and moving ahead.

The work of each day fits together into patterns of progress or problems requiring solutions. The manager measures milestones of progress against standards and indicators that can lead to a successful future. This gives a manager a sense of control over the program's destiny as potential problems are identified and resolved, as progress toward end results is accomplished, and opportunities are exploited.

The manager who looks ahead with the use of objectives stands in sharp contrast to the manager who never anticipates the future but waits for problems to arise. That manager then reacts in surprise, like a harassed firefighter running around "putting out fires." This manager lacks direction and focus and can be easily distracted by whatever operational trivia arises.

BENEFITS AND PITFALLS

Benefits

The objectives-oriented manager reaps a series of advantages by setting objectives.

Defines Tangible Results Desired. Setting objectives forces the manager to determine what specific results need to be accomplished in concrete, measurable, and time-limited terms.

Enables Assessment of Effectiveness. Setting objectives is geared to measurable results; it thus enables you to assess the effectiveness of organizations in terms of what is accomplished.

Sharpens Accountability. Setting objectives pinpoints each person's responsibility for results in measurable terms. Thus, everyone is able to see clearly whether performance is above or below expectation.

Provides Continuity. Setting objectives provides continuity by having officially approved goals and objectives determine where to go and what to accomplish. These goals and objectives remain in place for their designated time unless officially modified, regardless of changes in personnel.

Stresses Potential. Setting objectives helps to get beyond current difficulties and discomforts, whatever they might be, and focus on the potential of an organization and specified undertakings. It does this by compelling the manager to think of the future by setting objectives that indicate what the organization could be at its best.

Pitfalls

Although the setting of objectives possesses distinct advantages, a number of pitfalls exist that can undermine its effectiveness. Some of the ones most often cited are these:

Lack of Manager's Commitment. This is the most frequent cause of failure. Management commitment is imperative to the use of objectives as an effective tool of the program management process, since using them means taking much time and effort. This is not likely to happen if commitment is not present.

Poor Selection of Objectives. The process is often complicated by selecting and monitoring too many objectives at one time. This leads to overextending available resources and time limits of busy managers, and antagonizes many of them because they already resent the intrusion of management activity on their professional lives.

Lack of Skill in Formulating an Objective Statement. This is a frequent occurrence and one that is easily corrected.

Too Much Additional Paperwork. This can be overwhelming to many busy program managers. As one harassed manager complained: "Here I am worrying about tomorrow's meeting with an important client, and I have to submit my 'objectives' for what I want to accomplish over the next whole year. They want me not only to write out the objectives, but totell them why and how I plan to carry them out. Who has the time— even if I knew what I wanted to do?"

Rigidity and Inflexibility. This is an often-expressed complaint. Conditions change, but objectives put down in writing tend to be difficult to modify. This often generates a series of broken promises and missed opportunities when one is busy trying to meet targets for conditions that may have changed. It is imperative that a practical review-and-change process be built into setting objectives to keep them flexible and to permit adjustments as experience indicates. Otherwise, inflexible targets that are missed will compel managers to ignore them.

The Start and Stop Syndrome. Viewing objective-setting as a one-time event will result in killing it. It requires a continuity of effort to gain its advantages. A year or two may be necessary to become experienced in setting objectives and using them as a key tool in the management process.

WRITING MEANINGFUL OBJECTIVES

An objective is a specific description of an end result to be achieved. It should answer these questions:

—What is to be accomplished?

—When will it be accomplished?

—Who is accountable?

When managers are ready to write objectives for the program and unit for which they are responsible, the objectives should:

—specify a single end result to be accomplished, not describe the process involved;

—specify a target date for accomplishment;

—state the objective in measurable and verifiable terms so that it can be easily checked to see if it has been accomplished;

—develop an objective that is realistic, in that it has a fair chance to be attained in time but still represents a significant challenge; and

—formulate the objective in terms that are understandable and acceptable to the people involved.

In effect, objectives are concrete and operational and stand in sharp contrast to goal statements, which are by nature more abstract and philosophical. Several features stand out:

—They are statements of targets.

—They are achievable accomplishments.

—They are concrete indicators of attainable outcomes.

—They usually take place within the framework of goals.

—Their time span is usually one to twelve months.

—They are often accompanied by action steps to carry them out.

—They represent a joint commitment between managers and subordinates.

—They involve "reach" or "stretch" that encourage managers to progress toward or beyond levels of excellence.

An example of a stated objective is the American Red Cross "Program to Meet Certain Needs of Multiple Sclerosis Patients," which is used in its training program in program management:

Program Objectives

Objective 1. To teach by (date—one year hence) the Multiple Sclerosis Home Care Course to a minimum of 10 families of the bedridden and homebound patients.

Objective 2. To establish by (date—one year hence) at two locations monthly meetings of ambulatory persons with MS and their families to provide the Multiple Sclerosis Home Care Course, counseling help, and social event, including refreshments.

The above objectives are established to implement the following Program Goal: to provide a program of information and activities that will lead to better understanding and care of persons with MS. (American Red Cross 1976, 36)

DEVISING AND CHARTING ACTION PLANS

Our preceding discussion of setting objectives recommends fixing specific, attainable results to be accomplished. Five qualities of good objectives were offered. This section describes how to prepare action plans to carry out approved objectives.

What Is an Action Plan?

The action plan contains a series of steps that are specific segments of work or activity necessary to achieving objectives. Action steps are the most specific statements of intended accomplishments. Essentially they answer these questions:

—What work is to be done?
—Who is to do it?
—When is the work to be completed?
—How much will it cost?
—Where will the money come from?

The action plan fulfills three important needs: It describes how an objective will be reached and therefore increases the credibility and validity of the objective; it budgets the time and other resources required of those responsible; and it is used for monitoring progress toward the objective and its higher goal. The time span for an action plan is usually from one to twelve months.

Preparing Action Steps

To develop an action plan, start with a stated objective. For example, if the objective is to "conduct a weekend leadership training conference involving one hundred youth by May 15," the following kinds of action steps might be planned to meet that objective:

Action Steps	Completion Date	Person Responsible
1. Discuss conference with high school officials and request president of board of education to appoint a planning committee.	1/15	JK
2. Contact host hotel and obtain available dates and costs; check for discounts.	1/24	JK
3. Meet with planning committee chair to develop tentative agenda and set dates for committee meetings to plan conference.	1/31	JK
4. Arrange for planning committee to plan conference agenda, speakers, etc.	2/15	DG

It is important to put the action plan in writing and use it as a basis for reporting on progress and problems. The plan can save a great deal of confusion and misunderstanding later when trying to determine who was assigned to do what steps and when.

Charting Action Plans

Two fundamental management techniques that have been used for charting action plans and reviewing their progress are:

—The Gant Bar Chart, which has been used extensively for almost fifty years.

—The Milestone Chart, which emerged from the Gant Chart with a slight modification to make it easier and faster to check progress or problems.

The Gant Chart

The Gant Chart is a simple, linear chart that lists one step or task after another, with a bar visually indicating the passage of time. The chart takes each task and sets and charts a deadline for its completion.

Tasks of the action plan are usually listed numerically in the left-hand column of a chart, thus:

1. Task A.
2. Task B.
3. Task C.
4. Task D.

A time frame is then added on a horizontal plane, thus:

Task	Time Frame			
	Time 1	Time 2	Time 3	Time 4
1.				
2.				
3.				
4.				

The time frame is divided into appropriate units—months, weeks, days, or hours. One bar line is used to estimate the time required for completion. A second bar line can be used to chart progress and compares actual work status with set deadlines. The chart easily and quickly reveals delinquency and delays.

The bar line is charted like this:

Task	Time Frame
Task A.:	12/15 1/13 2/15 3/15 4/15
Deadline:	_____
(estimated completion)	
Progress:	_____

A memorandum accompanying the Gant Chart can explain the basis for any discrepancy between the estimated completion date and the actual work status. The virtue of the Gant Chart is that it facilitates planning and scheduling. It analyzes each step of the operation in carrying out the objective, finds the order in which they must be done, and then estimates the time necessary to complete each step and the operation in its entirety. A major disadvantage of the Gant Chart is that it does not indicate interdependencies between and among tasks, which would indicate readily what can happen when necessary actions are not taken in time. In complex situations, where precise scheduling of interdependent tasks and events is essential to avoid costly and significant delays, it may be necessary to use Project Evaluation and Reporting Technique (PERT).

Milestone Chart

The Milestone Chart is a modified Gant Chart that makes measuring progress easier and faster. It first describes the tasks to be performed, as in the Gant Chart. But then it breaks each task down into easily identifiable events or "milestones" that must be accomplished if the task is to be completed. A time date is assigned to each event. The milestones are identified by number and charted along a time frame. You then look for objective evidence to determine whether the event has been completed.

A Milestone Chart would look like this:

Tasks	Milestones and Timeframe
Task A.	Event 1 Event 3 Event 5 Event 7
Task B.	Event 2 Event 4 Event 6 Event 8

The numbers refer to specific milestone events, which can be listed on an accompanying memorandum with estimated dates attached to each one.

Case Examples of Gant Bar Chart and Milestone Chart

If the stated objective is to "conduct a weekend leadership training conference involving one hundred high school youth by May 15," then the Gant Bar Chart would look like this:

Task	Time Frame			
	Feb.	Mar.	Apr.	May
1. Discuss conference	10			
2. Contact host hotel	20			
3. Meet with planning chair		2		
4. Hold first meeting of		8		

A Milestone Chart for the above Gant Bar Chart would identify and chart the concrete events or "milestones" that must be accomplished for each task to be completed, as follows:

Task Event	Completion Deadline			
	Feb.	Mar.	Apr.	May,
1. Conference approved	10			
2. Hotel contacted; dates firm		1		
3. Planning committee appointed		15		
4. Conference agenda agreed on		29		
5. Conference committees appointed			6	

THE IMPORTANCE OF GAINING AGREEMENT AND SUPPORT

An action plan without agreement and support is a waste of time. Disagreements among those responsible for implementation can result in action steps being distorted, undermined, or not carried out. The most effective way to gain agreement is through a process of participation by those who are involved and affected by the steps of the action plan.

How you conduct the process of involvement is crucial to its success. You should be careful in two respects. Although you want to encourage the fullest staff participation, take the time to get the best person assigned to planning or implementing a specific step or activity. Avoid giving the assignment to a friend or to the person who mentioned it, unless that person has the best experience and skill for doing the specific activity. Second, pick people who are interested in the particular activity; this enhances their job satisfaction.

When seeking effective participation in the work plan, seek to get the job done smoothly with a minimum of friction. Several helpful hints include:

—Avoid surprise, minimize confrontation, and forget about coercion.

—Use questioning techniques. Ask simple questions: What do you think? Does this make sense? Is this right?

—Keep people informed; conduct periodic briefings; discuss status, problems, and progress.

Be aware that when you take the time to get good people involved, there may be accusations that you are too slow, indecisive, or too cautious. Counter by explaining your team approach to getting results, which means bringing in the people involved to sincerely obtain their advice and guidance and fullest participation.

18

Designing Program/Project Plans

RETHINKING PROGRAM DESIGN

Many programs are badly designed, ill-conceived, and fatally flawed. In the National Performance Review, the Government Accounting Office identified seventeen federal programs as high-risk activities especially vulnerable to waste, fraud, and mismanagement; the office of Management and Budget identified 104 federal programs on its high-risk list. The report *Rethinking Program Design* accompanying the National Performance Review (Office of the Vice President 1993e), reveals the severity of poor program design and its consequences in undermining the public's trust in government.

The report indicates that many government problems derive from the poor foundation upon which public programs are built—ambiguous goals, weak operational concepts, and careless implementation design. The report discusses ten objective criteria for determining what services the federal government should provide and what to discontinue. The formal development of a discipline of program design is recommended with suitable handbooks, training programs, and pilot project testing to validate concepts and gather experience.

The program design criteria discussed in the report are these:

—Identify clearly who benefits and how they benefit;
—Define and evaluate alternative of program delivery; determine most effective and least bureaucratic methods;
—Examine program compatibility with other programs;
—Assess cost-effectiveness and efficiency; evaluate costs and benefits;

—Evaluate consistency with accepted management principles;

—Ensure financial feasibility and affordability;

—Determine feasibility of implementation; provide for implementation in program design;

—Provide for program flexibility to adapt to changing conditions;

—Institute performance measurement and program evaluation; be prepared to remedy unintended negative consequences; and

—Build in cessation provisions wherever appropriate.

WHAT DOES A PROGRAM/PROJECT PLAN DO?

Essentially the program plan is a highly effective management tool for establishing a program/project and ensuring that it is clearly and properly designed. Once designed and approved, the plan serves as a basis for its effective management throughout the implementation and evaluation of program activity.

The program plan serves these three functions:

To Create and Clarify the Design of a Program. The manager must accomplish these tasks systematically:

—An early identification of problems to be resolved.

—Establishment of direction and purpose.

—Mobilization of resources.

—Definition of end products (outputs).

To Provide an Instrument for Obtaining the Necessary Review and Approval. This is done through a structure of prearranged clearance and decision points. It is important to know where in an organization the power resides, to enable new projects to get started, modified, or stopped. Most organizations have institutionalized systems for developing and approving programs as part of its program budgeting system.

To Provide an Objective Basis for Evaluation of Progress. This enables the manager to exert continuous control and to improve the program activity.

COMPONENTS OF PROGRAM/PROJECT DESIGN

Usually about seven components are taken into account in a design for establishing a new program/project or clarifying an existing one. Each of the components is described, though not all are included in every program design. What to include depends on the nature of the program and what the organization requires as part of its institutionalized procedures and systems.

Definition of Purpose

Purpose states the ultimate reason for the program, that is, what the program is expected to achieve if completed successfully and on time. One effective approach is to first describe the problem that needs to be resolved. Then shift the negative statement of a problem to a positive direction of what must be achieved to resolve the problem. For example, consider the following problem and purpose statement:

Problem: Population growth will outrun domestically produced cereal grain supply within three years.

Shift to purpose: Increase domestic production of cereal grains by X tons within three years to meet needs of growing local population.

The purpose of programs or projects is often linked to a goal statement that represents a higher programming direction to which the program/ project is intended to contribute.

Statements of purpose should be targeted to a specific audience or group. A specific time frame should be included; magnitude should be expressed whenever possible. Statements of purpose should be short so that they serve as a brief summary in concise language of what the program aims to accomplish.

Calculation of Inputs Desired

Inputs are the resources that are essential to producing certain desirable, definable outputs of end products. They are financial in terms of program costs, human in terms of staffing requirements, and material in terms of needed commodities and equipment.

It is useful to recognize two things: The amount of resources must be adequate over a sustained period, usually a year, to maintain stability; and good people with the right skills and expertise are essential to successful programs.

Definition of Outputs Produced

Outputs define the intended results and may contain dimensions of their magnitude that can be expected from good management of the inputs provided. In some instances, the output of a program/project can become the input of another one, for example, the kind and number of people trained: sixty trained agronomists within four years; or, the ridding of an area of all mosquitoes: the elimination of mosquitoes in Dade County.

Identification of Target Clientele

Knowing for whom the products or services are intended often determines how the program is designed and operated. This is referred to as "targeting" or "marketing" the program to a specific audience or clientele.

How a targeted clientele is reached depends on who they are and characteristics such as economic status, educational level, geographic location, physical capacities, and interests. It may be necessary to determine what the clientele need and want, and what they will accept and can afford.

Specification of Objectively Verifiable Indicators

Good program design should contain explicit and verifiable measures or indicators of results and expected progress. These indicators should be preestablished and agreed on during the process of design, review, and approval. Progress should be objectively verifiable so that discussions on progress will focus more on evidence than on opinion.

Indicators may be quantitative or qualitative. In some cases, where quantitative measures are not possible, objective observation of a qualitative change may still provide a measure of progress, for example: "Working relations among staff personnel are vastly improved this year; disagreements are greatly diminished." Quantitative measures are used extensively. They can be a wide variety of indicators, such as number of cars produced, number of patients seen, or number of persons who died from cancer or heart attack.

Indicators of Key Assumptions to Success of Program

Programs often depend on an event or action that must take place or a condition that must exist if a program is to succeed—but one over which the manager has little or no control. Experience reveals that programs often fail because uncontrollable external events can change to an unfavorable condition. One obvious example: a program to prevent AIDS by giving condoms to high school youths in a public facility depends on, or assumes the willingness of, public officials to provide money or authority to do so for a finite period of time. If public pressure causes certain officials to suspend the authority to do so, even if condoms are available from private sources, the program stops.

DESIGN FORMAT FOR EXPENSIVE PROGRAMS/ PROJECTS

The more expensive the program in terms of financial requirements and use of high-powered talent, the more justified is a complex design.

What is expensive and costly is, of course, relative. Military programs run into the millions and demand careful and complex design. But small programs in some nonprofit organizations may justify only simpler formats of program design.

It is necessary for organizations to decide what level of cost and complexity would justify the use of written program proposals and detailed design formats. One useful standard is to decide that program proposals should not be required to have a detailed and complex design format unless the program costs about four times the salary of the program manager. All lesser-cost programs could be entitled to use a simpler design format. The decision about program design format should consider the organization's tolerance for paperwork burdens and the possible cost/benefit that can be achieved. A minimum requirement, imperative for effective program management, is that every program, whatever the cost, should follow some form of design format and culminate in a written plan. This section discusses a more complex format for expensive projects that is based upon the use of a "logical framework." The next section will describe a simpler program/project design format.

Use of a Logical Framework Matrix

This framework for project design has been used for several decades in United States foreign assistance, with considerable effectiveness and numerous evaluations of its efficacy. The framework has a dual use: (1) to guide program staff to plan a program/project's design and (2) to set the stage for a later evaluation.

Using a logical framework matrix, program staff lay out a design that uses a hierarchy of objectives, progress indicators, and assumptions about necessary conditions for program success. When the program is to be evaluated, the basic information provided for the framework serves as a benchmark to determine whether the program's outputs have brought progress toward achievement of its purpose and higher goal. The evaluation also seeks to ascertain whether the design is still valid or should be changed in light of changing conditions or new knowledge or experience.

To develop the logical framework matrix, a special format has been developed by the Agency for International Development for its use in foreign technical assistance programs (U.S. Agency for International Development 1973, 45–61). This format provides a convenient reminder for recording the substantive steps in program design and makes it easier to comprehend the essential relationships. The Logical Framework Matrix Format is as follows:

	1 Narrative Summary	2 Indicators	3 Assumptions
A. Goal			
B. Purpose			
C. Outputs			
D. Inputs			

Instructions for Matrix Preparation

The instructions will refer to the rows designated at the left as A through D, and the vertical columns as 1 through 3. For example, cell A-1 would be Narrative Summary of Goal. In preparing an initial matrix, it may be more convenient to record ideas on separate sheets of paper for each major element of Goal, Purpose, Outputs, and Inputs that captures each of the vertical headings: Narrative Summary, Indicators, and Assumptions. These separate sheets can later be incorporated into a one-page matrix.

1. The Narrative Summary: Column 1 of the Matrix

1–A: Identify the goal to which the program is designed to contribute.

1–B: State the purpose that the project is expected to achieve if completed successfully and on schedule.

1–C: Describe the specifically intended kinds of results that can be expected from good management of the inputs provided, in a generally favorable environment.

1–D: Define the input of people, money, goods, and services that are essential to producing definable outputs of end products.

2. Indicators: Column 2 of the Matrix

2–A: Select explicit and verifiable measures or indicators of results and progress expected. These indicators should be preestablished and agreed upon during the process of design, review, and approval. Progress should be objectively verifiable so that discussion will focus more on evidence than on opinion.

Indicators should also be identifiable for Purpose, Output, and Input in cells 2–B, 2–C, and 2–D.

Examples of indicators can be seen in a Program for Malaria Eradication, as follows:

	1 Narrative Summary	2 Indicator
A. Goal	Reduce Mortality Rate	Death Rate
B. Purpose	Eradicate Malaria	Cases of Malaria Reported

C. Output	Eliminate Malaria Mosquitoes in House	Number of Houses Sprayed
D. Inputs	Spray Teams	Man-years of Spray Teams
	Vehicles	Number of Vehicles
	Chemicals	Tons of Spray

3. Assumptions: Column 3 of the Matrix

For each of the cells A-3, B-3, C-3, and D-3, specify the assumptions that must be realized if we are to obtain the conditions that will exist if the program achieves its purpose and outputs. To do this, identify the factors over which program personnel have little or no control, but which if not present are likely to restrict the progress of the program.

An example of assumptions can be gleaned from the same malaria eradication program, as follows:

	1 Narrative Summary	3 Important Assumption
A. Goal	Reduce mortality rate	Malaria is a significant contributor to death rate.
B. Purpose	Eradicate malaria	Malaria incidence is high.
D. Inputs	Spray teams	Significant portion of population will participate and allow work to be done.

PREPARING SIMPLER ONE-PAGE PROGRAM/PROJECT DESIGNS

For relatively simpler and much less costly programs and projects— down to the level of 100 percent unreimbursed volunteer effort with minimal out-of-pocket expenses—a short, one-page format may be entirely adequate and effective. One such simple, one-page format used by the American Red Cross (1976) contains these elements:

—Identification of needs
—Program goal
—Program objectives
—Action steps
—Responsible persons
—Resources required

19

Developing Performance Measures

GROWING ATTENTION TO PERFORMANCE MEASUREMENT

When Strategic Planning was introduced in the 1980s into public and nonprofit organizations, it devoted its primary attention to future intentions. It set strategic directions and goals and designed strategic initiatives to achieve them. This was a significant advance, but implementation faltered. Too often the performance results achieved bore minimal relationships to planned goals and objectives. Results were often disappointing.

In the search for better performance results, many experts recommend a fundamental shift in traditional managerial thinking. They suggest moving away from concentration on "inputs" that focuses on activities or resources, toward a performance-based management improvement approach that emphasizes "outcomes" and their measurement. This approach measures performance results against planned goals and objectives.

The emphasis on performance measurement was encouraged by the U.S. Department of the Treasury when they surveyed leaders in seventy-five American corporations, looking for good ideas for better management. Federal program managers, the Treasury officials concluded, could learn much from corporate best practice and particularly from the approach to performance measurement. The report indicated that "measurement of the effectiveness, efficiency and economy of products, services, and processes is the keystone for assessing current circumstances, planning strategic goals, and monitoring incremental and comprehensive improvements" (U.S. Treasury, Financial Management Service 1993, 12).

But when the Government Accounting Office (GAO), an arm of Congress, surveyed the existence of program performance measures in government, it found that two-thirds of the 103 agencies contacted already had strategic plans and more than three-quarters collected performance data. Although performance measures existed, their impact on results achieved were disappointing. The GAO discovered that fewer than half of these agencies were making substantial use of performance information in assessing progress toward strategic goals and objectives. The GAO's more detailed look at fourteen sample agencies found only a very limited application of performance information in program and policy decision-making. But when looking at federal programs that were judged to be successful, the National Performance Review (Gore 1993) noted that such successful agencies do measure their performance and act upon what they learn. They recommended that performance measurement be undertaken in the efforts to reinvent government.

Increasing Use of Performance Measures

For decades performance has been considered a primary criterion for judging organizations and has been a fundamental managerial concern. But efforts in the 1990s sharply expanded the attention to performance management improvement. By 1995, using performance measurement and standards became an accepted way of doing government business in more than a hundred federal agencies. Recent progress in government management improvement focuses both on the use of performance goals to support major objectives of strategic plans and on the use of service standards for customer satisfaction; and of course these practices overlap.

What Is Different about the New Situation?

Some say that we are learning how better to measure performance, although methodology needs further refinement. A deeper examination reveals a historic convergence in thinking and action of the powerful players in the game. This augurs well for achieving substantial progress in the measurement and improvement of performance in government and will have a ripple effect on the nonprofit management movement.

We witness the coming together of congressional, executive, and operating program management groups on a fundamental management premise: All parties agree that it is important to plan goals and objectives, measure performance against them, and then actually utilize such planning and data to manage for continuing improvement in results.

Congressional requirements now mandate both strategic planning and
performance measurement for all federal agencies and departments in
the Government Performance and Results Act of 1993. These legislative
efforts mesh with and strengthen the presidential and vice presidential
campaign to "reinvent government." Additionally, executives, managerial employees, and their staffs, as individuals and in teams, have been
mobilized and are being trained at all levels for extensive participation
in the improvement efforts, with visible progress. Some claim that the
leadership role of the Office of Management and Budget for implementing the Government Performance and Results Act is a crucial determinant of continuing success in performance improvement.

Experience further suggests that progress will be influenced substantially by the extent of White House interest and visible attention and
support of the president. This is positive in the Clinton administration,
with Vice President Gore in visible charge of reinventing government,
as it was positive with the Truman administration as witnessed by officials from the then Bureau of the Budget.

THE MANDATE OF CONGRESSIONAL ACTION

Congressional action with the passage of the Government Performance
and Results Act of 1993 embodies in legally mandated form essential
elements for "reinventing government" that have begun to stimulate
substantial efforts for improving the performance of government.

What the GPRA Proposes to Accomplish

The GPRA establishes for all federal agencies the mandatory use of
strategic planning and performance measurement in their efforts to
achieve results. Its purposes were clearly delineated in a report of the
National Performance Review:

1. Improve the confidence of the American people in the capability of the federal
   government, by systematically holding federal agencies accountable for
   achieving program results;
2. Initiate program performance reform with a series of pilot projects in setting
   program goals, measuring program performance against these goals, and reporting publicly on their progress;
3. Improve federal program effectiveness and public accountability by promoting a new focus on results, service quality, and customer satisfaction;
4. Help federal managers to improve service delivery by requiring that they plan
   for meeting program objectives and by providing them with information
   about program results and service quality;
5. Improve congressional decision-making by providing more objective infor-

mation on achieving statutory objectives and on the relative effectiveness and efficiency of federal programs and spending.

When President Clinton signed the bill he succinctly summarized it: "The law simply requires that we chart a course for every endeavor that we take the people's money for, see how well we are progressing, tell the public how we are doing, stop the things that don't work, and never stop improving the things that we think are worth investing in."

What It Requires Agencies to Do!

The law sets forth a set of specific, time-phased requirements at dates certain. All agencies are required to define their long-term goals, set specific annual performance targets, and report annually on performance compared to targets. The components are strategic plans, annual performance plans, and annual performance reports.

Agencies are being specifically asked to do these things:

—establish performance goals to define the level of performance to be achieved by a program activity;

—express such goals in an objective, verifiable, and measurable form;

—briefly describe the operational processes, skills, and technology and the human, capital, information, or other resources required to meet the performance goals;

—establish performance indicators to be used in measuring or assessing the relevant outputs, service levels, and outcomes of each program activity;

—provide a basis for comparing actual program results with established performance goals; and

—describe the means to be used to verify and validate measured values.

If an agency determines that it is not feasible to express performance goals for a particular program activity in an objective, quantifiable, and measurable form, exceptions may be authorized to develop alternative forms.

A most pragmatic feature of the legislation is the time-phased use of pilot projects over time sufficient to gain essential experience prior to the law's government-wide implementation. The pilots are designed to assess the benefits, costs, and usefulness of the plans and reports required in the pilot agencies, to detect any significant difficulties experienced by the pilot agencies, and to set forth any recommended changes to the provisions of the GPRA.

The GPRA Timetable

The law schedules pilot projects in each of the component areas of the legislation to be conducted in agencies designated by the federal Office of Management and Budget (OMB) prior to their government-wide implementation. The timing is staggered as follows: performance goal setting, measurement and reporting for fiscal years 1994–96; managerial accountability and flexibility for fiscal years 1995–96, and performance budgeting for fiscal years 1998–99.

At a later stage, pilot projects in performance budgeting will determine by 2001 whether the OMB director will recommend legislation requiring performance budgeting for all agencies.

Agencies are required to develop and submit strategic plans covering at least five years to OMB and Congress by September 30, 1997; to submit annual performance plans beginning with fiscal year 1999; and to begin reporting annually on performance budgets no later than March 31, 2000, if required to do so after the pilot experience is evaluated.

It is important to realize that performance planning in the late 1990s is in a pilot phase of experimentation and experience gathering and, by its very nature, necessarily so. It is expected that lessons learned will feed back ways to refine and improve both the system and substance of performance measurement well into the twenty-first century.

EMERGING ACTION DOCTRINE FOR PERFORMANCE MEASUREMENT AND IMPROVEMENT

There is emerging a body of "new" doctrine—new requirements, operating principles, and action steps—that is designed to guide and improve the management of program performance toward the achievement of better results; measurement plays a prominent role. Although evolving in the public sector, current doctrine will prove to be widely applicable in the nonprofit sector.

The claim for "newness" is only partially correct. Actually, the current efforts in performance management in the public and nonprofit realm have vintage roots. They build on three decades of improvements in program performance and the long span of management sciences with their goals and measurement models. Major federal developments that have occurred over time include Work Measurement and Program Budgeting, which developed in the 1950s and 1960s, with its systems thinking and project orientation. Systems analysis–oriented Planning-Programming-Budget System (PPBS) emerged in the 1970s, aiming to provide information on the outcomes (benefits or disbenefits) made possible by the use of inputs realistically estimated. The mid- to late 1980s introduced strategic planning to government and the nonprofits with its focus on change-oriented goals and objectives and its then-tenuous link to program budgeting and management, which is now being strengthened.

A Fundamental Management Premise

The essence of contemporary public performance management builds upon a long-known management premise of systems thinking; it combines goal models with systems models that perceive the public or nonprofit sector as a production system. Essentially, performance inputs are compared with the production of performance outcomes that are measured or at least assessed with the use of standards or benchmarks against the strategic framework of mission, goals, and objectives.

The managerial logic is clear, yet the development and use of performance management systems in public and nonprofit agencies have proven to be no easy task. Performance measurement that attempts to measure the significance, effectiveness, and efficiency of public and nonprofit programs is complex; indicators and measures of public and nonprofit outcomes often prove elusive in the absence of clear-cut "bottom lines" characteristic of private sector business. But the improvement of performance-based technology, system, and doctrine is under way and receiving priority attention in the public sector.

For those who desire to place current action doctrine and practice on performance management and its measurement in wider, historical, and scholarly perspective, a valuable book is *Public Sector Performance*, edited by Trudi C. Miller, particularly chapter 8 on management and accounting models.

Strategic Approaches to Performance Measurement

The contemporary approaches to results-oriented performance management are strategy-oriented; they place performance measurement in a strategic planning context of mission and selected strategic goals so that performance and its measurement focus on what is most important to an organization and on the desired results vital to its success.

New performance management embraces six dimensions, which to be most effective need to be integrated:

—the use of strategic planning to develop mission, goals, values and new initiatives;

—development of objectives and indicators to measure performance against the goals set; and comparisons of actual performance with standards established;

—identification of key environmental factors external to the agency and often beyond its control that could significantly affect the achievement of the general goals and objectives;

—assignment and identification of accountability for results achieved;

—linkage to budgeting by program accountability and program and project design; and calculation and control of required resources; and

—evaluation of results actually achieved, with a broadening of view to embrace systematic organization learning as well as traditional program and project evaluation.

These dimensions reflect many of the essential ingredients of the "strategic management system"; but recent efforts for better performance favor the semantics of "performance management for results" that occur in the literature on "reinventing government."

Action Concepts

Four action principles guide the new focus on performance management (*Mission-Driven, Results-Oriented Budgeting*, Office of the Vice President 1993c).

1. *Greater Use of Planning and Measurement to Improve Performance in Every Federal Program and Agency.* The Office of Management and Budget (OMB) through its leadership role encourages all agencies to make greater use of performance planning and measurement. Whether or not an agency is officially designated for pilot testing, it is encouraged to identify prototype sites, assess current status, identify benchmarks, formulate implementation milestones to cover its major mission areas, and make better use of currently available data. Agencies were encouraged to display performance measures in internal budget submissions and to tie performance to budget decisions.

The performance measurement effort is very significant. Differences in program performance—even small ones—can be important in people's lives. The Department of Treasury's Financial Management Service, for example, delivers 99.6 percent of its checks on time. But if this performance were to fall one-fifth of 1 percent, an additional 1.6 million Social Security or other checks would be late. This event could be serious for those who await the timely arrival of a government check when the rent is due.

Despite popular perception to the contrary, some federal programs are excellently managed; objective measures now exist to judge this. Organizations have established goals and standards for program achievements—the quantity and quality of goods and services the program will deliver—and can compare their performance with other programs, agencies, or organizations delivering similar goods and services. But many agencies and programs need to do more.

2. *Clear Assignment of Responsibility and Accountability.* Agency heads have the ultimate responsibility to lead strategic planning and performance measurement and assign them to line managers in programs for which they are accountable, not to staff or central agencies. The practice is to activate teams to establish program strategies, identify indicators and targets, and collect and use performance data. Such teams are widely representative; they include line managers, budget analysts, and strategic planners. They can have other program managers, outsiders, and even customer representatives and stakeholders. Representative teams are helpful to assure that performance information is simple, valid, and reliable.

3. *Clarity of Objectives of Federal Programs at Their Several Levels Is Strongly Recommended.* The results are to be incorporated into the development of agency strategic plans and program budgets, regional operating plans, and also at the microlevel of design and revision of operating programs and projects.

4. *Conduct of Budget and Management Reviews with Performance Objectives and Results as Key Elements.* The Executive Office of the President and individual agencies are encouraged to use performance information in program and policy decision-making and as an element of budget and management reviews. Efforts have been taken to reflect this in revised OMB circulars, agency budget guidance and review procedures, and training for budget, management, and program analysts. These efforts are increasing as agencies develop strategic plans, performance measures, and targets by scheduled deadlines. The budget and management analysts at the Office of Management and Budget are responsible for providing the feedback and oversight necessary for an effective system.

Challenges and Difficulties

Attempts to plan, measure, and manage for results, however, do not automatically create desired results without difficulties. They pose a series of challenges for program managers in the various agencies; the report of the National Performance Review (Gore 1993) pinpoints several:

Many Programs Encompass Multiple, Contradictory, Ambiguous, Changing, or Even Unfunded Objectives. Setting objectives requires choices that are not easy. They require careful consideration and possible trade-offs between competing objectives, between long- and short-term goals, or between innovation and certainty, or excessive risk. Establishing objectives confronts the limits and constraints of financial stringency; they are subject to the pressure of strong competing interests for limited resources.

Programs Are Diverse. Programs are as diverse as income security and national security, or Internal Revenue and Social Security, or health research. They involve different processes, produce different outputs that result in different outcomes, and thus require different performance measures. Some programs in agencies deal with a high volume of repetitive transactions and paperwork that can be converted to electronic processing, such as Social Security, the Treasury, and the Internal Revenue Service. These programs necessitate relatively less decision-making discretion, are more easily measured, and are vastly different but more certain in performance requirements than agencies performing less predictable diplomatic functions or scientific research.

Managers Need to Keep Performance Measurement Simple and Useful. The goal is to set few, relatively simple measures that tell managers how programs are performing, use that information to find potential problems and solutions, and stimulate continuous improvement. But too often measurement indicators produce numbers and quantities that do not produce valid indications of outcomes or results to answer the query "What results were actually achieved, how well, and how efficiently?"

The value of benchmarks as indicators is that they are drawn from actual practice in real organizations and not from abstract management models and can enable valid comparisons. This makes it easier to avoid the comparison of "similar categories but not really similar items," such as the obvious disparity of the workload and cost of maintaining residential rooms in military barracks with the benchmarks of the up-scale Ritz Carlton.

Outside critics have expressed other difficulties with the new thinking and practice on performance measurement and management. The biggest difficulty, claims Donald Kettl, in thinking about the problems of performance management is that reformers and managers alike far too often consider it simply a problem of measurement. Committing the government to performance-based management requires that officials identify and measure results. The more fundamental question Kettl raises is what to do with these measures. "Too often reformers pursue measurement for its own sake" (Kettl 1995).

Experience indicates that measurement often moves to that most easily measurable and ignores the significant factors that are difficult to quantify. In the realm of public affairs, measurement indicators often fall short of indicating the importance or effectiveness of outcomes; they more often count the number of actions or activities taken, which leaves the decision-makers uneasy about their value and ill-prepared to know what to do about them (Kettl and DiIulio 1995). "Body counts" in Vietnam is a dramatic example.

DEVELOPING PERFORMANCE AGREEMENTS WITH SENIOR LEADERSHIP

Government has been slow to set clear expectations for the performance of its top leaders. Generally, there have not been written agreements or any other systematic approach to link the goals of the president as chief executive to the performance of top political appointees and in turn to the civil servants below. The situation has begun to change.

Extensive Use of Performance Agreements

You now find a number of countries, states, and localities, as well as numerous private American corporations, using performance agreements with senior officials to set mutually agreed-upon objectives for organizational performance. We learn from the National Performance Review in its report on results-oriented budgeting (Office of the Vice President 1993c) that many senior officials in Australia, Canada, New Zealand, and the United Kingdom now have written agreements that are tied to agency-specific strategic plans. Senior officials in these countries claim that these agreements probably had a greater impact on organizational performance than any other single aspect of government reform. The agreements establish priorities, set understandings about expected performance, and grant specific delegations of authority.

In the United States, the first Status Report of the National Performance Review (Gore 1994) reported that the president signed five performance agreements with cabinet secretaries and leaders of two other agencies. A number of states and localities, from Ohio to Seattle to Sunnyvale in California, have developed some type of performance agreement with senior managers. As governments and nonprofits redevelop their human resources and reorient other management systems toward managing for results, performance agreements are part of the new improvement agenda. A missing link in the performance improvement chain has been supplied. Now recognized for entire organizations is the necessity to develop effective connections and achieve consensus among political officials, career executives, and program managers about the objectives and goals of the organization and to base accountability and incentive systems on progress toward the accomplishment of these goals and objectives.

Performance Agreements Can Empower, Not Just Obligate

Performance agreements can not only be vehicles for accountability; they can contribute to empowerment by granting, delegating, or clarifying decision-making authority to lower levels to achieve organizational and policy objectives. One concern is that excessive enthusiasm for quantitative precision and specificity can hamper the creativity, flexibility, and realism essential for sustaining improvement in achieving objectives.

The HUD Story

Performance agreements are only a piece of the quest for results. For performance-based management to be effective, it is necessary that a high-performing organization have a clear mission that is well-known and internalized by every single man and woman in the organization. That is why some agencies begin the performance process by developing a mission statement for the agency and by leading workshops all over the country to clarify the agency's values and mission. Then, based on the mission statement, senior staff establish performance agreements on program and management priorities that will guide the specific actions of each department and serve as the basis for benchmarks for agency performance. This is the approach of Secretary Cisneros at the Department of Housing and Urban Development, reported in some detail in the Status Report (Gore 1994) of the National Performance Review. One caveat: There is no single prototype for achieving performance; it is recognized that agency heads and managers need to use and blend multiple approaches that best suit their agency's needs and culture.

USING PERFORMANCE GOALS AND OBJECTIVES IN STRATEGIC PLANS: THE IRS STORY

Agencies have begun to include performance goals to support objectives in their strategic plans; the Internal Revenue Service's *Business Master Plan Strategic Extract, FY 1995–FY 2001* (U.S. Treasury 1994), is an excellent example. It implements the Government Performance and Results Act, which requires federal agencies to develop strategic plans linked to measurable outcomes and annual plans that specify performance goals, the actions to achieve the goals, and indicate accountabilities.

Use of Measurable Performance Goals in Support of Objectives

The objectives in the plan are first described and are then supported by individual performance goals that identify the performance indicators to be used in assessing progress. Note in the examples below that the Internal Revenue Service uses the semantics of "objectives" in ways others use the semantics of "goals" as described in this book and reverses the two labels.

A First Example of an Objective That Contains Supporting Goals

Objective 1. Increase Voluntary Compliance. "Our objective is to encourage and assist taxpayers to voluntarily file timely and accurate returns and to pay on time. Working toward voluntary compliance is the most efficient and cost-effective approach to collecting revenues prescribed by law" (p. 6).

There follows a description of the FY 2001 Performance Goals listed to support the first objective:

—collect at least 90 percent of the total tax dollars due and owing, through increased voluntary compliance and enforcement.

—achieve the recognition of the public, outside stakeholders, and IRS employees for the ethical conduct of IRS regarding fair and uniform application of tax laws, maintenance of highest standards of integrity, and confidentiality and security of tax information. (p. 7)

A Second Example:

Objective 2. "Achieve Quality-Driven Productivity through Systems Improvement and Employee Development. Our objective is to improve continually the quality of product and services we provide to our customers through the use of systems improvement tools and techniques and the development of a highly trained and diverse workforce. We do this to reduce the cost to both government and the public, provide improved customer service, and help improve voluntary compliance" (p. 11).

There follows the FY 2001 Performance Goals to support the objective:

—Reduce overall paper processing and handling.
  • increase the number of returns filed on media other than paper to 80 million;
  • receive all remittances electronically or by third-party processors;
  • reduce by 50 percent Service and taxpayer initiated, account-related correspondence.

—Provide a well-trained workforce that meets our diverse customer needs in fulfilling their tax obligations and reflects the diversity of the U.S. population as a whole.

—Increase the Service's productivity by 14 percent. (p. 11)

SETTING PERFORMANCE STANDARDS FOR
IMPROVING CUSTOMER SATISFACTION

The President's Call for Setting Customer Service Standards

President Clinton in 1993 issued an executive order that elevated the goal of improving customer satisfaction, one of the major principles for "reinventing government," to a high level of importance. Calling on public officials to change drastically the way government does business, the president set a standard for the quality of government service to be "equal to the best in business." It called for departments and agencies to identify and survey their customers, to post service standards, and to measure results against them; also to benchmark their performance against the best in business and to survey front-line workers on ideas for and barriers to reaching that standard.

By 1994 over a hundred federal agencies published fifteen hundred customer service standards in a report entitled *Putting Customers First: Standards for Serving the American People.* (Office of the Vice President 1994). Federal agencies have revealed their customer service plans as required by executive order. The service plans contain customer service standards, future plans for customer surveys, and the public or private standards used to benchmark against the best in business. The Office of Management and Budget (OMB) has helped agencies comply with the executive order by undertaking several initiatives in support of taking customer surveys: development of a resource manual, streamlined clearances to undertake customer survey research, and a training program in customer survey methods.

THE SSA STORY

The Social Security Administration is a fine example of the many ways government agencies have begun to use performance standards to elevate customer satisfaction with their agency's services. Its recent experience clearly illustrates what government is doing to improve its image and performance.

Social Security Administration plays a tremendous role in serving a large portion of the American public. It pays over $300 billion annually to 47 million beneficiaries; it maintains earning records for 131 million taxpayers. It has more than a thousand field offices; it operates probably one of the world's largest 1–800 free call services with about sixty million calls per year. With a maturing population, SSA's huge workload is estimated to increase by 26 percent by 2005.

An acknowledged trouble spot is disability claims. With a slow process, there have been backlogs of disability claims, hearings, and appeals. In 1993, the inspector general's report on overall SSA services showed "declining customer satisfaction for the fourth year in a row." It reported longer waiting times in offices and linked dissatisfaction among 1–800 callers to the number of attempts needed to get through. But aggressive efforts to improve have paid off.

With the achievement of its existence as an independent agency in 1994, the Social Security Administration placed a high value on customer service. It is reported that when the National Performance Review recommended that the agency set standards equal to the best in business, Commissioner Shirley Chater went one better and opted for world-class service equal to or better than anything in the public or private sectors. The SSA set and posted its customer service standards in offices across the nation. Seeking to improve, it then conducted a nationwide series of customer focus groups, and surveyed ten thousand customers in person or by phone and another twenty-two thousand by mail. Looking for further ideas for better service, SSA surveyed all its sixty-five thousand employees and organized discussion groups with many of them (reported in the status report of the National Performance Review, Gore September 1994).

Dramatic Progress in Disability Claims Processing

Additionally, reengineering teams began to scrutinize the problem-ridden process of handling claims from disabled Americans. The eighteen-member team of federal and state employees conducted more than thirty-six hundred interviews with frontline employees, managers, and executives as well as representatives from the medical community, legal aid advocates, and special interest groups. As revealed in the status report of the National Performance Review (1994), the team discovered that:

the average claim, before it is resolved, passes through the hands of 26 workers over 155 days. The actual work on the claim, however, takes only 13 hours, i.e. two work days. The rest of the time, it sits in a box, moves from office to office, or waits in the mail. But after 155 days, the process is only beginning. Most claims are rejected, prompting their reconsideration, involving more people, more processing, and more time. By the end of the full appeal process, the average claim is handled by 43 SSA employees over a span of 739 days. Although the disability program benefits only a fifth of Social Security recipients, it costs more to administer than all other Social Security programs combined.

When the team finished its work, they recommended a new system that promises to cut waiting times by 589 days, or nearly 80 percent. One significant insight emerged; no single office felt responsible for the entire process. One office would say that they did their job expeditiously, but they had to wait too long for another office to do its part of the job on the claim. Only when the team talked to customers were they able to focus on the entire problem in perspective, in which all the steps taken together served to create the long waits. They refocused the problem on the customer's needs and expectations and guided the recommended changes toward the promise of better customer service.

APPLYING BEST PRACTICE IN TELEPHONE SERVICE

As part of the federal government's effort to set and apply customer service standards in its campaign to improve program service, it looked to learn from business for the best in telephone practice. Ten government agencies and eight private companies cooperated to identify practices that can be applied in government to raise the level of service to equal the best in business.

Why Telephone Service?

The Federal Consortium Benchmark Study Report (Office of the Vice President February 1995) is significant for several reasons. First, the number of calls to government total in the many millions, with 1.7 million calls placed to the Social Security Administration on a single day, and 68.7 million calls to the Internal Revenue Service. Second, delivering services by telephone is cost-effective; it costs three times as much to answer the same query by letter than it does by telephone. And third, experts and citizens indicate that there is much room for improvement. We are told (but not how they know) that 25 percent of callers may give up without getting a response; fewer than 2 percent may abandon calls to the best companies. The report indicates that slow response and busy signals happen too often in the public sector, whereas world-class organizations answer in less than 15–20 seconds and rarely allow busy signals. In other ways the private sector has much to offer government in improving its phone service; it gives its employees extensive training and provides better-updated information more frequently to enable telephone staff to be more accurate and faster in their response to callers.

The Study Findings

Staff of the ten cooperating agencies reviewed a number of studies of world-class customer telephone service operations, identified benchmarking partners, talked to them over the phone, and made on-site visits. They talked to frontline employees, managers, and union officials. They discovered much similarity of common traits among industry's best organizations and reported these findings in their final report:

—All have strong corporate cultures which are totally focused on doing more than satisfying customers, on delighting them.

—The culture is based on guiding principles or values that have become ingrained throughout the organization—in senior managers and frontline and support employees.

—All work toward achieving employee satisfaction because it results in higher-quality performance.

—All commit the resources necessary to meet the customer service standards; this involves investing in hiring and training the right employees.

—In all, there is open communication between senior managers and employees.

—All continuously survey customers in order to understand how to improve services.

—In all, employees are empowered to handle calls to completion at the first contact.

—In all, employees are involved in all aspects of the calling-center operation and planning process through cross-functional teams.

The Report's Benchmarks

The report then proceeded to summarize the best practices identified that may be applicable to government. These benchmarks, to be used to assess one's own performance and to close the gaps identified, are discussed around major themes—leadership strategies, information management and analysis, planning, human resource management, process management, key measures for business results, and customer satisfaction. The report concludes with summarizing benchmark findings in ways that commit the key players; it does so in the voices and words of the customer, the customer server/satisfier, the team leader, and senior manager.

ESTABLISHING PERFORMANCE STANDARDS FOR EFFECTIVE LOCAL GOVERNMENT: THE ALLEGHENY COUNTY STORY

Within the last decade, a number of cities and counties with a population of at least one hundred thousand have begun to develop demonstration efforts to improve their management, productivity, and quality of services. A common thread woven throughout the effort was the establishment of a formal system for setting longer-term and annual goals, devising measurable program objectives and standards, formulating budgets based on the goals and objectives, and reporting on progress. The intent is to relate planning, budgeting, and performance measurement.

An example of excellent work done is the Allegheny County/Pennsylvania Program begun in 1991 as a local demonstration program to modernize county administration and organization. Financed with the help of five Pittsburgh foundations and county funds, the program was assisted by staff of the Coalition to Improve Management in State and Local Government, founded and directed for many years by the late Donald C. Stone, acclaimed as America's foremost public management expert and practitioner. The coalition prepared guidance materials useful to operating officials, derived from the best practice of experience, and organized conferences to consider results.

The Goals Program

The keystone of the Allegheny effort was the development and installation of a "Goals Program" in which the county's thirty-seven departments joined in a cooperative effort to prepare mission statements, set goals, develop work programs, and adopt performance standards and measurement to assess progress. The steps for implementing the goals and standards are described in the coalition's Management Guide No. 6–A, May 1991 (Donald Stone 1991b); a second part of the guide recommends the procedure to be used by a municipality in deciding what standards to select for priority attention.

A companion piece to the guide is *Standards for Effective Local Government: A Workbook for Performance Assessment*, prepared by the Southwestern Pennsylvania Regional Planning Commission (1990). This workbook enables government officials to apply the "Goals Program" to generally accepted municipal standards in twelve program areas and to determine how they rate in their performance. The important next step is to determine what improvements deserve priority attention, followed by the development of a work program with budget estimates to implement the selected priority areas.

The standards developed by the planning commission that are discussed in the workbook fall into twelve categories of municipal activity: general municipal management, financial management, personnel management, purchasing, police, fire, emergency medical services, emergency management, public works, planning/land use control, parks and recreation, and ethical standards for local government officials. These standards were field-tested by the staff, who were active in developing, refining, and producing the workbook. For each of the areas of municipal activity, evaluation factors were listed, with standards for effective performance described. The self-assessment rating scale determined whether the standard was met, was effective, and was verified. If the standard was not met, the reason was given: not relevant, no interest, lack of resources, or lack of administrative capacity/initiatives. The assessment provided opportunity for comments.

20

Budgeting for Program Accountability

ORIENTATION

In this generation—certainly over the last decade—program budgeting as a managerial tool has become the accepted way to conduct budgetary affairs. This is true for the multi–billion dollar higher education system, the small and large public agencies, the national private nonprofit organizations, and the corporations of the business sector. In fact, those who worked with the older types of budgets, such as the line-item budget, wonder how they were able to manage with such imprecise data and get away with it.

Essentially program budgeting is a management approach to budgeting. It presents the purposes and objectives for which funds are requested, estimates the costs of the programs proposed for accomplishing objectives, and offers the measures for assessing the accomplishments and work performed under each program.

The modern program budget is vital to all other functions of program management, such as planning, structuring, monitoring, controlling, and evaluation. Without the effective use of program budgets, it would be almost impossible to get the modern program management job done and have a solid basis for knowing how well you are doing.

Program budgeting has become so important to the modern organization that it can represent a specialized career pathway for those interested in either the public or private sectors.

Aims of Program Budgeting

Budgeting in an organization is a systematic design for planning, allocating, and controlling the use of resources. In organizations that use the program management approach, the dual aims of budgeting are to meet not only the program needs of institutions but also the needs of its organizational units. What it does is enable program managers and organization executives to:

—plan in advance for the acquisition and expenditure of moneys for needed resources, whether they be staff, equipment, or supplies;

—allocate money and authorize its expenditure for approved purposes; and

—monitor and control the expenditures of the authorized moneys.

There is a long-running debate whether to budget by organization units or by program. This is a false issue! Either approach allows incomplete accountability. Both must be done, for it is essential to provide money to organization heads and to hold them accountable for results. But the best way to do this is to budget their resources by program goals and activities and the other essential elements of a program budgeting system. It is therefore necessary that the program budget system have the capacity to develop program costs by program and organization and to be able to reconcile the two.

Evolution

Traditionally, institutions budget their resources to organizational units on what was called a "line-item basis." Under the line-item system, information was presented in two areas: a simple listing of source of income and a simple listing of categories of expenses, which usually were called "object accounts" for salaries, telephones, printing, travel, equipment, and the like. No effort was made to refer expenses to particular programs; rather, the reference was to particular organizational units. In effect, only by organization did you have answers as to where the money came from, in what amounts, where it went, and how much was spent.

Stimulated by the probe of the Hoover Commission at the federal government level in the 1950s, a movement emerged of institutions and individuals who wanted to know more precisely how funds were being used. Congress and the Bureau of the Budget in the Executive Office of the President were asking penetrating questions about the use of moneys, for which there could be no answers under the current budget procedure. Officials wanted to know about the programs for which money was being spent. They were concerned with purpose, result, and accomplishment. In effect, the concerns reflected an interest in both the substance of expenditures and what they bought, as well as its economic use and cost-effectiveness.

The "line-item budgeting" approach told you what you spent on salaries or postage stamps. But it did not allow you to determine what moneys were spent on what programs nor what was accomplished with the money.

Advantages

Program budgeting does have definite managerial advantages. It does help to manage more effectively by allowing:

Program Cost Identification. Identifies sources and uses of funds by programs and objectives, rather than by organizational unit and line-item category of account.

Better Cost Control of Programs. Knowing where the money is going helps control its use. It identifies which programs are most costly and can determine whether the benefits are sufficient to justify the cost.

Better Allocation of Resources. Provides the basis for effectively relating allocation of resources to goals and objectives. This enables resource allocation to areas that promise the greatest results and make the greatest impact.

Better Public Understanding. Tells precisely where the money is going and what various programs and their benefits cost.

Realistic Pricing for Cost Reimbursement and Fee Setting. Enables determination of what specific products and services cost, thus indicating feasible and realistic fee schedules and reimbursement costs when appropriate.

Essential Components of Program Budgeting

A full system of program budgeting in an organization relies on a number of major components of modern program management to make it work effectively. The components include:

Program Structuring. Program budgeting requires a program structure that can be reconciled with an organization's major organizational units.

Multi-Year Planning System. Program budgets usually require that multi-year plans be prepared and reviewed by top level decision-making authority. The most commonly accepted time frame is three to five years, although anything beyond one year is often acceptable. The multi-year plan should link each program to these items:

—stated goals and objectives;

—anticipated outcomes and accomplishments;

—identified resource requirements and sources; and

—established priorities.

Cadre of Designated and Trained Program Managers. The program budgeting system designates program managers with assigned responsibilities, preferably in writing, for coordinating and directing a particular program or programs. These program managers assume responsibility for the wise and effective use of the resources allocated to them. They are management executives variously designated as deans, directors, or chiefs; but usually they lack training in management.

Program budgeting requires that formal attention be given to the identification and recognition of the role of program managers. Ways should be established to incorporate their inputs into the decision and evaluation processes. The program budgeting system usually requires that program managers and decision-makers be supplied with data pertinent to the decisions they make.

System for Project Design, Review, and Approval. Program budgeting requires a system for originating, defining, planning, reviewing, and approving programs and projects.

Measures of Anticipated Outcomes and Accomplishments. Inherent in program budgeting is the measurement of outputs for comparison with inputs. By outputs we mean the measures that reflect results and performance. Inputs to programs are easy to identify: salaries, supplies, equipment, and the like.

Annual Budget or Annual Operational Plan. This reflects the financial and resource requirements of an organization's programs. The budget indicates:

—past year's actual expenditures;

—current year's estimated and actual expenditures; and

—next year's estimated expenditures.

Expenditures are listed by cost elements or "line items" for programs, objectives, or organizations. The annual budget seeks to reflect accomplishments for one year toward the multi-year plan. The multi-year plan provides the goals and objectives against which to assess progress and performance.

Program Feedback and Evaluation System. This component provides the data on what is really happening to your program as a basis for telling you how well you have done. The feedback system provides the data for assessing progress encountered in meeting goals and objectives and providing goods and services to an organization's clientele. A plan of special evaluation studies may be developed to probe and assess the changes that have occurred, the lessons to be learned, and the necessary adjustments to be made.

In summary, effective program budgeting requires a series of managerial components to be in place and working well, as follows:

—an organization and program structure that is clearly defined;
—a multi-year planning system that clearly establishes strategic direction, anticipated results, and resource requirements and priorities;
—a cadre of qualified and trained program managers;
—a system for project design, review, and approval;
—output measures of anticipated outcomes; and
—a feedback and evaluation system that indicates what is happening, the progress made, and problems encountered.

Major Tasks in Program Budgeting

A system of program budgeting includes managerial tasks that go beyond the financial considerations involved in computing program costs and income. The reason is simple. The program budget serves as the primary managerial instrument for dealing with the total span of management and accountability of program development and execution in an organization. The major tasks of program budgeting, in which the program manager should develop competence, are these:

—objective and goal setting;
—program cost determining;
—translating program budget into organizational budget; and
—designing central staff support for program budgeting.

ESTIMATING PROGRAM COSTS

Each program coordinator or unit supervisor is responsible for administering the budget process for the program activity under his or her jurisdiction. There are two simple tasks to master. One is to estimate the program costs and cast them into an "individual program budgeting schedule" for each program. The other task is to group and consolidate the program costs of a number of programs for which a particular organization unit is responsible and cast them into an "organization unit budget summary."

The Individual Program Budget Schedule

In essence, program managers are required to estimate their program expenses in advance of their disbursement. In most organizations a preprinted form is used, together with a set of instructions for its completion. The form presenting the program budget costs is designed to help the program manager develop the program budget and process its review and approval. In some situations, workshops and seminars are conducted for program managers who are new to program management responsibility.

Procedures for completing the program budget schedule are fairly simple. The largest item of expense for most organizations is the cost of salaries of the staff applied to the particular program being budgeted. Often staff do not work full time on any one program. It is then necessary to determine the percentage of staff time spent on the particular program. To make this estimate, the number of available work days in one year, that is, the total days less authorized holidays and weekends, is computed. In the federal government, the number of workdays for one year is usually 260 days. Then the number of days that staff will work on the project is calculated. If a staff member will work on the project for 130 days, then the budgeted time for that person will be 50 percent or half a working year.

In addition to the estimate of salary expenses, it is necessary to estimate all other expected expenses. To help calculate what expenses will likely occur in the program, the preprinted program budget schedule usually lists categories of expense as follows:

01	salaries (prof.)	09	transportation
02	salaries (clerical)	10	promotion
03	telephone	11	postage/freight
04	insurance	12	retirement
05	repairs	13	social security
06	equipment	14	rent
07	supplies	15	personnel training
08	outside service		

Help in making cost estimates can be found in previous submissions or in average cost tables often prepared by budget staff and made available to program managers as part of the budget process.

In many nonprofit organizations where income may not be ensured over the program duration, an additional column is included to cite the source and amount of anticipated income. The categories often used are these:

Income

01	membership	05	rent
02	group fees	06	vending

03   program fees   07   services
04   food services   08   contributions

Some organizations provide detailed instructions for prorating administrative, overhead, or fixed costs to particular programs. This normally should be done by support staff in appropriate staff offices such as accounting and budgeting; the burden for doing it should not fall on the program manager.

The Organization Unit Budget Summary

An organization is in need of knowing its program costs according to the operating unit responsible for its performance. Thus, after a program budgeting schedule is completed for each of an operating unit's programs, the unit executive is required to complete a consolidated program budget summary. This is done by grouping all individual program budget summaries into an organizational budget summary that includes all the programs under the operating jurisdiction of an organizational unit. This budget summary is again done on a preprinted format that lists all the pertinent programs and itemizes the key expense categories. For those organizations that include categories of income on their budget schedules, the organization unit summary adds columns that indicate whether there is a gain or deficit of the expense and income for a particular program.

WHAT TO EXPECT FROM CENTRAL STAFF SUPPORT

To be effective in an organization, program budgeting needs guidance and support from a central staff unit. This central unit can do five things:

—design the process for formulating, executing, and controlling the program budgeting system;
—educate personnel on how to carry out the process;
—provide essential data helpful to budget makers;
—review and evaluate proposals and approved programs; and
—take the lead in preparing for the chief executive the annual call for estimates.

Designing the Process

Central staff usually design the detailed budget process, including forms, deadlines, data flows, and review and approval requirements and procedures. This includes instructions and guidance for the annual call for budget estimates. Central staff work with top management to include the annual budget guidance for the entire organization and the policy guidance and assumptions that are to be made in developing program cost estimates.

Educating Personnel

It is very common for workshops and seminars to be conducted to help program managers and staff prepare their budget submissions. The training programs can quickly develop essential budget skills and serve as a delivery system for providing essential data helpful to program managers.

Providing Essential Data

The program budget requires a significantly greater amount and kind of data than required for the traditional line-item budget. The central staff unit can be very helpful in developing and furnishing data about current operations as well as past experience.

A helpful central staff unit could develop, maintain, and make accessible various information data banks that contain such data as:

—ratios, standards, and averages for calculating costs, such as case load, average productivity, or teaching load;

—performance data and indicators that can be useful in assessing performance effectiveness, such as anticipated outputs and outcomes; and

—comparative cost data, which include comparisons with past years, with other organizations, or with national averages.

The data bank must be updated and monitored to ensure that the information is timely and accurate and useful to the program manager. Unfortunately, this process is time-consuming and beyond the scarce time available to individual program managers.

Reviewing and Evaluating Proposed Programs

Central staff take the lead in designing and administering a process for the review and approval of proposed programs within the organization. Consolidated budgets of major operating units are usually approved at two levels: the top management policy level within the organization and a higher echelon of authority, such as the board of directors in a nonprofit independent-sector organization. Or, the budget could be reviewed by a central budget unit like the Office of Management and Budget, representing the president, or a central budget unit representing the governor or mayor, before being passed on to Congress or to similar authorities at lower jurisdictions of governance.

Preparing Annual Budget Guidance

Central staff prepare for the chief executive and the senior staff the annual guidance to the organization for the preparation of the program and organizational budget submission. Annual guidance offers significant trends having an impact on the organization, major directions the organization intends to go, and whatever guidance and instructions are essential to preparing realistic and effective program budget submissions.

USEFUL REMINDERS FOR EFFECTIVE PROGRAM BUDGETING

A number of points that have emerged from experience with program budgeting deserve careful consideration.

Time Constraints and Necessary Lead Time

Simply stated, the implementation of a new program budgeting system cannot be accomplished overnight, nor will a system be fully usable the first time it is put into practice. Sufficient time must be allowed to accumulate essential expertise and experience throughout the organization. Adequate time is required to:

—design a budget process, with its attendant forms, instructions, and policy guidance;

—conduct training programs for unit heads and their key employees and provide informal tutoring and counseling sessions as needed;

—increase the time allowed for budget preparation the first time program budgets are prepared to enable staff to ask questions and get help if needed; and

—consider a pilot or transition year to uncover "bugs and kinks" and errors in process or data and to generate competence and confidence in using the tasks and techniques of program budgeting.

Senior Commitment

It is necessary to secure the broad commitment of senior management staff to the fundamentals of program budgeting. They must be convinced of the need for a system and declare publicly their intention to use and support a program budgeting process.

Fear and Resentment

Many employees fear and resent the role and practice of the central budget authority. It is true that program budgeting does generate greater control of expenditures and stricter accountability. Most program persons would like to have their funds allocated and then to be left alone. No one seems to like the prospect of having a central authority, who usually has little program experience, making decisions that so vitally affect their programs.

The tensions that crop up between operating officials and program budget personnel are serious enough to merit special attention. One approach is to face the concern directly and attempt to reconcile differences before issues are magnified from inattention. One technique is to create an advisory task force on program budgeting to handle any special issues, concerns, or disputes on the new program budgeting process or substance. The task group could be composed of representatives of top management, program personnel, and budget personnel to promote active participation in the design and improvement of the program budgeting process. This would gain their active involvement and acceptance.

EXPERIMENTAL TRANSITION TO PERFORMANCE BUDGETING

As part of the Government Performance and Results Act of 1993, Congress has established the requirement that the director of the Office of Management and Budget evaluate the feasibility of a new kind of "performance budgeting." Performance budgeting would go further than program budgeting by including the dimension of performance measurement, with its emphasis on using measurable progress indicators against planned goals in the budgetary decision process.

The director would designate not fewer than five agencies as pilot projects in what is called "performance budgets" for fiscal years 1998 and 1999. Such budgets shall "present for one or more major functions and operations of a designated set of agencies, the varying levels of performance, including out-come related performance, that would result from different budgeted amounts." The law indicates that at least three of the agencies be selected from those previously designated to develop performance plans and performance reports in pilot projects for performance measurement.

The pilot projects to develop performance plans would establish performance goals for program activities and express such goals in objective, quantitative, and measurable form. The pilot projects would also establish performance indicators to be used in assessing relevant outputs or service levels and outcomes for each program activity. This would provide a basis for comparing actual program results with established program goals; performance reports would be required to compare the actual results with intended results expressed in planned goals.

After a reasonable period of accumulated experience, the director of the Office of Management and Budget will analyze the pilot projects in performance budgeting, and by March 31, 2001, will recommend to the president whether to include a performance budget to be required as part of the annual budget containing performance plans and performance reports.

The scheduled use of pilot projects to gain experience can provide a sound basis for determining the feasibility of requiring performance budgeting. But some observers already worry that the precision about program cost and workload performance measurement will provide ammunition to congressional and other enemies of specific programs that make it easier to identify work and budget amounts they wish to cut, as experience with previous programs in work measurement demonstrated. Other observers are critical in another direction; they fear that government downsizing both in agencies and in the Office of Management and Budget will undermine the capability for guiding and operating a technically demanding transition to performance budgeting.

21

Organizing Program and Responsibility Structure

DIVIDING UP THE TOTAL PROGRAM: DESIGNING PROGRAM STRUCTURE

An early and essential step in program management for an organization or a component thereof is to define and classify the primary areas of its functional responsibility into a series of program categories. When these program categories are added together, they constitute the total work program of the entire organization. The end product is called the "organization of the program structure" or, in simpler terms, "program structure." Program categories and any subcategories usually possess succinct descriptive labels that indicate the products and services of an organization.

Building Blocks of Program Structure Defined

What Is a Program? There appears to be general agreement among experts on the definition of a program. The following statement appears to be representative: A program is a group of interdependent or related activities conducted by an operating group that mutually contribute to the realization of a common goal or objective. Some experts refine the definition further by agreeing in general with the above definition but adding a second dimension to the definition in operational terms. They aim to clarify what programs are designed to accomplish by indicating that programs seek to create, continue, increase, or improve an organization's capacity to provide specific services or products to identifiable clientele. A third aspect is sometimes added to reflect the perspective of systems thinking. From the systems point of view, programs are "systems of action" to allocate and use resources. These resources, which are called inputs, are designed to stimulate activity that generates results in service or product. These results are called outputs, and thus you have the basis for doing systems analyses of the relationship of input to output or for performing cost-effectiveness and cost/benefit studies.

What Is a Project? Many people ask: "What is a project, and how does it differ from a program?" In many organizations, a program consists of a series of projects, that is, it is the larger arena of activity into which individual projects fit. In effect, a program is usually an aggregation of projects. But in other organizations, the words "program" and "project" are the same and may be used interchangeably. This book often uses "program/project" to indicate the lack of difference between the two terms in most situations.

What Is a Program Category? Grouping programs into categories establishes a program classification structure that attempts to place under a succinct caption those program activities that serve the same or similar goals or objectives. Program categories usually have subcategories to indicate that broad areas of functional activity need to be subdivided further to achieve a desired level of program management and accountability.

There are no exact or precise guidelines to follow in classifying program structure. Often the category designation is whatever best describes and communicates what the organization does to and for a target clientele group. In organizations that use a program budget, the program structure for an organization reflects its budgetary needs and therefore parallels the budget structure.

A program structure is never cast in concrete. It can and usually should be reviewed and revised as experience indicates. Experts recommend that the number of categories should be limited if they are to facilitate and be useful for top management review and control. But the number is never precisely defined. The answer to the query "How many is best?" often provokes the typical American response, "I.A.D.," that is, "It all depends."

Years ago, when the author was responsible for training officials from many third-world countries and the European continent, the customary practice was to debrief them before their return home. The final query was usually "What American management characteristic, feature, or notion impressed you most and may be most valuable to your practice of management back home?" The answer of one Middle Eastern official was stunningly simple and yet brilliantly insightful. He said that he talked to a wide variety of America's top management leaders in both government and the private sector as part of his scheduled on-site training visits during his stay in America. Before he met with so many American managers, his formal management training in the United States gave him so many great answers to his management problems at home. But whenever he asked the top management officials for answers to his management problems, they almost always responded with a three-word phrase: "It all depends." At first, he felt the American managers were not very smart, but then he realized they were saying something quite significant. He understood that there can be no absolute or universal answers to management problems; answers to specific problems depend on local situations and circumstances. Of course, management knowledge and experience can help guide management courses of action. But the ultimate response to a management problem is: "It all depends."

How Program Structure Is Used in Program Management

Program structure provides the basic framework for program managers to accomplish their jobs and defines areas of jurisdiction and responsibility. The steps undertaken in using program structure include the following:

Identify and Classify the Program Areas or Categories and Subcategories. Program areas best describe the major kinds of things that your organization does to provide its product and service. In addition to a listing of the major product and service, include those activities that are in support of primary programs such as administrative or institutional.

Designate a Program Manager for Each Program Area or Group of Categories. This provides coordination and supervision, which in simplest terms is program management defined.

Indicate That the Responsibility for Coordination and Supervision Covers the Full Range of Program Management Functions. The identification of these managerial responsibilities is often contained in written job descriptions; if not, they should be put in writing.

Assign Titles for the Program Manager Designation. They will vary in different institutional settings. For example, educational and health institutions resist the label of manager; they more often are comfortable with titles of "head, director, dean, or chair." Sometimes they use the designation of team leader, task force director, or project director. Industrial settings tend to use the designation of manager more frequently. But whatever the label, the range of managerial responsibility remains the same.

Although the program managerial responsibility may be similar in all institutional settings, the way that program management tasks are carried out usually varies from organization to organization. Some organizations use formal and complex program management systems that are precisely prescribed as to form, format, and working method. Others are less formal in that they avoid or seek to greatly simplify paperwork. The

degree to which program management tasks are formally prescribed depends, of course, on the scale of size and cost of a particular program
and the general significance of the results desired. The greater the extent
to which large amounts of money and people are involved and results
are important to the organization's top management, the more likely it
is to encounter formal and intensive paperwork requirements and review
processes.

Examples of Program Structure

A most widely known and accepted program structure in the area of
higher education is the one proposed by NCHEMS/WICHE. The acronym
stands for the National Center for Higher Education Management Systems and the Western Interstate Commission for Higher Education (Ohio
Board of Regents Management Improvement Program 1974a, 30–31):

Primary Programs

1.0 Instruction
    1.1 General Studies
    1.2 Technical Education
    1.3 Baccalaureate General
    1.4 Baccalaureate Professional
    1.5 Master's Program
    1.6 Graduate Professional
    1.7 Doctor's Programs
    1.8 Medical Programs

2.0 Organized Research
    2.1 Institutes and Research Centers
    2.2 Individual or Project Research

3.0 Public Service
    3.1 Departmental Continuing Education
    3.2 Organized Extension Continuing Education
    3.3 Organized Extension Community Service
    3.4 Campus Community Service
    3.5 Agriculture Extension Service

Support Programs

4.0 Academic Support
    4.1 Libraries
    4.2 Museums and Galleries
    4.3 Audio/Visual Services
    4.4 Computing Support
    4.5 Auxiliary Support

5.0 Student Services
    5.1 Social and Cultural Development
    5.2 Supplementary Educational Service

5.3 Counseling and Career Guidance
5.4 Financial Aid
5.5 Student Support
6.0 Institutional Support
   6.1 Executive Management
   6.2 Financial Operations
   6.3 General Administrative Services
   6.4 Logistical Services
   6.5 Physical Plant Operations
   6.6 Faculty and Staff Services
   6.7 Community Relations
7.0 Independent Operations
   7.1 Institutional Operations
   7.2 Outside Agencies

A second example illustrates the simpler program structure of the American Heart Association's National program, as reflected in its *Goals and Subgoals: Fiscal Years 1978–82* (1977):

Program Categories

1. Research

2. Professional Education

3. Community Program

4. Public Relations

5. Fund Raising

USING TRADITIONAL CONCEPTS OF ORGANIZATIONAL STRUCTURE

Program managers need to know how to design organization structure and understand the pattern of structure around them. This means knowing how authority and responsibility are formally distributed into patterns of hierarchy to accomplish specified goals and objectives. In simplest terms this answers the query: Who is responsible to whom for what area of responsibility? This is commonly called "organization structure."

Organizing Concepts Identified

Five organizing concepts govern the design of traditional organization, sometimes referred to as "functional organization." These concepts provide particular characteristics to an organization.

Specialization. Individuals assigned to a job are given concentrated duties and responsibilities requiring a specific or specialized set of skills and knowledge. That is why traditional or functional organization is commonly described as organizing work into "related bundles or packages of skill."

For example, looking at an organization chart, you will note that the chart has boxes containing key related functions such as finance, personnel, and training or program services. People working in organizational units with these labels are given specific, concentrated, and related duties requiring special skills or knowledge.

Clear Vertical Authority. This defines superior/subordinate relationships from the top of the organization down to the lowest level. At the top of the structure the ultimate source of power is identified. Throughout the organization, the lines of authority create a pattern of hierarchy, and formal channels of communication are delineated.

There is a principle of management important to the traditionalist that calls for "unity of command." It states that every subordinate should have only one superior to whom he or she is directly accountable and through whom orders and directions should flow. The unity of command concept helps every employee know to whom they should listen and who is available for guidance, consultation, and support.

Defined Horizontal Relationships. These are the linkages and contacts among peers, colleagues, and fellow workers who normally have no authority over each other. They tend to be somewhat equal in terms of authority and influence. These relationships among equals tend to create difficulties in situations where a worker's job depends to some extent on what others do and yet the worker has no authority over the others' behavior. If they cooperate, that is fine. But if they do not, the ensuing problem must be resolved by taking it to higher levels of authority.

In many situations, work requires a high degree of interdependence among units and employees. Close cooperation is needed to get the job done on time and to enable differing types of experts to work together. If the necessary cooperation is not forthcoming, the use of new or special team devices like project organization or task forces may be justified. These team structures are discussed later.

Clarification of Program and Support Relationships. As organizations grow, they tend to establish units of "staff support" specialists, which are usually analytic or service-oriented in nature. They are advisory rather than decision-making. These staff specialists usually perform support tasks such as planning, budgeting, accounting, and personnel. They are usually assigned or available to support and service program officials who are called "line officials." As program "line" officials, they are placed in positions of direct flow of authority within an organization's hierarchy of power. Thus, program managers tend to be decision-makers; staff support specialists tend to be advisors.

The organizing concept is that staff specialists are established to serve program managers by performing tasks for which program officers lack the specialized knowledge or skill or the time to perform. In the smaller organization, program managers usually perform the tasks of staff specialists in addition to their own. Larger organizations almost always have units of staff specialists who are available to advise and work with program officials. In some situations, staff specialists may actually be loaned or assigned temporarily to a program manager in special project or task force arrangements.

Workable Span of Supervision. Formal organization structure determines the number of individuals or units who are responsible to a particular manager. The primary concern is that not too many units or individuals report to any one program manager. The reason is that each of the program manager's subordinates should have sufficient time and attention for guidance, consultation, and support from his or her superior.

The span of supervision is never a precise number; an old-fashioned "rule of thumb" is that the number should be less than seven. Actually the number depends on the best calculation of the time and attention needed by each subordinate. Factors to consider are:

—similarity or dissimilarity of functions performed;

—geographic or physical nearness or distance;

—level of complexity or simplicity of functions performed; and

—need for direction, support, and guidance by subordinates.

Strengths of Traditional Organization

In essence, the traditional organization structure does provide a number of strengths to the organization. Primarily it is a stable organization where everybody has the security of a "home base" to which they are assigned on a permanent basis. This secure assignment offers each person a clearly defined work environment where assigned tasks are clear, reporting and accountability channels are simplified, communications and decisions tend to follow the chain of command, and power and authority are formally defined. Traditional structure thus provides a more permanent environment where technical and professional personnel update and refurbish their professional competencies and catch up on developments in their respective fields.

What Are the Weaknesses?

Although traditional organization is widely prevalent throughout government, the private sector, and the nonprofit world, its weaknesses and limitations are often clearly apparent. But weaknesses are not necessarily fatal flaws. They need to be understood in terms of their consequence and impact on one's ability to meet goals and objectives. If the weaknesses are serious and if organizational problems continue to persist, they often can be resolved within existing organizational arrangements by initiating newer team devices like project organization or task forces, or process reengineering and new information technology. These are some of the weaknesses common to traditional organizations:

Excessive Specialization. Traditional organizations concentrate their specialists to gain the advantage of specialization, but this can have disadvantages. One important one is that few specialized individuals can see the overall picture and thus adequately appreciate or understand other approaches or perspectives. It is often hard for specialized individuals or units to know or appreciate how other functions fit into an organization's higher mission. This situation can be dramatically expressed in terms of hospital organization, where a specialized doctor in a field like thoracic surgery may differ with the decision of an oncology cancer specialist. In many situations the high-technology scan x-rays can be interpreted differently or are not definitive. Does the patient go with the surgeon to start exploratory surgery or allow the cancer specialist to start radiation therapy? Unfortunately, in medicine there is no patient manager or coordinator who reconciles and coordinates diverse specialists. The family doctor or the internist could do so, but in practice they do not or will not. They almost never have the authority to coordinate or reconcile.

Narrow specialization often promotes a sharp competition for resources. Each specialist feels that his or her specialty deserves the highest priority in acquiring resources. The conflict among specialists often throws the decision up to higher levels where the individuals are too far removed from the reality of their decisions.

Insufficient Coordination. Many situations and problems involve more than one unit or function. Someone has to see to it that coordination and consultation occur to assure proper involvement of the right people and the dovetailing of interdependent activities and tasks. One way organizations try to cope with multiple unit involvements is to set up committees. But committees tend to proliferate in attempts to improve coordination. This situation worsens as the organization grows larger and more complex.

Inadequate Communication. Often there is limited provision made for horizontal communication. More often communications go up and down in an organization, but less frequently do people in organization units keep their horizontal colleagues—those at their level—fully informed. It takes time and effort, which are scarce, and there is little reward for doing so.

Limited Opportunity for Sharing. Traditional organizations, which are organized on functional lines, have limited opportunity to share resources, people, and ideas because each functional unit becomes its own complete identity and becomes very competitive and protective of its resources and "turf." Such organizations can degenerate into a series of feudal kingdoms that try to exist on their own, go their own way, and in effect live apart from the organization.

Overly Centralized Decision-Making. Functional organization tends to push decision-making up the hierarchy of power. The very shape of functional organization—which is narrow at the top and wide at the bottom—often pushes decisions away from operational centers to higher levels because they claim that only people at the top see the entire organization and its full interests.

But centralized decision-making has three possible disadvantages that a program manager must be careful about.

1. Time delay: It delays matters to push decisions up for action and then wait for the decision to be made and transmitted back.

2. Lower-quality decision: Often operating people know more about local circumstances affecting the decision than do officials at higher levels. Thus, when decisions are finally made they may lack direct relevance to current problems. Or, decisions at higher levels may be made for special political or economic reasons or may be adversely influenced by special viewpoints or interests of higher-ups or board members. These reasons and influences may be at the expense of effective program performance.

3. Diminished job satisfaction and hampered employee growth: When jobs are limited in decision-making authority, they fail to respond to employee wants and needs for growth.

Fragmented Service to Clients. This is a very serious limitation. Specialized groups, who each work on a particular set of services, may often be only a part of the service a client needs. This compels the client to go to different places, at different times, to get a problem solved or their needs serviced. There often is much referral of clients to other people and places, but it takes a tremendous effort and increased time and cost to get this done.

One device that is increasingly used in the human service organization is the information and referral system or office that undertakes the job of referring clients or service providers to other places to obtain needed service. There is increasing interest in establishing "one-stop centers" akin to the supermarket in the food business.

Excessive Levels of Review. In a hierarchical structure, there often exist intermediary levels of review between the operating personnel and high-level decision-makers. Sometimes certain middle-management levels can be justified, where continuing review and coordination creates demonstrable program benefits. More often the intermediary level of management creates problems of extra paperwork requirements and meddling interference that make it more difficult for program officials to do their job. A constant complaint of people at the operating program level is that they waste too much time responding to queries and prods from people who are too far removed from the reality of their specific job situation and yet not high enough in the hierarchy of power to make decisions.

NEWER ORGANIZATIONAL THINKING AND PRACTICE

In an era of profound change and severe financial stringency, rigid and outmoded organizational structures are substantially changing. The pressures for speed dictate reductions in decision response and processing times. The frequency of change compels flexibility and agility. The availability of new information technology enables units and individuals in diverse locations to communicate more easily among themselves and with outside customers and suppliers—at times, almost instantaneously.

In response to new realities, newer patterns of organizational redesign are coming into wide use; their characteristics are:

—flatter structures with fewer levels and less pyramidal hierarchy; these structures tend to eliminate and transform what's left of middle management;

—fluid structures that are temporary and shifting; they include projects, teams, alliances, and joint ventures and involve staffing arrangements that include temporaries, part-timers, flex-timers, and contractors: they all encourage flexibility to accommodate the need for constant adaptation to change; and

—reengineered lateral processes that cut across, integrate, and improve horizontal and interdependent tasks; these processes when redesigned enable units and individuals to work together on sequential tasks to pursue and achieve higher quality, decrease processing times, increase cost-effectiveness, and raise customer satisfaction.

Reducing Management Layers

Too many layers of organizational structure is an important cause of slow management response to changing conditions and resource constraints. Excessive layers clog the gears of change. Current thinking by experts like Tom Peters recommends that no more than five layers of management are necessary regardless of organizational size. Otherwise, "Good intentions and brilliant proposals will be dead-ended, delayed, sabotaged, massaged to death, or revised beyond recognition or usefulness by the overlayered structure at most large and all too many smaller firms" (Peters and Waterman 1982). It is difficult to cite any particular number of levels, other than the general admonition that fewer levels are most desirable.

As middle managers are caught in the squeeze for reducing layers of structure, they are slowly beginning to be recognized as the people who can make an organization's strategic initiatives work. Middle-level program managers, those who are left, are changing their role and becoming strategic program managers. They are the ones who implement strategic intent and directional goals. Although goal-directed, they are action-oriented; their program management is fast-paced and flexible in response to strategic initiatives. The review and control they do is for their own program and action plans. They operate as teams of expertise assembled for specific tasks.

The pressure to limit the number of layers tends to be accompanied by a desire to cut central staffs and assign more of their functions to program action groups. This produces a state of anxiety for central strategic planners as their role changes to advisor and facilitator to line program managers. One national nonprofit organization capitalizes on the trend of an expanded strategic role for decentralized program managers by providing a qualified strategic planning consulting service to the line managers of local affiliates, at modest fees for a one-time consultation or a continuing one.

Using Fluid and Temporary Arrangements

Organizational arrangements are becoming transitory, flexible, and constantly changing. Ad hoc projects, task forces, or teams are formed to handle specific tasks or problems as they arise and then are disbanded or modified as situations change. Mergers or strategic alliances and affiliations are accomplished to work together for particular goals and objectives, whether it be to gain a government contract, enhance distinctive competencies and competitive advantage, or generate savings through efficiencies of scale.

Staffing of an organization is becoming more flexible. When Charles Handy predicted that by the year 2000 half of the working population would be working outside the traditional organization, people thought it absurd. But by 1994, more than 35 percent of Americans in the work force are either unemployed or are temporary, part-time, or contractual workers; the number is more like 50 percent in Europe (*Fortune*, October 31, 1994).

Handy's idea of a shamrock organization, which is being widely practiced, develops a blueprint for identifying core activities and hiring "core workers" and outsourcing everything else by using temporary employees, part-timers, or contracts, as work and workload ebbs and flows. Workers are encouraged to think of their current job not as a career but as just one part of a lifetime pattern of wages, contracts, charity work, and study, with the possibility of consulting and teaching.

Reengineering Lateral Processes

The movement to reengineer processes, most popular in the private sector, is being applied widely in government and gradually is finding its way in the nonprofit organization. Processes are simplified to meet the contemporary demands for quality, service, speed, flexibility, and lower cost; this is the theme of reengineering. Processes in organizations tend to become complex, costly, and time-consuming. Though reengineering has no set formula or recipe, some recurring ideas of approach are apparent (Hammer and Champy 1993):

Several Jobs Are Combined into One. Often one person is assigned as "process manager," who is the single point of contact for the steps in the process. This person may do the entire process, if feasible, or be responsible for the end-to-end process and outcomes and works with others on process activities.

Workers Make Decisions. Rather than go up the hierarchy for decisions, workers make more of their own decisions. They are encouraged to make continuous lateral improvements in processes that save time and effort. Work processes are sequenced so that there is the most natural flow to achieve greatest speed, highest quality, lowest cost, and best satisfactory outcome for the customer.

22

Using Team Structures

A number of organizational structures have emerged over the years to remedy the limitations and weaknesses of traditional functional organization. These structures are variously labeled "project organization" or "task force." As organizational units, they tend to be small in size. Small groups of persons are made responsible for achieving clearly defined results. They operate with greater than normal independence from the levels of organizational hierarchy. Experience indicates that results take less time and tend to be more creative.

Organizations of the future, experts predict, will be greatly "atomized" into smaller team groups. Much, if not all, of their work will be done in teams that are somewhat independent and self-reliant. The IBM corporation pioneered the "team oriented" approach with units called "independent business units" to handle specific tasks such as developing and marketing a new personal computer. It grants these units funds and has them report back, but it gives them more freedom than its established divisions and terminates them when their mission is complete. IBM, like many other corporations, uses the team device to handle a great number of tasks that may be transient but require a variety of skills and expertise that must be drawn from different units that are independent of each other. When IBM installs a large computer system in an account over a weekend, to keep its disruption to a minimum, it draws talent from all pertinent organization units to establish an installation team. A team leader is appointed and the required installation planning is completed and assigned. The intent is to get the job done quickly with the least number of possible flaws and problems.

In essence, the team structures deal with new tasks or issues that span the responsibilities of several units or levels or fall between the neat lines of bureaucratic responsibility. In these situations it is often not clear who should do what and certainly is not clear who should take the initiative or act as coordinator and leader. Setting up the new but temporary team structure with a designated leader can meet quickly any real need that does not fall clearly into one of the organizational boxes of the functional organization.

Many excellent organizations today expect their program managers to bring the right people together in a team arrangement when the conditions are ripe for such action. Being busy is no excuse to avoid participation in a team effort in many successful organizations; teamwork is an expected work style.

WHEN TO USE TEAM STRUCTURES

The question often arises: What conditions prompt and justify the use of team-oriented structural arrangements? The structures have no available cookbooks that contain precise recipes governing their creation and establishment, but many helpful fundamentals drawn from experience do exist. The essential point to know is that traditional forms of functional organization, which tend to be overcentralized in command and control, tend to cope inadequately with fast-moving and quickly changing situations. Even the frequent response of creating decentralization tends to be insufficient.

Certain conditions occur in the work situation that do underscore the limitations and weaknesses of traditional functional arrangements. Those conditions, which seem to respond effectively to team structures, are:

—required high quality end product: when one must attain a high quality end product in a limited period of time within specified budgetary resources;

—complex problem-solving: when one attempts to solve new or complex problems;

—rapid response needed: when a rapid response to a problem situation or emergency is required, when consequences grow more serious over time, or when extremely tight deadlines must be met;

—need for experimentation and innovation: when experimentation with innovative ways of doing things is necessary; and

—urgently desired client satisfaction: when client satisfaction is an absolute must.

UNDERSTANDING THE TEAM APPROACH

When establishing a team-oriented structure like project organization or a task force, members of teams are brought together to work on interrelated tasks designed to achieve clearly defined results. The ideal is when team members know what to do and how to work well together. Be aware that whenever you create a project group or task force, you essentially are establishing a structure that depends for its success upon teamwork.

Characteristics of the Team Approach

In recent years the extensive use of team efforts has produced a pattern of characteristics that can easily be identified. Team efforts are usually:

—small in number of members;

—diverse and different in terms of members' background, skill, and knowledge;

—formed by members drawn from various parts of the organization or, in special instances, members selected from the outside;

—a group that works together on a specific and defined task;

—a group whose members work on tasks interrelated to tasks of other team members;

—a group that reports to a leader, however labeled;

—a group that tends to be flat in hierarchical structure of power with no superiors or subordinates; often there may be seniors and juniors working together with a focus on task, not on authority;

—temporary in duration as a team effort, with starting and completion times established; but its team mission may be a continuing one; and

—targeted to a client or customer, inside or external to the organization.

Potentially, the team effort aspires to be fairly self-sufficient and independent of close supervision. It tends to do the full spectrum of the managerial framework of functions—from planning to implementation, and sometimes evaluation. Small team efforts can be fast moving, with a bias for getting things done at a high level of excellence and with dispatch. When they work well, they can be effective in harmonizing a group's interaction to achieve great results.

The hospital setting offers a splendid example of the team effort. Good examples are the surgical team for by-pass surgery or even the out-patient clinic. The structural unit is the team or group mobilized from the medical services for the needs of an individual or group of patients. The team leader is the designated physician, with other members supplying different skills to be drawn upon as needed.

Strengths of the Team Approach

A Shared Big Picture. Everybody knows the work of the whole, its over-all expected result and outcome, and accepts responsibility for it. They all share in the contribution to success. It thus overcomes the functional insulation and parochialism of only looking at one's fragmented piece of action and being inconsiderate of other's interests in achieving the end result. Assuming responsibility for total outcome and feeling a share in its success creates greater commitment, pride, and a disposition to work well with others. And, of course, success begets success.

For the sports fan, just think of your favorite team and speculate how it puts into practice the essentials of the team approach. The generalities of management language will come to life. It will also highlight that "structure" is an insufficient condition without "strategy" and "game-plan."

Receptivity to Innovation. Team approaches are highly receptive to new ideas and new ways of doing things. When what we are trying to do is something that has not been done before or is something we do not know how to do, we need to identify and mobilize those particular skills that can help us innovate. Often we do not know when and where the particular skills will be needed, nor do we know for how long or in what volume. We need the flexibility of a team structure.

Weaknesses of the Team Approach

No Automatic Organizational Clarity. The team effort does not possess clarity of objective, roles, or relationships unless the leader creates it. If the leader is poor, heaven help us!

High Managerial Effort. Team efforts require a high level of managerial effort to make them work. By this we mean that a team demands continuing attention to its management processes in such ways as:

—defining and clarifying relationships among team members;

—assigning members to jobs and clarifying what the job entails; and

—communicating to ensure that personnel understand their role and job, and carry it out well.

Thus a large amount of effort from all members is expended keeping things running. The team must work constantly to explain to itself and to others in the organization a number of essential things, such as what it is trying to do, what it is working on, and what it has accomplished.

Instability. Teams are temporary and essentially unstable. This can be a strength if you are trying to innovate and do things differently. But the temporary nature of the team effort often makes it difficult for the careers of team members. They may not have a job to go back to when the temporary team effort is concluded. Or they may be overlooked when opportunities arise in their career progression if they stay away from their home base too long.

Why Do Teams Fail? And They Do!

Primarily, teams are disappointments because they do not impose the self-discipline required to compensate for the flexibility and freedom characteristic of carrying out the team task. This is true whether one is engaged in a new way of doing things, problem-solving, or attaining a high quality product within a limited time frame. Lacking are the usual guidelines for responsibilities, roles, and relationships. They must all be carved anew and rearranged until grooves and channels are set. Not all people are able to work in such unstructured and unfamiliar circumstances; many people find it difficult to cope with such freedom.

The greatest limitation is size. Teams work best with a limited number of members. Peter Drucker, in his wisdom, refuses to give precise numbers, but he does go back into history to note that the early aborigine hunting bands numbered five to fifteen persons. He further notes that the sports teams of today contain limited numbers: baseball, nine; football, eleven; and basketball, five. They perform with a limited but specified number of substitutes and support staff.

What Can We Conclude about Organization Structure?

First, realize that there is neither a universal nor a perfect design principle, as experts like Peter Drucker tell us. What the experts do agree on is the need for organizational simplicity. The simplest organization structure that will do the job is the best one.

Second, what does emerge from the growing use of team-oriented efforts is that they are not a full substitute for the traditional functional organization. Most organizations will use both approaches simultaneously. The functional organization with its hierarchy of power remains the basic organizational mode. But the establishment of teams is used frequently to compensate for the limitations in traditional functional structure. The organizational issue of the future will be when and how often it will be necessary and justifiable to use the team-oriented structures. We realize that team structures make for complications in organizations, but they do have substantial rewards when properly created and used.

GUIDELINES FOR DESIGNING A TEAM

To be effective as a group, each team's design should pay attention to these guidelines:

—Clear and sharply defined objective: The objective of the team must be clearly understood by each member of the team, and must guide the work of the whole team.
—Leadership: One person is designated leader for making decisions and giving commands.
—Clarity of individual role and contribution: Members of the team must know exactly the nature of their role and what tasks they are expected to do and when.
—Clarity of group's interactions and interdependencies: It is important for the group to know how the group will interact, and which interdependencies are critical.
—Entire group responsibility: It is important that the entire group assume responsibility for the whole task and final outcome above and beyond their individual role and contribution.
—Easy and informal communications: Group effectiveness depends on the ability to communicate directly and quickly, which maximizes face-to-face contact and minimizes formal reporting.

Of course, the team leader is the person who must ensure that the above guidelines are clearly understood by each member of the group and that they are effectively put into practice.

CHOOSING AMONG TEAM ALTERNATIVES

When the overall or parent organization decides to initiate a new activity that meets the prompting conditions for using a team structure, it can choose to organize from among several structural alternatives. It can:

—assign the new responsibility to an existing organizational unit;
—set up a separate single-purpose project organization unit; or
—establish a temporary task force.

Use of Existing Organization

The existing organization can choose to pick one of its units to take responsibility for planning and carrying out the new activity. In that situation, the newly designated leader would have to obtain the cooperation of the various other organizational units to handle support functions such as personnel, accounting, and procurement.

Possible advantages include:

—specialized personnel already on board can be used;

—personnel and equipment available in the parent organization can be shared;

—if new workload is small in relation to regular workload, it may be squeezed in by being absorbed by current staff;

—participation in new activity can increase skills;

—integration of staff of new activity into existing organization is easier after activity is ended.

Possible disadvantages include:

—current staff may not be oriented to cope with innovation, change, uncertainty, and pace of the new activity; and

—new workload may be large in relation to normal workload, and new work or regular work may suffer.

Setting Up a Separate Project Organization

A second alternative is to set up a separate single-purpose organization unit to plan and carry out the project. One key advantage is that the leader is free to choose members of the team for their qualifications and suitability without being restricted by the staffing and procedures of the parent organization. If the leader chooses staff from the current organization, they usually sever their connection for a set period.

The possible disadvantages include:

—recruitment may be difficult because of the limited time of employment;

—procedures have to be established anew;

—it is more difficult to tap the experience of the parent organization; and

—it is difficult to integrate project staff back into the parent organization when the project terminates.

Use of Task Force

A task-force organization may be created to plan and carry out a temporary activity that demands a degree of urgency. Personnel from functional organizations are assigned to the task force on either a full-time or priority part-time basis. In most cases, they continue to receive administrative support from their home organization. In some cases task-force personnel are on loan to the task-force director and operate completely under his/her direction. Usually task-force personnel follow their regular "home" or parent organization's way of doing things, even though they are under the task-force leader's direction. As potential conflict is extremely probable, it is essential to clarify how things are expected to get done.

The advantages include:

—rapid establishment, and
—flexibility in operation and ease of modification to meet changing conditions.

The disadvantages include:

—difficulty guiding and controlling the activities of a task force arrangement for a large program;
—an inefficient way to manage a long-term effort; and
—more difficulty obtaining support from functional organizations for task-force arrangements.

The task force is most suitable for small or medium-size activities that can be accomplished in a limited time, normally less than six months.

Part 7

LEARNING FROM EXPERIENCE

23

Controlling and Monitoring Performance

WHY CONTROL?

Nobody likes controls. The very word "control" bothers people, and it should. It suggests obedience and conformity. But controls are necessary to make program management work.

Up to this point in the program management process, the emphasis has been on a set of intentions to guide future behavior such as determining goals and strategies, setting objectives, developing action plans, and preparing program budgets. The common characteristic of these tasks is that they are plans for action to take place in the future. They are not actions, only guides to action.

But plans and intentions, even when beautiful and elegant and conceived by the most qualified staff, do not automatically self-execute. But they can self-destruct. The reason is obvious: Plans depend on people and external events, and both can be uncertain and unpredictable. The ideal condition is to provide adequate assurance that work is done properly as planned and in timely fashion. Setting controls is the realistic way to do this.

So often things go wrong: people make mistakes or get sick and are not available. Or they are in conflict with schedules or other events they must attend. Family requirements intervene; rain or snow can act as deterrents. No one can anticipate all problems, blockages, or obstacles despite the most strenuous effort to do so. No matter what we do, experience tells us that things can and do go wrong. In fact, folk culture has labeled the perennial problem condition "Murphy's Law," whereby "whatever can go wrong, will."

Because many of the "wrongs" can create serious trouble to the success of a program/project, the wise and prudent course is to set up management controls to provide timely feedback on what is happening, or not happening, to know what problems are happening or likely to occur. This makes it possible to keep on track the actions we plan and to establish contingency plans, or just simple alternatives, to handle the unexpected that does go wrong. A simple example is to set up alternate dates or places for an outdoors art exhibit in case of rain.

Management controls in program management have only one reason for their existence: to alert us when we are about to get into trouble in sufficient time to take necessary corrective action. The essence of the control approach focuses on measures to provide early warning signals and the raising of "red flags" to alert us before trouble hits. The controls are designed to anticipate and prevent problems as much as possible, rather than wait until someone or something has "messed up" and the damage is done.

Unfortunately, in too many situations, managers disregard problems as being the "normal way things happen around here" until strong client response forces corrective action to be taken. In effect, they expect the client to do their management job, and too often they get away with it. But remember what happened to the American car industry with its poor quality and multitudinous problems. It suffered financial disaster. The Japanese car industry penetrated the American market with superior quality cars and forced an American response. American car producers that deliver verified "quality" and "customer satisfaction" are reaping just rewards.

USE OF THE TRADITIONAL CONTROL MATRIX

The tendency of some quality-conscious program managers is to attempt to control everything in their quest for excellence. But it is not feasible in time or cost to exert control in every situation. Total control would frustrate everyone with excessive reports, meetings, and paperwork. Rather, the issue is how to selectively determine where to put control emphasis to get a quality job done and yet do it within reasonable amounts of effort compared to the benefit gained.

To do this, we suggest the use of a "control matrix" to help understand what control entails and to serve as a guide to the key steps in carrying out a program control process. The control matrix, adapted from a discussion of control by George L. Morrisey (1977) divides into two parts. Part One is devoted to the elements of what to control: time, resources, quality performance, and quantity. Part Two focuses on the steps constituting the control process: establishing standards, monitoring performance, and taking corrective action. Part One of the matrix is contained in Exhibit 23.1; Part Two of the matrix is contained in Exhibit 23.2.

Exhibit 23.1
Matrix of What to Control: Part One—Elements

ELEMENTS	Likely to Go Wrong	Why	How and When Will You Know	What Will You Do
1. TIME				
2. RESOURCES				
3. QUALITY PERFORMANCE				
4. QUANTITY				

Exhibit 23.2
Matrix of How to Control: Part Two—Process Steps

Establishing Standards	Monitoring Performance	Taking Corrective Action
Specify:	Use:	Determine:
—end results	—charts	—self-correction
—time frame	—staff meetings	—intervention
—measurable	—reports	—further examination
	—inspections	—revised standards
	—walk arounds	
	—progress reviews	

WHAT TO CONTROL: ELEMENTS

We first examine our objectives, program design, and plan of action to reveal what it says or implies about the four basic elements that are important to control: time, resources, quality performance, and quantity. We aim to identify and anticipate problems that will require corrective action regarding one or more of these basic elements.

To avoid scattering your efforts, concentrate on identifying only those problems which are most serious in consequence and where the payoff for corrective action is the greatest. This is referred to as "concentration on the critical few" rather than being preoccupied with the "trivial many." Be concerned with those problem situations where a substantial investment of time, energy, and talent produces the greatest contribution to the program's objective and end result.

For each basic element, ask these fundamental questions:

What Is Likely to Go Wrong That Is Critical to Success?

Do not attempt to identify all problems; rather, identify what is most likely to happen and only those deemed critical to your program's success. It is not necessary to set up controls for minor problems because they can be treated as a normal part of monitoring and supervision.

Why? What Are the Probable Causes?

Knowing why something went wrong and its probable causes is important to its correction. Some attempts have been made to place the causes of problems into categories. The category labels are not important. Use them only if you find them helpful in probing for problem causes and taking corrective action. Following are some categories of probable causes:

Uncertainties. These are judgments of reasonable expectations of the future that are, of course, subject to wide fluctuation and change. We make our best projections, forecasts, or predictions and thus make judgments of what will likely occur. But there can be no assurance that the estimated or assumed will take place. These events are beyond the control of the program manager. Examples of uncertainties include such items as absenteeism, accidents, errors, or emergencies affecting workload.

Unexpected Events. These situations are not reasonable or probable expectations, but do create significant consequences that justify the existence of contingency plans when they occur. Unexpected events might include acts of nature, such as storms or floods, loss of a major supplier, or death of a major executive.

Failures. These causes are problems that are beyond the control of the accountable program managers but have an impact upon their work. They could include computer breakdowns, inability of staff to supply necessary work components on time, or failure to get required approvals.

Human Errors. This is the situation where human performance, under the jurisdiction of the program manager, goes wrong. People make mistakes all the time. It could be an "honest error," which can happen from time to time among the best of us. Or it could be "incompetence," where a pattern of errors occurs that indicates willful or gross negligence or an inability to perform the work.

How and When Will You Know?

It is important to calculate in advance the means whereby you will be able to know what is going wrong quickly and with the least expenditure of time and effort. Two process steps discussed in Part Two of the control matrix are designed to accomplish the earliest and easiest identification of problems. One is the establishment of standards or indicators, and the other is the systematic monitoring of performance and identifying the variance from standards.

What Will You Do?

After you know what problems will likely occur, the question is what corrective actions should be taken and in what time. Potential corrective actions must be concrete and feasible so that they can be quickly accomplished. They should work so that people will get accustomed to achieving fast results.

HOW TO CONTROL: PROCESS STEPS

In Part Two we focus on how to carry out the control process by taking three fundamental steps:

—establishing standards or indicators about what is likely to go wrong that is critical to the program's success;

—monitoring performance against the standards by which we observe what is happening and how work is progressing in an effort to spot variance from the standard; and

—taking corrective action to ensure the achievement of planned objectives and end results.

Establishing Standards

In our attempt to gain control, we are concerned with developing standards as gauges by which we can measure performance in achieving objectives. The standards give us something to measure against. Unfortunately, standards are imperfect units of measurement; in fact, there are few "perfect ones," particularly in the public and nonprofit sector. Everyone realizes the limitations of many standards by which we are measured in life, such as grades in school or even "SAT" scores, which are scholastic assessment tests. Yet we tend to tolerate and use them because they have practical utility, although we seek to make the measuring devices more relevant and valid.

Without some type of standard or indicator, there is no clear way of knowing whether we are achieving our objectives. It is easier to accept the limitations of standards when we realize that they are primarily indicators or "red flags" to cue us to potential problems.

Measurable indicators are often expressed as one of the following:

—Numbers: as in hours or units.

—Dollars: as in costs or revenues.

—Percentages: as in errors, defects, or breakage.

—Time Lapse or Lag: as in preparation time or backlog.

—Episode or activity unit: as in a contact, a treatment, or an interview.

—Material unit: as in a meal or a finished product.

—Completion point: as in milestones accomplished or problems overcome.

Standards, to be effective gauges of performance, must be both understood and accepted by the three organizational levels most concerned with the particular program's performance: the responsible program managers, their superiors, and their subordinates. Since the subordinates do most of the work toward achievement of the objectives, it is neither fair nor realistic to expect them to meet performance standards that they do not understand or are unwilling to accept. An effective way to gain understanding and acceptance is to secure active participation of those affected in setting the standard prior to its approval.

Monitoring Performance

Monitoring performance is defined as "determining actual versus planned performance." In the program management approach, there can be no valid program measurement without recourse to the built-in indicators contained in the preparation of program plans.

A variety of feedback and monitoring mechanisms can be used effectively and adapted to gaining timely information to achieve program control. Some of the most commonly used are:

Visual Devices, Charts, and Graphs. These are often favored to express control information. Simple visual displays that are used frequently are Gant Bar Charts or Milestone Event Charts.

Written Reports. Regular written status or progress reports are frequently required. But they tend to be widely resented and often the least useful of the feedback mechanisms because of the time and cost involved in preparation and reading. When and if used, they should be brief (one or two pages), outlined rather than long narratives, and prestructured so that only essential information is presented.

Staff Meetings. These are useful devices to help program staff communicate with the boss and each other. But as a control device, they are often inefficient because staff have trouble keeping to the main topic and rarely want to publicize their problems or variations from agreed-upon standards.

Periodic Progress Reviews. A necessary ongoing control device is the periodic progress review that can be conducted monthly, quarterly, or for whatever period is important to the program cycle. The program manager can be informed of progress or problems and in turn is in a position to notify superiors of program progress or any serious problems.

Taking Corrective Action

As we mentioned earlier, the only reason for controlling as a management function is to enable us to take the corrective action to ensure the achievement of our objectives. This does not necessarily mean that someone has done something wrong or is incompetent. We should clearly realize that performance standards are best estimates; some variation is to be expected. The important thing is to know what to do, not whom to blame.

Three kinds of corrective action can take place when you have determined that action is appropriate:

Self-Correcting Action. Some variances from standards are acceptable in that they tend to work themselves out over time. For example, a low weekly output of placements in nursing homes, from a Veterans Hospital, could balance out over a month or two. Or, low output by a staff member can be self-corrected as soon as the information is available to all concerned. If not corrected, then intervention may be necessary. If an individual knows what is expected and is informed factually that performance is inadequate, then it is wise to give sufficient time to permit self-correction before intervening.

Operating Action or Intervention. When corrective action is necessary, you can allow the responsible staff member to do the operating work that constitutes the corrective action. Or you can do it yourself. Or you can get technical assistance from within or without the organization. It is desirable to enable the responsible staff member to make the corrective action so that learning and development can take place.

Revision of Standards. This kind of corrective action leads to a survey that examines the management activities that developed the standard, such as the setting of objectives or devising time schedules or action steps. The aim is to decide whether the standard or indicator needs revision and, if so, to make the necessary modification.

KEY QUESTIONS FOR EVALUATING CONTROL MEASURES

To assure that the control measures are effective means to identify the significant variances against planned performance requirements, these are some key questions to ask:

Are the significant problems that can impact the success of the program likely to be identified by the monitoring devices selected? Or should several of the devices, like the reports, visual charts, or progress reviews, be prestructured to focus directly on the main standards and their possible variances? This could assure that main events and schedules are monitored and that data are fed back into reviews.

Does the control method identify the problem in sufficient lead time to enable timely corrective action to be taken? Finding out something is wrong when it is too late to do anything about it is a waste of everybody's time and can undermine the entire control effort.

Are the time and effort required to identify problems justified by the value received? You should carefully consider how much time and effort are involved when you, as manager, ask for feedback on any element of program performance. Written reports can take much effort when perhaps a brief face-to-face verbal report may suffice. Control measures rarely should exceed 5 to 10 percent of a manager's monthly man-hours. Every effort should be taken to simplify and curtail the extent of written controls.

Is there a danger of overcontrolling? Are the controls producing a negative impact? Staff tend to resent the person who is always looking over their shoulders to find something wrong. How much controlling is excessive certainly depends on the situation and the consequences of error. Be sensitive to the negative morale and resentment engendered by overcontrol and the stifling environment it creates, which can thwart innovation and creativity.

Another dilemma of overcontrol is that it can delay getting the job done. So much time can be taken in reviews and safeguards that the main job is seriously impaired. Sometimes a fair risk of variance can be undertaken to get on with the job and make corrections as they are indicated.

NEW THINKING: ARE CONTROLS ACCEPTABLE AND ACHIEVABLE IN AN AGE OF EMPOWERMENT?

A fundamental problem facing managers is how to exercise adequate control in organizations that are working to expand their flexibility, innovation, and creativity. Some say control and creativity are not compatible in the new liberated managerial culture, where employees are increasingly being empowered to decide and do more on their own. They are urged to be entrepreneurial in search of higher quality at lower cost; they are encouraged to make process improvements and to do more to respond to customer needs and expectations. Yet employees are expected to do these creative things—somehow—in a controlled, systematic way. Difficulties have begun to surface.

Consequently, some organizations are moving away from the traditional fundamentals of control as performed in the 1950s and 1960s, when managers exercised control by telling people precisely how to do their jobs and then monitored them constantly to avoid surprises. New managerial paradigms are emerging to ease the apparent tension between control and creativity.

The Broadening of Control: Emergence of a Creative Control Grid

Organizations recognize that they face a fundamental issue: What do you do to reconcile the tension between creativity and control? The concern is that controls set too narrowly and monitored too closely hamper innovation and creativity and generate much resentment and resistance among employees. Tools are emerging to reconcile the conflict. Robert Simons (1995) points out that measures and standards that measure progress against achievement of goals and objectives are only one element of control. If you wish to be effective in achieving control but not to hamper creativity, three additional ways are important. Suggested is the use of a blend of four levers of control.

Diagnostic Control Systems. The first lever is the "diagnostic control system," or use of critical performance variables, which builds clear targets and standards of performance that can serve as indicators of performance progress. The diagnostic system of performance variables, which most closely resembles traditional control systems, enables the organization to scan and detect what can go and is going wrong and yet keep performance within preset or expected limits. Managers monitor goals and targets and measure progress toward benchmark standards. Feedback enables managers to adjust inputs and processes so that results match goals, objectives, and benchmark standards.

Diagnostic control systems are proving to be of help, but they are not sufficient to assure effective control. Managers claim that they create pressures that can lead to control failures. Dangers arise when managers are held accountable for performance goals and then empowered employees go off on their own to achieve them. Studies indicate that some employees display exemplary performance, but others abuse the system.

What sometimes happens is that employees under pressure of demanding goals become "creative"; they manipulate financial and production data by false accounting entries to enhance their reported performance. It became apparent that additional levers of control are necessary.

Belief Systems, or "Core Values." The second lever is the use of core values as belief systems. Organizations have long used belief systems that articulate the values and directions that top managers desire their employees to embrace. They draw employee attention to core values about levels of performance with statements about "pursuit of excellence" and how individuals are expected to behave in their internal and external relationships, such as having "respect for the individual."

Statements of core values promote commitment to an organization's belief systems. The managers who use their mission and core values to guide patterns of acceptable and desirable behavior discover a powerful level of control.

Boundary Systems, or "Risks to Avoid." This lever specifies and enforces the rule of the game; it helps employees do right under pressure or temptation. Conventional wisdom tells us not to engage in negative thinking, but experts tell us of the power engendered by negatives. They suggest: Tell them what not to do rather than telling them what to do. This allows innovation, but within clearly defined limits.

Boundary systems are stated in negative terms or as minimum standards of ethical behavior and codes of conduct. They indicate activities that are "off-limits" and underscore what risks to avoid. They make clear the line between acceptable and unacceptable behavior; they forewarn of what is likely to go wrong. In effect, core beliefs inspire, promote, and commit, while boundary systems provide the constraints to organizational behavior and protect against potentially damaging behavior.

Interactive Control Systems, or "Concern for Uncertainties." Interactive controls track data about strategic uncertainties, identify major patterns of change, and encourage creative ideas to resolve outstanding issues. New information technology makes access to such strategic data much easier and enables employees throughout the organization to share constantly changing information that affects their decisions and operations in matters of strategic importance to the organization. This promotes dialogue and discussion to encourage organizational and individual learning and change.

The interactive control system operates in these ways:

—identifies patterns of changing information and trends that top managers have identified that will affect the success of the organization;

—ensures that the information is significant enough to demand frequent and regular attention from operating managers at all levels of the organization;

—arranges for the data generated to be communicated and interpreted in face-to-face meetings of superiors, peers, and subordinates; and

—serves as a catalyst for an ongoing review and debate about underlying data, assumptions, and action plans.

Collectively the four levers of control reinforce each other. They provide measures of effective control that guide employee behavior, but provide proper limits and boundaries to avoid the dangers inherent in promoting creativity and empowerment.

24

Evaluating Program Performance in a Learning Organization

THE WHAT AND WHY OF EVALUATION

Evaluation is a systematic means of finding out how well you are doing the things you set out to do and the probable reasons for their success or failure. It usually is a deliberate, scheduled, and analytical process that seeks to accomplish specific aims. Its primary purpose is to examine systematically what you have been doing in the past or what you are now doing in order to improve your performance in the future. It searches to identify lessons learned and makes them available for use in current or future planning. It tries to provide the basis for better informed decisions that can resolve issues of continuing, modifying, expanding, contracting, or terminating program activity.

Why Do People Resist Evaluation?

People frequently are afraid of evaluations. In part because they seem so difficult, complex, and time-consuming—and sometimes they are. But also they are resented because evaluations often have negative and punitive connotations. Unfortunately, evaluations are used to punish people whose programs do not measure up to expectation. This is regrettable, for the evaluation process should be viewed as a constructive effort to develop information and knowledge that can guide action to bring about program improvement. As program managers gain practice and experience in the conduct of evaluations, like all other management skills, they will become competent and confident. Evaluations will become easier to do, particularly if top management provides the positive perspective of evaluation as a knowledge-building activity for program improvement rather than one of punishment.

What Does Evaluation Do?

As a basic management tool, evaluation helps to improve programs by providing answers in three dimensions: effectiveness, efficiency, and significance.

Questions regarding effectiveness include:

- Is the program fulfilling its purpose?
- Have we reached our goals and objectives?
- Are we moving in the right direction?
- Should we change our priorities?
- What are reasons for success or failure?
- What lessons did we learn for the future?

Questions regarding efficiency—a matter of how much effort and money are used to achieve a beneficial result—include:

- Do the benefits gained justify the cost and effort?
- Are there more efficient ways to achieve the same goals and objectives? By more efficient we mean less costly, less complex, or less time-consuming.

Questions regarding significance—a matter of providing a greater benefit than the specific output—include:

- Does the program make a significant difference to anyone, or could it disappear without a ripple?
- Will the output produced contribute to a greater economic or social advantage of the target clientele served? For example, if learning English is an output, is there evidence that the learning of English by the foreign-born helped them get a better job or eased their cultural adaptation to American customs and practices?

What Is an Annual Evaluation Plan?

The experts suggest that every organization should have an evaluation plan. But what you evaluate and how much and when depend on local conditions and available resources. Evaluation does take time and effort and cannot just be fit in as another thing to do on one's busy schedule. It takes planning and considerable effort to do it well and requires top management support to enable the resources to be mobilized and to provide assurance that the evaluation results will get a fair hearing.

Being required to prepare an annual evaluation plan compels you to face up to the dilemma of what to do about evaluation. The issue is to decide what to evaluate and when. You cannot do everything each year. Certain matters are normally evaluated each year, but others can be staggered over years. Yet others require evaluation at certain periods each year. Some can be fit into varying times when you and staff are the least busy.

The annual evaluation plan will recommend to higher authority what you plan to evaluate and when. It will request approval and any resources essential to its performance. Normally, an evaluation plan will schedule performance appraisals for both individuals and organization units to be conducted annually. In some organizations, an annual plan will also select certain clientele and evaluate their impact and response to specific programs and services.

Additionally, the organization should take at least one program or project and examine its performance in terms of its effectiveness, efficiency, and significance. This is what is called an ad hoc or special program evaluation study. If resources were unlimited, and they never are, it would be ideal to evaluate all programs and projects in depth. But this is not realistic.

Be selective, choose an area of work that is important, and fit its evaluation into your schedule so that it will prove to be the least disruptive to an already burdened schedule. In large organizations, programs and projects are evaluated every year. If programs are not subjected to intensive evaluation, they receive some degree of review as part of the program budgeting process.

PERFORMANCE REVIEW AND APPRAISAL

Employees and managers at all levels have a legitimate need to know how their performance compares with their superior's expectation. This is a powerful way to communicate between manager and employee and develop a commonality of shared responsibility and direction. But too often the performance appraisal activity takes a negative turn and generates a vast amount of fear and hostility. In the absence of feedback on how one is doing, unsatisfactory performance can continue. Or misunderstandings and resentments can fester and even grow worse. The review and appraisal process must be handled well to gain its advantages and not provoke unnecessary embarrassment and irritation.

Common Inadequacies of Performance Appraisals

A number of criticisms have been directed at current efforts at appraisal. In fact, no one seems to be happy with the appraisal process they are subjected to in their organization. Some of the common inadequacies follow:

—Judgments on performance are usually subjective and impressionistic. They often reflect one's feelings toward another person rather than an objective review based on concrete performance data.

—Ratings by different managers are usually incomparable. What is considered excellent by one manager may be seen as much less so by another. People do have biases and prejudices.

—Managers are urged to give performance feedback freely and often. But raters often tend to procrastinate and delay their feedback because they wish to avoid the emotional confrontations that might occur when criticism is offered.

—Raters may not have the time, nor do they always take the time to do a thorough review and appraisal. Ratings therefore are often superficial and do little to improve work performance.

Guidelines to Performance Review

Admittedly, review and appraisal are difficult activities to do. There are no easy answers; but experience does provide some helpful guidelines:

Guideline 1. Base the review of performance on objective data that reduce the personal bias. Tailor the data directly to the work to be performed. Use the following techniques as a more objective basis for performance review:

—Clearly defined written job description or task list.
—An agreed-upon set of objectives and work plan.

These techniques will enable the appraisal to be an objective assessment of results achieved rather than just a subjective assessment of personality traits.

Guideline 2. Avoid performance appraisals that depend solely on personal traits or qualities of personality. Work traits and qualities are often used and can be helpful, but when used alone they tend to produce defensiveness and hard feelings. People resist and resent comments on their personal behavior. They find it hard to change their work behavior based on generalities; it is hard enough to change even with specific data. When people are rated on personality traits, they tend to "clam up," which precludes adequate feedback and discussion. It is decidedly preferable to relate performance to work behavior that is results-oriented, measurable, observable, and understandable. That is another good reason for taking the time to set objectives and work plans that do contain clear-cut results in measurable, time-bound dimensions. Of course, the process is made easier if the objectives and work plans have been pre-

viously accepted by the person being rated. If that person also participated in setting the objectives and work plans, then the task is further
simplified.

Guideline 3. Make the performance review interview a constructive
work session. Do it face-to-face in four parts:

—Review progress. Ask what progress has occurred. Compare progress to date
  with results specified in set objectives and work plans.

—Discuss current problems. Ask what are the main problems. Help to resolve
  key problems that are blocking progress toward achieving objectives.

—Do future planning. Ask what changes or revisions in any element of the objectives or work plan are necessary. Come to agreement on any changes to be
  made. This is an opportunity to ensure that objectives and work plans are
  realistic and feasible and tied to actual work performance.

—Do staff development planning. Identify and discuss activities to be undertaken during the year to improve performance and contribute to the employee's growth and development. Include, if possible, training opportunities
  and professional conferences.

Guideline 4. Restrain from "zapping" your assistants. Make the appraisal interview a positive one; avoid sharp confrontation and excessive
criticism. Make the session one of genuine interaction, rather than a one-
sided attack.

—The executive role should be one of openness and receptivity by listening,
  responding, counseling, and advising. It should not be one of aggressive in-
  terruption and continuous chatter. Take time to really listen. Let there be a
  true interaction of points about objectives and work plans and the work and
  problems involved. Allow some give and take to occur in settling differences.

—Try to build a feeling of shared responsibility and common experience. Build
  a common framework of contribution to shared goals and objectives and values. It is "we" and "us," not "you" or "I."

—Recognize and commend progress and results. Practice short, succinct praising.
  People appreciate sincere commendation and will flourish in a positive environment.

DESIGN OF TRADITIONAL EVALUATION STUDIES

Evaluation studies are in-depth analyses of ongoing or completed
strategies, programs, or projects that are examined for their effectiveness,
efficiency, and significance. Since they can be undertaken for a variety
of reasons, it is important that a number of key questions be asked initially to clarify the study's basic design.

- What is the study to be done?
- What is to be learned?
- Who wants to know?
- How is the study to be done?
- Where is the study to be done?
- When is the study to be done?

The answers to these questions will help to shape the study design to reflect realities.

Criteria for Designing a Study

Evaluation studies help management make decisions. Therefore, you should keep in mind these criteria:

Objectivity. Evaluation activities must keep subjectivity to a minimum and be based upon objective evidence. Otherwise they will not be taken seriously.

Timeliness. Evaluation studies must be available to decision-makers on a timely basis so that they can take meaningful action.

Operationally Useful. Findings and conclusions produced by the study must be useful to decision-makers.

Understandable. The study's substance and conclusions should be written so that they can be understood by users of the study's results.

Validity. The design of the study should provide for the identification, collection, and processing of reliable data.

Steps in Designing and Conducting an Evaluation Study

You will find familiar many of the early steps in designing an evaluation study. They have been identified and discussed along with previous functions of the program management process. This is another reminder that the program management process is an integrated set of managerial functions that are interdependent. For example, evaluation is a managerial function that depends on the goals, objectives, work plans, program plans, and so on of other functions of the program management process. You measure progress against the standards previously set as the management process unfolds. If no goals, objectives, and program plans exist, it is necessary to develop them; otherwise there can be no objective basis for assessing progress.

The first four steps of an evaluation design tell what the strategy, program, or project is all about:

—define the need or problem;

—determine goal and objective;

—identify target clientele group; and

—establish evaluation criteria (or indicators of progress).

Normally, these steps will have been taken by program managers as they performed their managerial role in such functions as setting objectives, designing program or project plans, and devising work plans and milestone events. They all have been previously discussed. But if your organization does not do these things, it is necessary to develop them for the particular program you intend to evaluate.

The next three steps pertain to the conduct of the designed evaluation study:

—identify data needed, sources, and collection methods;

—arrange for data collection; and

—analyze and interpret data for findings and conclusions.

The final step is to prepare the evaluation report and arrange for its presentation, in which you specify progress, indicate constraints and problems, and propose forward action.

Useful Checklist for Designing an Evaluation Study

The following checklist for planning an evaluation study is excerpted from the *Evaluation Handbook* of the United States Agency for International Development:

Objectives

—What is the study (not program) objective?

—Does the study have a potential for providing new (and needed) information? A new Method? Technique? Procedure? Policy?

—Will the final results be important or significant for the program or project?

Methods

—Are the techniques, instruments, or modes of inquiry appropriate to the study design?

—Will the methods require adaptation to local conditions?

—Are there sampling problems?

—If interviewing or opinion-survey techniques are to be used, have the questions been reviewed for meaningfulness in local language and culture? Good taste? Religious connotation?

—Will the methods gather more data than are required? Less? That is, are they efficient, economical, and effective in terms of the goals of the study?

Data Processing

—Are the procedures for the statistical manipulation of the data stated clearly? Is there a clearly conceived plan for the analysis that will be done once the data have been collected?

—Have statisticians or ADP system experts been consulted regarding the programs to be used?

—Are the analytical procedures likely to produce meaningful statements?

Analysis and Interpretation

—Have a wide variety of potential findings been considered?

—Does the logic or design of the study permit clearly stated generalizations?

Costs

—Are the costs for the evaluation study reasonable for the various categories (personnel, travel, supplies, overhead, etc.)?

—Are there luxury or unnecessary items in the budget?

—Are the total costs proportional to the scope or importance of the study? Is the study worth the investment? Will the study cost more than the study might save?

General

—Will the study answer the questions it set out to answer?

—Will it produce explicit and usable results?

—If it is not completed, will there be salvage value?

—If the study is completed—THEN WHAT?

(U.S. Agency for International Development 1972, 40)

ANALYSIS AND INTERPRETATION OF EVALUATION FINDINGS

A common dilemma confronts the evaluator after volumes of data have been produced about the program. On what basis do you decide what is good or bad? We all have been exposed to numbers in findings—say, fifty interviews have been conducted this month—but is this enough? How do we really know, when there is no absolute standard of perfection of program effectiveness available to us?

To test and measure the effectiveness of a program or project beyond the achievement of its immediate objectives, it is necessary to have a basis or rationale for judgment. To help develop a creditable rationale and to be able to defend it, we must realize that the essence of evaluation is "change and comparison." What we attempt to do is discover what changes have taken place as the result of a program or project. We then assess the changes we have identified by subjecting them to a series of comparisons.

To provide a basis for assessment, we provide three rather simple modes of analytic design that have one characteristic in common: they are all based upon comparison.

- Model A: Before and After Comparison.
- Model B: Comparison of Planned Versus Actual Performance.
- Model C: Comparison with "Ideal" Standards.

Model A

The basis of Model A is a comparison of program outputs at two points in time. It thus requires collection of data at two ends of a continuum; one is before a particular point in time, and the other is after a particular point in time. You may wish to collect data to develop time trends over the months or years between the two points in time. The line between the two points represents what effect the program and its objective have on the data.

The steps in this simple model are:

—collect relevant information for the "before" part of the study, commonly referred to as "benchmark" data;

—collect relevant information for the "after" part of the study;

—compare the two sets of data; note the trends; and

—seek reasons to account for the differences.

Model A can be illustrated thus:

TIME   TIME

X ———————————————————————————————— Y

Program

Model B

This model is based upon a comparison between what you planned to accomplish and what you actually accomplished. This model also requires data at two ends of a continuum. You plot the starting data, when the program initiates, at one end. The planned output is plotted at the other end of the continuum that constitutes the date of the program's completion or a preselected time period.

In this model the steps are to:

—establish objectives to indicate planned performance;

—select appropriate measures of progress;

—collect data to indicate actual performance;

—compare actual performance with planned performance as reflected in objectives and measures of progress;

—seek reasons to account for the differences; and

—draw conclusions.

Model B can be illustrated thus:

TIME   TIME

X = Actual _____ Y = Planned

Program

Model C

This design is different in that actual performance is compared with ideal or external standards as opposed to standards set by the organization itself. Ideal standards reflect the consensus of external groups, whether they be governmental or professional. Examples of external standards are those that may be set by the United Way for agencies that receive its funding or those set by the government in its regulations. In this model, the ideal standards are a substitute for planned program objectives.

In summary:

Model A tells us how a program is doing now compared to some previous time.

Model B will tell us how close a program is coming toward meeting its planned objectives.

Model C will tell us how well a program is doing compared to an accepted norm.

PREPARATION OF AN EVALUATION REPORT

An evaluation report can be prepared in many formats. It can be formal, with a detailed content outline and a written report. Or it can be rendered informally, with a brief oral presentation at a staff meeting. This discussion on evaluation reports is designed for those situations where a formal report is expected.

Your report could affect important decisions about your program's future. Just remember that decision-makers are busy people and will appreciate reading well-organized, easily understood material that is succinctly summarized. Narrative summaries or abstracts are helpful necessities. One influential decision-maker once asserted, "Give me your findings and conclusions on one page, and I'll read the report if I have to."

Outlines of evaluation report content are never standardized. Funding agencies often prescribe their own content requirements, and organizations often have their prescribed format and content traditions. The evaluation report, in addition to a front cover or title page, usually contains five sections, as follows:

- Section 1. Summary
- Section 2. Background Information Concerning the Program
- Section 3. Description of the Evaluation Study
- Section 4. Results
- Section 5. Conclusions and Recommendations

The front cover or title page provides the following for identification purposes:

- Title of the program and its location
- Name(s) of the evaluators
- Name(s) and titles of people to whom the report is to be submitted
- Period covered by the report
- Date the report is submitted

Section 1: Summary

The summary is a brief description of the evaluation report that explains why the evaluation was conducted and lists its key findings and conclusions. Recommendations for follow-on action should be included. In some situations, a detailed implementation plan is also included.

Section 2: Background

This section describes how the program was started and how long it has been in operation. It states the goals of the program and describes what was intended to be accomplished.

Section 3: Description of the Evaluation Study

This section sets a frame of reference for the study and clarifies its intent and limits. Also contained is a description of the methodology for the study. Sometimes the methodology is detailed in an appendix or a concluding section.

If the evaluation was designed to provide information for a particular decision or a focused set of issues, then this should be clearly stated. Who is conducting the study should also be included.

Section 4: Results

This section offers the findings and outcomes of the data collected and analyzed and the investigations undertaken. In effect, this is what the evaluation found out.

Section 5: Conclusions and Recommendations

This section presents the conclusions that are to be drawn about the effectiveness, efficiency, and significance of the strategy and program. Uncertainties should be indicated. Recommendations for any modifications should be briefly and succinctly stated. In some situations, the implementation plan is made part of the section on conclusions and recommendations.

CREATING AN ORGANIZATION OF LEARNERS

Overcoming Learning Disabilities

The decade of the 1990s made clear that many organizations, like some children, have learning disabilities. They fail to learn enough from experience, despite the presence of traditional program evaluation studies. This does not suggest that you immediately stop doing evaluations as a waste of time and money. What is meant is that traditional, one-by-one evaluations are necessary but insufficient to learn from experience; they do not provide enough understanding to deal successfully with a rapidly changing world. One reason is that organizations break work and problems apart to make complex tasks more manageable. They act as if the world was made up of separate, unrelated forces. This makes for easier program management, but the cost is that they lose the sense of the "big picture." They often fail to see the interactions of their fragmented actions and the consequences and are not able to grow, change, and respond when they must.

Many successful organizations now operate as "learning organizations." They take steps to understand the interconnections of the forces that affect them and continually strive to learn what to do and how to deal with them.

These learning organizations no longer have one person and the top team learning for the entire organization, with everyone else following the top strategists. Learning organizations work to create learners from all persons at all levels. They create an organization where people "continually expand their capacity to create the results they truly desire, ... and are continually learning to learn together" (Senge 1990). Working together they learn how to produce extraordinary results.

The Learning Organization Movement

Spearheaded by Dr. Peter Senge and colleagues at the Center for Organizational Learning at MIT's Sloan School of Management, a movement has emerged for understanding what makes for organizational learning and for developing a worldwide community of organizational learning practitioners. A new type of management practitioner is emerging, they believe, that combines personal learning with broader collective learning action in organizations.

These new practitioners are learning to apply five "component technologies" that converge to create learning organizations. Each technology is developed separately, but in concert with the others each adds an important capability that enables organizations to learn and flourish. The fundamental technologies, or disciplines as they are labeled, are discussed in *The Fifth Discipline: The Art and Practice of Learning Organizations* (Senge 1990). The strategies and tools for building a learning organization are contained in *The Fifth Discipline Fieldbook* (Senge et al. 1994). The *Fieldbook* shares more than a decade of experience of learning-organization principles and methods for creating learning organizations.

Systems Thinking

This first component technology stresses that events that may be distant in time and space may be connected and have an influence on the others. These interconnections are usually hidden from view. Senge says that you can only understand the whole picture or the system by contemplating the whole, not any individual part of the pattern, and by discerning the parts' significant influences and relationships.

Be aware that human efforts are also systems, bound together by interrelated actions that affect others. We tend to see and focus on pieces, or snapshots, of isolated parts of the system, which is what particular individuals or groups are doing. It is hard for us to know what is really happening among all the players in the game.

Systems thinking as a body of knowledge, with new tools that have been developing for the past fifty years, can be of help. Experience shows it can be learned. In fact, some people are talented "linkage masters" in that they readily discern the interrelationship of diverse forces. They can detect problems and consequences, exploit opportunities, and rapidly mobilize information and expertise for solutions. The *Fieldbook* discusses a number of the tools and methods for achieving constructive learning and change, many rooted in the "system dynamics" understandings developed by Jay Forester at MIT over the last forty years.

Personal Mastery

This component discipline is considered the foundation of the learning organization for an important reason: an organization's ability to learn can be no greater than that of its employees. Personal mastery encourages each of an organization's individual employees to grow and learn; they are urged to commit to lifetime learning that enables them to take action and realize the results that matter to them.

Personal mastery seeks to clarify and deepen vision, urges the focus of energies, develops patience, and strives to see reality objectively. These noble aims are demanding but not impossible.

Organizational learning practitioners approach personal mastery as a "discipline" that offers a series of practices and principles that can be learned and applied. Not surprising, few persons develop full personal mastery, with the daily distractions and disruptive immediate events that take priority. Yet experience shows personal mastery offers many potential rewards to individuals and organizations.

Fostering personal mastery in an organization cannot be forced or compulsory. But leaders can serve as role models and reinforce the idea that personal mastery is valued in an organization.

Mental Models

Experienced managers realize that many best ideas never get put into practice. Organizational learning explains that new insights often fail to move into action because they conflict with people's view of the world, that is, their "mental models." Images held in a person's mind of how the world works limit us to familiar ways of thinking and acting and cause us to resist new approaches that may lead to better results. This happens even when pilot project experiments demonstrate superior results from the new approach. The mental models determine how we take action. They affect what we do and what we do not do, because in part they affect what we see. What we see shapes how we act. But one problem with mental models is that they can exist below the level of awareness. If they remain unexamined and unchanged long after the conditions have changed, the mental models will no longer reflect reality. This can have serious consequences; it freezes organizations in outmoded thinking and practice. A dramatic example is what happened in the automobile industry in Detroit. The mental models of automotive decision-makers reflected the American desire for style, long after they began to lose market share to vehicles from abroad that offered performance quality and controlled cost.

Now that we know that mental models can impede learning, the emphasis is on the use of mental models to accelerate learning. Large business organizations have taken the lead. Royal Dutch/Shell helps its managers clarify their assumptions and discover contradictions or outmoded images. They were able to think through new strategies based on new assumptions and to design scenarios of alternative future trends. The new strategies proved very useful. But what also emerged was a new set of shared mental models that enabled decision-makers the flexibility to feel they could question their own views of reality and change them when necessary.

The Hanover organization (one of the best performing companies in the property and casualty insurance industry today) approached organization learning a bit differently. Their approach combined vision, values, and mental models; the aim is to bring people together to develop the best possible mental model to face any situation at hand. They gradually identified a set of core values, particularly "openness," "merit," and "localness," as an approach to managing mental models.

"Openness" they considered to be the answer to the problem of "playing games" that concealed real views and motives that often served self-interests and hurt the organization. They emphasized the "merit" of making decisions in the best interests of the organization rather than reflecting bureaucratic politics where the object is to get ahead and gain personal advantage. As the values took hold, the belief evolved that decision-making processes could be vastly improved if people became better able to discuss their different ways of looking at the world.

Hanover soon realized that people learn most when they possess a sincere sense of responsibility for their actions and believe that they can influence the circumstances under which they live. This recognition compels organizations to extend the maximum degree of authority and power from the top levels of organizations. It means moving decisions down the organization hierarchy and giving local decision-makers the freedom to act, to try out their own ideas, and to be responsible for producing results. The move to extend power and flexibility out to local decision-makers they called "localness."

Changing people's mental models and action patterns and putting the new values into practice have been difficult to do. But organizations like Hanover are convinced that their substantial investment in developing skills and appreciation of mental models and inculcating values like openness, merit, and localness have produced substantial benefits.

Shared Vision

A fourth discipline, shared vision, is vital for the learning organization; it gives focus and energy to learning. Organizational learning practitioners mean by "shared vision" a compelling idea that creates a commonality of purpose that pervades an organization and gives coherence to diverse activities. For the learning organization, it is expected that shared vision generates and expands the ability to create. When the vision is compelling, people become excited about what they truly want to accomplish.

"Vision" is a familiar concept today in institutional management. But all too often a statement of vision is conceived in the front office and imposed on an organization. Although this may work, writing a vision statement can only be a first step in building shared vision. For a shared vision to be really effective, it must be one that many people are truly committed to because it reflects their own personal set of values, concerns, and aspirations. Visions do not become an organization's vision until they become connected to the personal visions of people throughout the organization. One man's vision that worked was President Reagan's view that "government is the problem, not the solution." One may not agree with its accuracy or merit, but it has been powerfully effective because it really resonates with the mental models and values of vast multitudes of people.

Shared visions, when they take hold in an organization, accomplish many things: they uplift people's aspirations; they exhilarate; they compel acts of daring and courage. They can change employees' relationship from "their organization" to "our organization." Shared visions foster experimentation and risk-taking; they promote a commitment to the longer-term. Organizational learning practitioners offer a tempting set of inducements.

The discipline to "build shared vision" entails four dimensions familiar to those working with strategic planning:

An Image of the Future. This presents a picture of the future you wish to create. It states where we want to go and what it will be like when we get there.

A Code of Values. This governs how we will behave—with each other, our clients, and our community—on our journey to the future.

A Longer-Term Mission or Purpose. This represents the fundamental reason for the organization's existence. It describes what we are here to do together.

A Set of Realizable Goals. This identifies what people commit themselves to do. Goals pinpoint the directions to take and specify what changes are to be made.

Team Learning

Progressive organizations have increasingly begun to use teams for mobilizing diverse efforts to get their work done. The team players must know how to work together. We recognize this quality on the playing field when we see our favorite football team win when they all play well together at their peak performance or lose when some members fail to do their part.

Team learning is becoming the process for developing the team's capacity to create the results its members truly desire. Many important decisions are now made in teams, or teams are used to translate decisions into action. How the team learns to do its job can be crucial not only to the team's success but also to the organization's strategic concerns.

Team learning within organizations has five essential dimensions. One is the need to think insightfully about complex issues. This is not an easy task but one that is becoming extremely important, as public and nonprofit organizations are compelled to deal with increasingly complex issues in an environment of profound and rapid change with severe financial constraints.

A second dimension is the need for innovative and coordinated action. Outstanding teams achieve states of "operational trust" wherein they complement each other in dependable, competent ways.

Third, there is the need for teams to develop the skill to work with and through teams. More often, senior executives make decisions in teams but then get other teams to carry out the decision.

A fourth dimension involves mastering the practice of dialogue and discussion in working teams. This involves a "dialogue" of free and creative exploration of complex and subtle issues, a deep listening to one another, and suspension of one's views. Also involved is "discussion," a different mode of conversation, that presents and defends ideas in a search for the best view to support decisions that must be made at this time. Team learners are aware that the free-wheeling mode of "dialogue" differs from the taking and rejecting of positions in "discussion."

Team learning practitioners cite the experience of a famous scientist, Werner Heisenberg, formulator of the Uncertainty Principle, who claims that conversations with others had a profound effect on his learning. He recalls the power of collaborative learning, where "collectively we can be more insightful, more intelligent than we can possibly be individually."

Bibliography

American Council of Voluntary Agencies for Foreign Service. *Evaluation Sourcebook for Private and Voluntary Organizations*. New York: 1983.

American Heart Association. *Goals and Subgoals: Fiscal Years 1978–82*. Dallas, TX: 1977.

American Red Cross. *Program Administration Participants Workbook*. Washington, DC: 1976.

———. *Corporate Planning: Corporate Direction 1979–85*. Washington, DC: 1978.

———. *Executive Summary: Strategic Plan, FY 1987–88–FY 1990–91*. Washington, DC: 1987.

Ansoff, Igor H. *Strategic Management*. New York: John Wiley and Son, 1979.

Barry, Bryan W. *Strategic Planning Workbook for Nonprofit Organizations*. St. Paul, MN: Amherst H. Wilder Foundation, 1986.

Belasco, James A. *Teaching the Elephant to Dance: Empowering Change in Your Organization*. New York: Crown, 1990.

Bennis, Warren G. *Beyond Bureaucracy*. San Francisco: Jossey-Bass, 1993.

Bennis, Warren G., and Bert Nanus. *Leaders: Strategies for Taking Charge*. New York: Harper and Row, 1985.

Berg, Norman A. *General Management: An Analytical Approach*. Homewood, IL: Richard D. Irwin, 1984.

Bielefeld, Wolfgang. "Funding Uncertainty and Nonprofit Strategies in the 1980s." *Nonprofit Management and Leadership* 2, no. 4 (Summer 1992).

Business Week. "The New Breed of Strategic Planners." September 17, 1984, 62–78.

———. "Who's Excellent Now?" November 5, 1984, 76–88.

———. "Middle Managers: Are They an Endangered Species?" September 12, 1988, 80–88.

Carver, John. *Boards That Make a Difference: A New Design for Leadership in Nonprofit and Public Organizations*. San Francisco: Jossey-Bass, 1990.

Cohen, Steven, and Ronald Brand. *Total Quality Management in Government: A Practical Guide for the Real World*. San Francisco: Jossey-Bass, 1993.

Crosby, Philip B. *Quality without Tears*. New York: McGraw-Hill, 1984.

———. *The Eternally Successful Organization*. New York: Penguin Books, 1988.

Crowder, Nancy L., and Virginia A. Hodgkinson, eds. *Compendium of Resources for Teaching about the Nonprofit Sector, Voluntarism, and Philanthropy*. 2d ed. Washington, DC: Independent Sector, 1991.

Davis, Stanley M. *Future Perfect*. New York: Addison-Wesley, 1987.

Delp, Peter, et al. *System Tools for Project Planning: Nine Categories of Analytic Technique*. Bloomington, IN: International Development Institute, Indiana University, 1977.

Dionne, E. J., Jr. *Why Progressives Will Dominate the Next Political Era*. New York: Simon and Schuster, 1996.

Drucker, Peter F. *Management: Tasks, Responsibilities, Practices*. New York: Harper and Row, 1973.

———. *Managing the Nonprofit Organization: Principles and Practices*. New York: Harper Collins, 1990.

Duke University. *Shaping Our Future: A Young University Faces a New Century*. Durham, NC: Strategic Planning Committee, 1994.

Fahey, Liam, and Robert Randall. *The Portable MBA in Strategy*. New York: John Wiley, 1994.

Galbreath, Jay R., and Edward E. Lawler III. *Organizing for the Future: The New Logic for Managing Complex Organizations*. San Francisco: Jossey-Bass, 1993.

Gore, Al. *Creating a Government That Works Better and Costs Less: Report of the National Performance Review*. New York: Plume, 1993.

———. *Status Report of the National Performance Review*. Washington, DC: Government Printing Office, September 1994.

Hammer, Michael, and James Champy. *Reengineering the Corporation*. New York: Harper Business, 1993.

Hammer, Michael, and Steven A. Stanton. *The Reengineering Revolution: A Handbook*. New York: Harper Business, 1995.

Hanna, Nagy. *Strategic Planning and Management: A Review of Recent Experience*. World Bank Working Paper No. 751. Washington, DC: International Bank for Reconstruction and Development, 1985.

Hardy, James M. *Establishing Operational Goals: The Key to Future Directions*. New York: Association Press, 1972.

Heath, Daniel, ed. *America in Perspective*. Boston, MA: Houghton Mifflin, 1986.

Hickman, Craig, and Michael A. Silva. *Creating Excellence: Managing Corporate Culture, Strategy, and Change in the New Age*. New York: New American Library, 1984.

Higgins, J. C. *Strategic and Operational Planning Systems*. London: Prentice-Hall International, 1980.

Hodgkinson, V. A., K. D. McCarthy, and R. D. Sumariwalla. *The Nonprofit Sector in the Global Community*. San Francisco: Jossey-Bass, 1992a.

Hodgkinson, Virginia A., Murray S. Weitzman, Christopher M. Toppe, and Stephen M. Noga. *Nonprofit Almanac 1992–1993: Dimensions of the Independent Sector*. San Francisco: Jossey-Bass, 1992b.

Howlett, Michael J. "Strategic Planning in State Government." In *Managing Non-*

profit Organizations, edited by Diane Borst and Patrick L. Montana. New York: AMACOM, 1977.

Janus, Irving, and Leo Mann. *Decision Making*. New York: Free Press, 1977.

Kanter, Rosabeth Moss. *The Change Masters*. New York: Simon and Schuster, 1983.

Kast, E., and James E. Rosenzweig. "Program Management: Weapons and Space Systems." In *Theory and Management of Systems*, 2d ed. New York: McGraw-Hill, 1967.

Kearns, Kevin P. "From Comparative Advantage to Damage Control: Clarifying Strategic Issues Using SWOT Analysis." *Nonprofit Management and Leadership* 3, no. 1 (Fall 1992).

Kearns, Kevin P., and Georgine Scarpino. "Strategic Planning Research: Knowledge and Gaps." *Nonprofit Management and Leadership* 6, no. 4 (Summer 1996).

Kearns, Kevin P., Robert J. Krasman, and William J. Meyer. "Why Nonprofit Organizations Are Ripe for Total Quality Management." *Nonprofit Management and Leadership* 4, no. 4 (Summer 1994).

Kettl, Donald F., "Building Lasting Reform." *Inside the Reinvention Machine: Appraising Government Reform*, Donald F. Kettl and John J. DiIulio, Jr., eds., 1995.

Kettl, Donald F., and John J. DiIulio, Jr., eds. *Inside the Reinvention Machine: Appraising Government Reform*. Washington, DC: Brookings Institution, 1995.

Knauft, E. B., Renee A. Berger, and Sandra T. Gray. *Profiles of Excellence: Achieving Success in the Nonprofit Sector*. San Francisco: Jossey-Bass, 1991.

Kouzes, James M., and Barry Z. Posner. *The Leadership Challenge: How to Get Extraordinary Things Done in Organizations*. San Francisco: Jossey-Bass, 1987.

Kreitner, Robert W. "Designing Organizations." In *Management: Problem Solving Approach*. Boston: Houghton Mifflin, 1980.

Liebschutz, Sarah F. "Coping by Nonprofit Organizations during the Reagan Years." *Nonprofit Management and Leadership* 2, no. 4 (Summer 1992).

Lippert, Gordon L. *Organization Renewal*. 2d ed. Englewood Cliffs, NJ: Prentice-Hall, 1982.

Lorange, Peter. *Implementing Strategic Planning*. Englewood Cliffs, NJ: Prentice-Hall, 1982.

Mattessich, Paul W., and Barbara R. Monsey. *Collaboration: What Makes It Work*. St. Paul, MN: Amherst H. Wilder Foundation, 1992.

McMurtry, Steven L., F. Ellen Netting, and Peter M. Kettner. "How Nonprofits Adapt to a Stringent Environment." *Nonprofit Management and Leadership* 1, no. 4 (Summer 1991).

Miller, Trudi C., ed. *Public Sector Performance*. Baltimore: Johns Hopkins University Press, 1984.

Mintzberg, Henry. *Rise and Fall of Strategic Planning*. New York: Free Press, 1994.

Moe, Ronald C. "The Reinventing Government Exercise." *Public Administration Review* 54, no. 2 (March/April 1994).

Morris, Lynn Lyons, ed. "How to Present an Evaluation Report." *Program Evaluation Kit*. Center for Study of Evaluation, University of California, Los Angeles. Beverly Hills, CA: Sage Publications, 1978.

Morrisey, George L. *Managing by Objectives and Results*. Reading, MA: Addison-Wesley, 1977.

Morrisey, George L., Patrick J. Below, and Betty L. Acomb. *The Executive Guide to Strategic Planning*. San Francisco: Jossey-Bass, 1987.

Naisbitt, John. *Megatrends: New Directions Transforming Our Lives*. New York: Warner Books, 1984.

Naisbitt, John, and Patricia Aburdene. *Megatrends 2000: Ten New Directions for the 1990s*. William Morrow, 1990.

Nakamura, Robert T., and Frank Smallwood. *The Politics of Policy Implementation*. New York: St. Martins, 1980.

National Association of Realtors. *Strategic Plan for 1989*. Washington, DC: 1988.

Nutt, Paul C., and Robert W. Backoff. *Strategic Management of Public and Third Sector Organizations*. San Francisco: Jossey-Bass, 1992.

Odiorne, George S. *Management by Objectives: A System of Managerial Leadership*. New York: Pitman, 1965.

Office of the Vice President. Accompanying Reports of the National Performance Review. Washington, DC: Government Printing Office, 1993.

———. *Creating Quality Leadership and Management*, 1993a.

———. *Improving Customer Service*, 1993b.

———. *Mission-Driven, Results-Oriented Budgeting*, 1993c.

———. *Reengineering Through Information Technology*, 1993d.

———. *Rethinking Program Design*, 1993e.

———. *Strengthening the Partnership in Intergovernmental Service Delivery*, 1993f.

Office of the Vice President. *Putting Customers First: Standards for Serving the American People*. Washington, DC: Government Printing Office, September 1994.

Office of the Vice President. *Serving the American Public: Best Practices in Telephone Service*. Federal Consortium Benchmark Study Report. Washington, DC: Government Printing Office, February 1995.

Ohio Board of Regents Management Improvement Program. *Planning: Universities*. Columbus, OH: 1974a.

———. *Program Budgeting: Universities*. Columbus, OH: 1974b.

Ohmae, Kenichi. *The Mind of the Strategist*. Penguin, 1982.

Osborne, David, and Ted Gaebler. *Reinventing Government*. New York: Addison-Wesley, 1992.

Paul, Samuel. *Strategic Program Management*. Management Development Series No. 19. Geneva: International Labour Office, 1983.

Peter F. Drucker Foundation for Nonprofit Management. *How to Assess Your Nonprofit Organization with Peter Drucker's Five Most Important Questions*. User Guide by Constance Rossum; Participant's Workbook by Peter Drucker. San Francisco: Jossey-Bass, 1993.

Peters, Thomas J. *Thriving on Chaos*. New York: Knopf, 1988.

———. *Liberation Management*. New York: Alfred A. Knopf, 1992.

Peters, Thomas J., and Robert H. Waterman, Jr. *In Search of Excellence: Lessons from America's Best Run Companies*. New York: Warner Books, 1982.

Petersen, Glenn R. Executive Director, American Red Cross Massachusetts Bay. Letter to author, December 16, 1988.

Porter, M. E. *Competitive Advantage: Creating and Sustaining Superior Performance.* New York: Free Press, 1985.

Public Administration Service, Publication No. 91. *Work Simplification.* Chicago, IL: 1945.

Radin, Beryl A. "Varieties of Reinvention: Six NPR "Success Stories." *Inside the Reinvention Machine: Appraising Government Reform,* edited by Donald F. Kettl and John J. DiIulio, Jr.

Ramo, Simon. *Cure for Chaos: Fresh Solutions to Social Problems through the Systems Approach.* New York: David McKay, 1969.

Rivlin, Alice M. *Reviving the American Dream: The Economy, the States, and the Federal Government.* Washington, DC: Brookings Institution, 1992.

Rowe, Alan, Richard O. Mason, and Karl E. Dickel. *Strategic Management and Business Policy: A Methodological Approach.* Reading, MA: Addison-Wesley, 1985.

Salamon, L. M., R. M. Kramer, and B. Gidron, eds. *Government and the Third Sector.* San Francisco: Jossey-Bass, 1992.

Selby, Cecily. "Better Performance from Nonprofits." *Harvard Business Review* 56, no. 5. (September-October 1978): 92–98.

Senge, Peter M. *The Fifth Discipline: The Art and Practice of the Learning Organization.* New York: Doubleday, 1990.

Senge, Peter M., Art Kleiner, Charlotte Roberts, Richard B. Ross, and Bryan J. Smith. *The Fifth Discipline Fieldbook: Strategies and Tools for Building a Learning Organization.* New York: Doubleday, 1994.

Shaplin, Arthur. *Strategic Management.* New York: McGraw-Hill, 1985.

Simons, Robert. "Control in an Age of Empowerment." *Harvard Business Review* (March-April 1995): 80–88.

Singer, Mark I., and John A. Yankey. "Organizational Metamorphosis: A Study of Eighteen Nonprofit Mergers, Acquisitions, and Consolidations." *Nonprofit Management and Leadership* 1, no. 4 (Summer 1991).

Southwestern Pennsylvania Regional Planning Commission. *Standards for Effective Local Government: A Workbook for Performance Assessment.* Pittsburgh: Spring 1990.

State of Ohio. *Toward a Working Ohio: Executive Summary: A Strategic Plan for the Eighties and Beyond: Investing in Ohio's People.* Columbus, OH: September 1984.

Steiner, George A. *Strategic Planning: What Every Manager Must Know.* New York: Free Press, 1979.

Stone, Donald. *Improving Local Services through Intergovernmental and Intersectoral Cooperation.* Paper No. 5. Pittsburgh: Coalition to Improve Management in State and Local Government, 1991a.

———. *Improving Management in Pennsylvania Municipalities: Implementing Goals and Standards.* Guide 6–A. Pittsburgh: Coalition to Improve Management in State and Local Government, 1991b.

Stone, Melissa M. "The Propensity of Governing Boards to Plan." *Nonprofit Management and Leadership* 1, no. 3 (Spring 1991).

Stone, Melissa M., and William Crittenden. "A Guide to Journal Articles on Strategic Management in Nonprofit Organizations, 1977 to 1992." *Nonprofit Management and Leadership* 4, no. 2 (Winter 1993).

Stone, Susan C. *Strategic Planning for Independent Schools*. Boston: National Association of Independent Schools, 1986.

United Way of America. *Strategic Management and United Way*. Alexandria, VA: 1985.

Unterman, I., and R. H. Davis. "The Strategy Gap in Not-For-Profits." *Harvard Business Review* 60, no. 3 (May-June 1982): 32–40.

U.S. Agency for International Development. *Evaluation Handbook*. 2d ed. Washington, DC: Office of Program Evaluation, 1972.

———. *Project Evaluation Guidelines*. 2d ed. Washington, DC: Office of Program Evaluation, 1973.

———. *Design and Evaluation of Aid-Assisted Projects*. Washington, DC: Office of Personnel Management, 1980.

U.S. Navy, Public Works Center. *FY 1994 Strategic Plan*. Yokosuka, Japan: 1994.

U.S. Treasury, Financial Management Service. *Performance Measurement: Report on a Survey of Private Sector Performance Measures*. Washington, DC: January 1993, 12.

U.S. Treasury, Internal Revenue Service. *Strategic Management System Handbook*. Washington, DC: 1985.

———. *Business Master Plan Strategic Extract FY 1995–FY 2001*. Publication 1822 (8–94). Washington, DC: 1994.

———. *Strategic Business Plan FY 1994 and Beyond*. Document 7382 (Rev. 9–93). Washington, DC: 1993.

Walter, Susan, and Pat Choate. *Thinking and Acting Strategically: A Primer for Public Leaders*. Washington, DC: Council of State Planning Agencies, 1984.

Walton, Mary. *The Deming Management Method*. New York: Dodd, Mead, 1986.

Waterman, Robert H., Jr. *The Renewal Factor*. New York: Bantam Books, 1987.

Weisbrod, Burton A. *The Nonprofit Economy*. Boston, MA: Harvard University Press, 1988, 1991.

Wheelen, Thomas L., and J. David Hunger. *Strategic Management and Business Policy: A Methodological Approach*. Reading, MA: Addison-Wesley, 1985.

Zemke, Ron, with Dick Schaaf. *The Service Edge*. New York: New American Library, 1989.

Index

Action plans, devising and charting, 241–45; gaining agreement and support, 245–46; Gant chart, 243–44; Milestone chart, 244–45; preparing action steps, 242

Administrative rationality, 231

Agency for International Development, 251–53

American Heart Association, mission, 124

American Red Cross, 77, 126–27

Ansoff, Igor H., 46, 47–49

Assessments, strategic, 105–20; of environment, 111–16; of program performance, 108–11; of strategic implications, 116–20

Bennis, Warren, 58–62

Budgeting by program, 272–82; aims, 272–73; essential components, 274–76; estimating program costs, 276–78; major tasks, 276

Change mastery, 44–57; Ansoff's categories, 47–49; applying renewal factor, 50–53; commitments and practices common to successful leaders, 54–57

Chief Executive, general manager of strategy, 35–43; how to establish proper climate, 42–43; personal involvement, 41–42; playing multiple roles, 38–41

Chief Planner, as expert advisor, 90–92

Competitive advantage, 135–37

Complexity and risk, assessing, 113–14

Control, 305–15; new thinking and emergence of creative controls, 313–15; use of traditional control matrix, 306–10

Control measures, key questions for evaluating, 312

Creating Excellence (Hickman and Silva), 62–63

Customer satisfaction, 197–204; follow-up to service failure, 199–200; guiding principles, 200–204; performance standards, 266–68; server-customer interface, 198; special role of recipients, 198–99

Decision Making (Janus and Mann), 89–90

Decision-making, raising quality of

decision-making procedure, 85–87;
essential conditions, 85–87; special
organizational arrangements, 87
Duke University Strategic Plan, 135–
37, 138

Environmental scanning, 111–16; assessing complexity and risk, 113–14;
calculating competitive advantage,
114; checklist for reading the environment, 115–16; detecting trends,
112
Evaluation, 316–27; annual evaluation
plan, 317–18
Evaluation, strategic management system, 96–101; guiding concept, 96;
major mistakes, 97–98; Steiner Report Card, 98–100
Evaluation studies, 320–27; design criteria, 321; evaluation report preparation, 325–27; findings and
analysis, 323–25
Executive Committee. See Planning
Council

Facilitative planning approach, 90–91

Goals, establishing, 124–29; how to
write, 126–29; use of sub-goal statements of possible outcomes, 127–29
Government and nonprofit sector, interdependence of, 175–89
Government downsizing, 17, 153–54;
savings and cutbacks in personnel,
153–54; undermining employee morale, 149; weaken monitoring of
liabilities, 160–61
Government Performance and Results
Act (1993), 256–58

IBM Corporation, 295
Implementation matrix, 131–32; exam-
ple in strategic plan of state of
Ohio, 131–32
Information technology, 208–10; elec-
tronic bulletin boards, 209; informa-

tion superhighway and Internet,
209–10
Informed opportunism, 51, 52–53;
pragmatic strategy (combining analysis with intuition), 53; stochastic
shock, 53
Institutionalization, 96–97
Internal Revenue Service, 68–69, 88,
92–93, 94, 95, 137, 264–65
Issues management, 77–80; process,
79–80; top management role in, 79–
80

Janus, Irving, 89–90

Leaders (Bennis and Nanus), 58–59
Leadership Challenge, The (Kouzes and
Posner), 54–57
Leadership practices, 54–57; challenging the process, 55; enabling others
to act, 56; encouraging the heart, 57;
inspiring a shared vision, 56; modeling the way, 57
Leadership roles, multiple, 38–41; ar-
chitect of vision, 39; director of strategic system, 40; guardian of top
quality performance, 41; mobilizer
of major resources, 41; molder of
corporate culture, 40; sage of the
environment, 40–41
Limits, era of, 14–20; complexity factor, 17–18; financial constraints, 14–
15; promise of strategic
management, 20–21; ripple effect of
severe limits, 18–20; short-term focus, 16–17; tough choices, 16
Logical framework matrix, 251–53; instructions for preparation, 252–53

Management by Objectives (MBO),
rise and decline of MBO movement, 236–38; shift in doctrine and
practice, 13. See also Objectives
Mental models, (Senge), 329
Mission statements, 122–24
Murphy's Law, folk culture, 305

Nonprofit sector, 18–19; international research, 18; professional growth, 18; reliance on government, 18. *See also* Strategic competence, nonprofit organizations

Objectives, 236–46; benefits and pitfalls, 239–40; new doctrine for setting objectives, 239; objective-oriented manager, 238–39; writing objectives, 240–41
Office of Management and Budget, federal, (OMB), 258, 260, 261
Ohio strategic plan, state of, 131–32
Organizational learning, 327–32; component technologies, 328–32; mental models, 329; personal mastery, 329; shared vision, 324; systems thinking, 328–29; team learning, 332
Organizational structure, traditional, 287–89; newer organizational thinking and practice, 292–94; strengths and weaknesses of, 289–92
Organizational values, expressing, 129; components of value statements, 129

Performance agreements, with senior leadership, 263–64
Performance appraisal, 318–20; common inadequacies, 318; guidelines, 319–20
Performance criteria, 228–32; acquiring sufficient resources, 230; administrative rationality, 231; efficient use of inputs, 229; providing customer focus and satisfaction, 229–30; quality output, 228–29; satisfying powerful interests, 231–32
Performance measurement, 254–71; best telephone service practice, 268–69; congressional mandate: Government Performance and Results Act, 256–58; performance goals in strategic plans, 264–65; performance standards in customer satisfaction, 266–68; performance standards in local government, 269–71

Performance monitoring methods, 310–11
Planner, chief, 90–92; facilitative approach, 90–91; functions of, 91–92
Planning Council (or Executive Committee), 87–88; primary functions, 88
Powerful interests, satisfying, 231–33
Program budgeting, components of, 274–76
Program costs, estimating, 276–78
Program management, modern, 213–23; benefits and pitfalls, 220–23; operational concepts, 215–17; source, 214–15; strategic role of program managers, 219–20
Program managers, 224–38; learning areas for reinvention and transformation, 235; managerial functions, 226–28; new role for senior executives, 233–34; responsibilities of, 225–26
Program performance, assessing, 108–11; assessing balance (of supply, demand, and resource), and checklist, 109–11; profiling supply and demand, and checklist, 108–9
Program plan (or project plan), 247–53; components of program plan: inputs desired, 249; objectively verifiable indicators, 250; outputs produced, 249; purpose, 249; target clientele, 250
Program structure, 283–94; examples, 286–87; how used, 285–86

Reinventing government, 143–61; Brookings Institution appraisal, 147–50; critical commentary, 150–53; Federal National Performance Review, 143–47; fundamental approaches, 153–57; guiding strategies, 144–45; widespread quality movement, 158–59
Renewal Factor, (Waterman, Jr.), 50–53
Response behavior, strategic, 46–49; Ansoff's categories (stable, reactive,

anticipatory, exploring, and creative), 47–49

Silva, Michael A., 62–63
Situation audit, strategic, 105–7; con-
tent, 106–7; process, 107; purpose,
106
Small Business Administration, 161
Social Security Administration, 266–68
Span of supervision, 289
Specialization, 287–88
Staff support units, 288
Standards, establishing, 309–10, 266–
71
Steiner, George, 97
Stochastic shock, 53
Strategic assessments, 105–20; situa-
tion audit, 105–7
Strategic balance (of supply, demand,
and resource), 109–11
Strategic Business Plan of the U.S.
Navy Public Works Center, 132–33
Strategic capability, chief executive's
role, 35–37; dimensions of, 37
Strategic competence, nonprofit organizations, 162–74; Arizona study
of nonprofits, 164–68; experience
with mergers, 168–72; response to
financial stringency, 162–64; strategies used by service providers, 166–
67
Strategic consulting service, in-house,
92
Strategic initiatives, 130–31; what they
accomplish, 130–31
Strategic management explained, 20–
32; aims, 28–29; characteristics, 26–
27; evolution, 22–23; pay-off, 29–32;
problems in practice, 6–7; quick
view, 20–22; trends in effective
practice, 7–12; types of strategy, 22
Strategic management support group,
92; functions, 93
Strategic management system, descriptive model, 67–72; designing,
67–77; preparing to start formal
system, 80–82
Strategic operational service group,
focus and function, 93–95

Strategic Planning (Steiner), 97–98
Strategic Planning and Management
(Hanna), 90–91
Strategic plans, preparing components
of basic version, 122–32; mission
and purpose, 122–24; new initiatives, 130–31; organizational goals,
124–29; provision for
implementation, 131–32; values, 129–
30
Strategic plans, preparing special features in expanded version, 133–38;
Duke University Strategic Plan, 135–
37; expressing distinctiveness, creating competitive advantage, 134–37;
providing fiscal outlook, 138; stating measurable progress indicators,
137
Strategies, private sector, applied to
public concerns, 190–210; customer
satisfaction, 192–214; experience
with mergers, 168–72; information
technology, 208–210; streamlining
and reengineering, 204–8; total
quality management, 192–97
Strategy formulation, 71
Strategy implementation, 71–72
Streamlining and reengineering, 204–8;
new ways to calculate process
costs, 206–7; productivity and employee involvement, 207–8; reengineering work processes, 205
System design, strategic management
system, 71–77
Systems thinking (Senge), 328–29

Teams or team approach, 295–97;
characteristics, 297; design guidelines, 300; strengths, 298; weaknesses, 298–99
Total Quality Management (TQM),
192–97; fundamental concepts, 193–
95; new quality responsibilities and
tools of analysis for program managers, 195–97
Trends, in effective strategic management practice, 7–12
Trilateral interdependence, of federal,
state and nonprofit organizations,

179–83; an institutional approach, 182–83

Turbulence, escalation of: patterns of (novelty, speed, predictability, and complexity), 45–46; scale of (steady, shift, drift), 46

University of Maryland Law School, strategic plan, 137

Values: expressing organizational, 129–30; typical value statement, 129
Vision: communicating, 61–62; criteria for effective, 59–61
Visionary executive, 62–63

Waterman, Robert Jr., 50–53
Welfare state, rise and decline in America, 176–89; greater use of states as problem-solving laboratories, 180; growing reliance on nonprofit sector, 179; half-century of government growth, 176; historic shift to state responsibility, 177–78; retrenchment in Reagan years and beyond, 176–77
World Bank (International Bank for Reconstruction and Development), 90–91
WOTS-UP Analysis, 116–20; defined, 116–17; presenting findings and results, 118–20

About the Author

JACK KOTEEN is a strategic management consultant and trainer who was formerly a member of the faculty at the University of Maryland and at the Graduate School of the U.S. Department of Agriculture. Mr. Koteen was also Director of the Office of Development Administration in the U.S. Department of State, and has been a consultant for the Agency for International Development.